D1328181

THE JOHN HARVARD LIBRARY

Bernard Bailyn
Editor-in-Chief

THE JOHN HARVARD LIBRARY

PROBLEMS OF MODERN DEMOCRACY

POLITICAL AND ECONOMIC ESSAYS

BY

Edwin Lawrence Godkin

Edited by Morton Keller

THE BELKNAP PRESS OF
HARVARD UNIVERSITY PRESS

CAMBRIDGE, MASSACHUSETTS

1966

Contents

Harvard 5.36

6-13-67

Introduction

During the last decades of the nineteenth century many Americans of education and social sensibility came to despair of the state of the Republic. After the Civil War American public life, in their estimation, underwent a precipitous and disastrous decline. Shocked by what they saw around them—gross politicos, venal machines, empty campaigns—they set themselves the task of restoring the purity of American politics. They joined municipal movements against city machines; they declared their political independence from the Republican party by supporting Grover Cleveland against James G. Blaine in 1884. The name attached to them in that year—Mugwump—best identifies these genteel reformers and their distinctive political attitude.[1]

The great Mugwump spokesman was Edwin Lawrence Godkin, editor of the *Nation* and the New York *Evening Post* and the most distinguished journalist of his generation. His cool, acerb leaders summed up the Mugwump sense of the nature and direction of

[1] *Mugwump* supposedly derived from the Algonquian Indian word for *chief*. It was used before 1884 to designate an important (and, increasingly, a self-important) person. In the wake of the 1884 convention the Republican press attached the word, with suitable intonations of irony and sarcasm, to the respectables who bolted to Cleveland. Gerald W. McFarland, "The New York Mugwumps of 1884: A Profile," *Political Science Quarterly*, 78 (1963): 40–58, and Geoffrey T. Blodgett, "The Mind of the Boston Mugwump," *Mississippi Valley Historical Review*, 48 (1962): 614–634, describe the Mugwumps of two major cities.

American public life. "To my generation," wrote William James, "Godkin's was certainly the towering influence in all thought concerning public affairs, and indirectly his influence has certainly been more pervasive than that of any other writer of the generation, for he influenced other writers who never quoted him, and determined the whole current of discussion." Godkin's close friend Charles Eliot Norton said of him: "He did more than any other writer of his generation to clarify the intelligence and to quicken the conscience of the thoughtful part of the community in regard to every important political question of the time." Charles W. Eliot magisterially observed in 1899 that Godkin's *Nation* "has had a decided influence on my opinions and my action for nearly forty years." [2]

To have "determined the whole current of discussion"; to have shaped the thinking of "the thoughtful part of the community": these were Godkin's great contributions as an editor and publicist. In over two thousand articles and editorials he held up what seemed to educated Americans the truest mirror of their time.

In the late 1890's, when depression, farmer and labor unrest, imperialism, and war swept across the American scene, Godkin culled from his periodical writing those pieces that best conveyed his growing unease with the American experiment in government. *Problems of Modern Democracy* (1896) and *Unforeseen Tendencies of Democracy* (1898) were his final, and unhopeful, legacy to his reading public.[3] Because *Problems of Modern*

---

[2] Rollo Ogden, ed., *Life and Letters of Edwin Lawrence Godkin* (New York, 1907), I, 221; James to Henry L. Higginson, Feb. 8, 1903, in Henry James, ed., *Letters of William James* (Boston, 1920), II, 182; Norton to Leslie Stephen, June 3, 1902, in Sara Norton and Mark A. de Wolfe Howe, eds., *Letters of Charles Eliot Norton* (Boston, 1913), II, 322; James F. Rhodes, *Historical Essays* (New York, 1909), p. 270. There is an acute analysis of Godkin as "the severest critic of the Gilded Age" in Vernon L. Parrington, *The Beginnings of Critical Realism in America* (New York, 1930), pp. 154–167. The best survey of Godkin's career, and of the literature on that career, is William M. Armstrong, *E. L. Godkin and American Foreign Policy, 1865–1900* (New York, 1957), chap. 1.

[3] Godkin also published *Reflections and Comments, 1865–1895* (New York, 1895), a collection of nonpolitical essays. He intended to write the volume on government for the

Democracy is made up of articles drawn from the thirty-year range of Godkin's editorial career, it is the more revealing book. It remains the best entry to the opinions of one of the most influential of all American publicists.

2

Godkin brought to his judgment of post–Civil War American life a perspective that was very much the product of his origins and youth. He was born on October 2, 1831, in Moyne, County Wicklow, Ireland. His were Protestant, not Catholic, parents in a place where the distinction was important. His father, James Godkin, was a Presbyterian minister at a distance both from his Catholic neighbors and, as an active spokesman for Home Rule, from the British authorities in Ireland as well.

Not surprisingly, Godkin always was sensitive to matters of national and ethnic identity. He did not hesitate to declare himself an Irishman, and he remained a staunch advocate of Home Rule. But he never looked upon the Irish Catholics who figured so prominently in the politics of New York as in any sense compatriots. There was something of the passion of old hatreds in his response to the American Irish. Soon after he came to the United States he observed: "The mass of Celts is now too large and unwieldy for American temperament to permeate it," and with the passage of years his distaste for them only deepened.[4]

As an editor Godkin frequently faced attacks questioning his Americanism. This was one of the few forms of criticism that ruffled his composure. He complained in 1865: "I am an American citizen, am as American in feeling as any man in the country . . . My children were born here. I want to die here, and I protest

---

American Science Series that included William James's *Psychology* and Francis A. Walker's *Political Economy*, but the manuscript never was completed. Henry Holt, *Garrulities of an Octogenarian Editor* (Boston, 1923), p. 293.

[4] Ogden, ed., *Godkin*, I, 183.

in these days of negro suffrage, against being cried down on this score." [5] But the accusations may have hurt because they came so close to the truth. James Bryce's observation that Godkin was "not an American at all but a European, and indeed a European who never became thoroughly Americanized" was echoed by others who knew him. Matthew Arnold found him "a typical specimen of the Irishman of culture." [6] And at the end of his life Godkin gave up his American residence to live in England.

He was raised and educated as an Anglo-Irishman. He went to Queen's College, Belfast, in the 1840's, which gave him a solid grounding in classic English Liberalism. Godkin recalled of his college days: "John Stuart Mill was our prophet, and Grote and Bentham were our daily food." [7] The diet was a strong and unforgettable one. It committed him to a set of political, economic, and philosophical beliefs that were always to condition his reactions to public issues. His stubborn loyalty to the idea of democracy (after he had condemned nearly all its works) and his profound belief in the economics of laissez-faire (after it had passed out of fashion in England itself) were testimony to the persistence of his youthful intellectual inheritance.

Liberalism was far from being a purely theoretical set of social beliefs in the 1840's and the 1850's. Godkin found in its precepts a call to action. He took up the study of law at Middle Temple in the early 1850's, but soon was roused by English indifference to the Hungarian and Italian struggles for national independence. In 1853, when he was only twenty-two years old, he left off his legal studies to write, with small learning but great passion, a

---

[5] Godkin to Charles Eliot Norton, July 29, 1865, Godkin Mss (Houghton Library, Harvard University). In 1862, when he was seeking an editorial position, Godkin feared that his Irish origins would hurt him: "How would my being a foreigner affect my position if I were prominently and openly an editor? There is a sort of feeling, I fancy, in America, against foreigners connected with the press." Godkin to Charles Loring Brace, Jan. 7, 1862, Godkin Mss.

[6] James Bryce, *Studies in Contemporary Biography* (New York, 1903), p. 368; Ogden, ed., *Godkin*, II, 1.

[7] Ogden, ed., *Godkin*, I, 11–12.

History of Hungary that celebrated the movement for liberation from the Austrian yoke. The book appeared concurrently with a visit to London by the flamboyant Hungarian leader Kossuth, and made for Godkin a quick and outsized reputation in English journalistic and literary circles.

On the strength of his fledgling success he was sent as a correspondent by the London *Daily News* to report on the Crimean War. From 1853 to 1855 he returned dispatches crackling with a Churchillian verve and dash. They revealed that his staunch commitment to freedom did not preclude a sense of the propriety of a stratified social order. Scotch Highlander troops were fortunate enough, he reported, to be led by officers "who are looked up to . . . not simply because of their military rank, but because of their greater intelligence, better education, and higher station in society." Godkin himself apparently suffered from the rigidities of the English class structure; he said after the Civil War that returning to England "would be going back into an atmosphere that I detest and a social system that I have hated since I was fourteen years old." But his social difficulties in England served only to whet his ambitions. Henry Holt said of him: "He cared as much for social position as for intellectual position." [8] The ambivalence implicit here appeared in his observations on society at large. To the end he remained faithful to the principle of democracy; but increasingly he criticized the specifics of democratic practice.

For one so young, so able, so ambitious, the New World beckoned invitingly. Godkin's early sense of the United States came from Tocqueville; and the open, free, opportunity-filled society across the ocean irresistibly drew him. Although he was offered the editorship of the *Belfast Northern Whig*, in 1856 the twenty-five-year-old migrated to America. He came with the intention of devoting himself not to the trade of journalism that had

[8] *Ibid.*, I, 73; II, 140. Holt, *Garrulities*, p. 293.

won him such quick recognition but rather to the more prestigious and rewarding profession of the law.[9]

Upon arriving in New York, Godkin became an apprentice in the law office of David Dudley Field. He joined the bar in February 1858. But despite so promising a beginning—Field was in the first rank of American attorneys—Godkin quickly lost interest in the law. He continued as a correspondent for his old London newspaper, the *Daily News,* and published letters describing a trip through the South. He moved easily into New York and Boston literary-intellectual circles; his friends soon included Frederick Law Olmsted, Charles Loring Brace, William Cullen Bryant, Charles Dana, George W. Curtis, Charles Eliot Norton. He became an editorial consultant to the New York *Times,* and in 1859 married the granddaughter of Senator Samuel E. Foote of Connecticut.

He had come to America at a time when the law, set against the excitements of political controversy, seemed humdrum indeed. Genteel, educated northeasterners in the late eighteen-fifties were engrossed in the politics and the ideology of anti-slavery; and Godkin's Liberal heritage made it easy for him to respond to the prevailing tone. On the evening of his first day in America, in November of 1856, he attended a Frémont rally in New York's Academy of Music. He found in the 1856 presidential campaign a politics not of privilege and place but of democratic purpose and of public morality: "in a few days I became aware that themes were under popular discussion which had never been so discussed—the rights and wrongs of slavery, the equality of man, the provisions of a written Constitution, the position of leading

---

[9] Tocqueville may well have been the source of Godkin's choice. *Democracy in America* commented on "the small influence of the American journals" and editors. But though in England "lawyers do not occupy the first rank," in America their special skill "ensures them a separate rank in society, and they constitute a sort of privileged body in the scale of intellect." In consequence "they form the highest political class and the most privileged portion of society." Tocqueville, *Democracy in America* (Vintage Books, New York, 1958), I, 283, 287–288. These were important considerations for Godkin.

public men on questions which were half moral and only half political or legal." He told his English readers after the 1856 election that "the reign of men has gone by and the era of principles begun." Almost half a century later he still vividly recalled the heady political air at the time of his arrival:

> The State was still in a stage in which men were admired and had influence. There were still worshippers . . . of Andrew Jackson, of Calhoun, of Daniel Webster, of Henry Clay, and of Silas Wright . . . the air was full of the real 'Americanism.' The American gospel was on people's lips and was preached with fervor. Force was worshipped, but it was moral force: it was the force of reason, of humanity, of human equality, of a good example. The abolitionist gospel seemed to be permeating the views of the American people, and overturning and destroying the last remaining traditions of the old-world political morality. It was really what might be called the golden age of America.

The frailties of democratic politics—officeholding by the corrupt and ignorant, "the little arts that can influence the feelings of the uneducated"—did not, as in later years, fill him with despair. They marred but they did not transform a political environment ultimately so moral and committed: "It is undoubtedly a proud boast for any country that its political system can not only permit such saturnalia without injury, but be positively strengthened by their violence." [10]

It was of the utmost importance to Godkin's career as the great observer-critic of the Gilded Age that these were the conditions of his introduction to American politics. His initial observation of the nature—and the possibilities—of American public life led him to drop the law and assume the engaged and influential role of the journalist. These stirring antislavery years gave him a yardstick by which to judge American political behavior thereafter. The form of the political process in the postwar years would not be so very different from that of the fifties. But the content of

---

[10] New York *Evening Post*, Dec. 30, 1899; Louis Filler, "The Early Godkin," *Historian*, 17 (1954): 57; Ogden, ed., *Godkin*, I, 169–179.

Godkin's first confrontation—passionate involvement in a cause that touched the deepest wellsprings of his Liberalism, a cause defined and furthered by the best educated and most distinguished Americans of his time—would not outlast the era of the Civil War. Then ways of politics that once had been unpleasant but unavoidable realities became the measure of a people's fall from grace.

3

The Civil War, and the end of slavery, were for antislavery intellectuals at once a culmination and a beginning. They expected that the moral fervor of the antislavery crusade and the war would continue to shape the politics of the nation. And those who had lent force and distinction to the assault on slavery might with reason expect to play a significant part in postwar public life. Ralph Waldo Emerson dwelt on the enlightening effect of the great conflict: "It is plain that the War has made many things public that once were quite too private . . . at some moment, on the old topic of the days, politics, [the American] makes a distinction he had not made; he discerns a little inlet not seen before." James Russell Lowell had a similar sense of possibility: "What splendid opportunities has not our trial revealed even to ourselves! . . . Here at last is a state whose life is not narrowly concentrated in a despot or a class, but feels itself in every limb; a government which is not a mere application of force from without, but dwells as a vital principle in the will of every citizen." [11]

A mood of heightened expectation prevailed especially among men of Godkin's age and stamp. His intellectual godfather John Stuart Mill sharpened his sense of the possible by writing to him: "the great concussion which has taken place in the American

[11] Edward W. Emerson and Waldo E. Forbes, eds., *Journals of Ralph Waldo Emerson* (Boston, 1914), X, 116; James R. Lowell, *Writings* (Boston, 1890), V (*Political Essays*), 212.

mind must have loosened the foundations of all prejudices, and secured a fair hearing for impartial reason on all subjects such as it might not otherwise have had for many generations." Godkin was receptive to the possibilities of this time of hope. He told Olmsted during the war: "Affairs are every day more curious and interesting, and I am duly thanking Heaven that I live here and in this age." To his friend Charles Eliot Norton he declared in February 1865: "The intellect and education of this country have for three generations run into law, divinity, or commerce. Ought we not to try and do something to turn the tide into politics?" [12] Henry Adams, serving in England as secretary to his father, the American ambassador, felt the same stirrings. He wrote to a friend: "We want a national set of young men like ourselves or better, to start new influences not only in politics, but in literature, in law, in society, and throughout the whole social organism of the country—a national school of our own generation." George W. Curtis of *Harper's Weekly* spoke on "Political Infidelity" some fifty times during the 1864–1865 lecture season, telling his listeners: "we are mad if the blood of the war has not anointed our eyes to see that all reconstruction is vain that leaves any question too brittle to handle. Whatever in this country, in its normal condition of peace, is too delicate to discuss is too dangerous to tolerate. Any system, any policy, any institution which may not be debated will overthrow us, if we do not overthrow it." [13]

It was in this ambience that Godkin cast about for a venture suitable to his abilities and ambitions. He wrote staunch pro-Northern letters to the English press, and toward the end of the war did some work for the New York *Times*. Olmsted tried to interest him in a joint ranching venture in California, but Godkin could not commit himself "unless for a very certain gain."

[12] Mill to Godkin, May 24, 1865, in Hugh S. R. Elliot, *The Letters of John Stuart Mill* (London, 1910), II, 35; Godkin to Olmsted, n.d., Godkin Mss; Ogden, ed., *Godkin*, II, 47.
[13] Ernest Samuels, *The Young Henry Adams* (Cambridge, Mass., 1948), pp. 145–146; Edward Cary, *George William Curtis* (Boston, 1894), p. 187.

With Olmsted's support he sought especially to establish "a weekly newspaper of a high order" along the lines of London's *Spectator* or *Saturday Review*. In the spring of 1865 Godkin came into contact with groups of wealthy men in Boston, New York, and Philadelphia who wished to see a new journal that would take up the cause of the emancipated slaves in the spirit of William Lloyd Garrison's *Liberator*. George L. Stearns of Boston, Richard P. Hallowell of Philadelphia, and James M. McKim of New York were the prime movers in the project; behind them were Wendell Phillips and Garrison himself. Godkin was not their first choice to create the new magazine; they approached George W. Curtis and Whitelaw Reid before him. But in many ways he was ideal for their purposes. His journalistic skills were extensive and evident; he had been active in the abolitionist cause; he had the cachets of a background in English journalism and a solid grounding in English Liberalism.[14]

A capital of $100,000 was raised, and in July 1865 the New York *Nation* began its long career with Godkin as its first editor. The magazine's prospectus reveals Godkin's desire to emulate the dispassionate, literary tone of the great English journals and his backers' wish to further the cause of the freedmen. A stately dedication to "the discussion of the topics of the day, and, above all, of legal, economical, and constitutional questions, with greater accuracy and moderation than are now to be found in the daily press" coexisted with a pledge to "the earnest and persistent consideration of the laboring class at the South . . . with a view to the removal of all artificial distinctions between them and the rest of the population." [15]

[14] Ogden, ed., *Godkin*, I, 224, 229–230; Frank Luther Mott, *A History of American Magazines* (Cambridge, Mass., 1957), III (1865–1885), 331. Frank P. Stearns, *The Life and Public Services of George Luther Stearns* (Philadelphia, 1907), pp. 334–336, is an account of the *Nation's* founding highly critical of Godkin. See also James M. McPherson, *The Struggle for Equality* (Princeton, N.J., 1964), p. 322.

[15] Ogden, ed., *Godkin*, I, 236, 240; text of prospectus in Gustav Pollak, comp., *Fifty Years of American Idealism* (Boston, 1915), pp. 7–8.

At first the differing ambitions of Godkin and his backers did not conflict. They shared a melioristic purpose that was widespread among intellectuals in the immediate postwar years. George W. Curtis and Thomas Nast made *Harper's Weekly* a strong voice for the principles to which the *Nation* dedicated itself. In 1864 Godkin's close friend Norton became editor of the *North American Review,* and sought to create a magazine that would be "one of the means of developing the nation, of stimulating its better sense, of holding up to it its own ideal." [16]

The very name of the *Nation*—with connotations of force and vigor that the more flaccid term "Union" did not convey—emphasized the journal's initial commitment to a vigorous democratic nationalism. Its first pages celebrated the "triumph of American democracy," the resolution of "the great strife between the few and the many, between privilege and equality, between law and power, between opinion and the sword." The magazine proclaimed: "We see the principle of nationality under democratic forms asserting itself with a grandeur of military strength, a unity of political counsel, a dignity of moral power, before which the empire of Caesar, of Charlemagne, and of Napoleon dwindle into insignificance." Confidently it expected that the next quarter of a century would have "a wondrous story to tell" of moral and intellectual progress, progress spurred by "the rapid growth of the community in intelligence, experience and self-possession." [17]

The postwar mood of ebullient confidence survives in the first selection of *Problems of Modern Democracy,* "Aristocratic Opinions of Democracy." There Godkin celebrated the "force . . . originality . . . vigor and concentration" displayed by American democracy when it faced its great wartime test. He

---

[16] Mott, *American Magazines,* II (1850–1865), 246.

[17] *Nation,* 1 (1865): 5, 39; 7 (1868): 247. The contrast between the early and later *Nation* is laid out in some detail in Alan P. Grimes, *The Political Liberalism of the New York Nation, 1865–1932* (Chapel Hill, N.C., 1953), and Richard C. Sterne, "Political, Social and Literary Criticism in the New York *Nation*: 1865–1881; A Study in Change of Mood" (unpub. diss., Harvard University, 1957).

rejected aristocratic critiques of democratic manners and morality, and spoke of a national future of great material strength
"controlled and directed to a very high order of cultivation, both
intellectual and aesthetic, and perhaps richer, more varied, and
more original in many of its manifestations than any that has been
seen in modern times."

He was confident that men of his type had an important role to
play in the new society. In 1867 he wrote to his old journal, the
London *Daily News:* "I can honestly say that I am unable at this
moment to mention a single man who, being fortified by culture
or character for a political career, has been shut out from it by
popular dislike of his mental, or moral, or social excellences."
He found that "the value of knowledge in politics is every year
more highly estimated; and the deliverances of men of special
training in social and political questions have an influence which,
in my opinion, they have never before had." [18]

Godkin's early writing in the *Nation* exuded a vigorous
optimism. He championed congressional reconstruction; the
Republicans were "the party of good government, of virtue, of
knowledge, and understanding"; the Democrats represented "the
most ignorant and vicious elements in the community." It was
essential for Negroes to take an active role in postwar southern
society, and thus restore the South to a place in the life of the
nation at large: "The true way to prevent 'sectional feeling' and
'sectional agitation' is to abolish sectional institutions, to make
the bases of society and government the same in all parts of the
Union, in other words to render it thoroughly democratic." [19]

The precepts of democratic nationalism determined Godkin's
initial response to postwar northern society as well. He had a

[18] *Below,* pp. 65, 52; Ogden, ed., *Godkin,* I, 314–316, 319, 321–322. For similar
declarations by Godkin see his "The Democratic View of Democracy," *North American
Review,* 101 (1865): 103–133, and "The Tyranny of the Majority," *ibid.,* 104 (1867):
205–230.

[19] "Congressional Reconstruction," *Nation,* 4 (1867): 150; "Republican Aims," *ibid.,*
5 (1867): 354–356; "The Essence of the Reconstruction Question," *ibid.,* 1 (1865): 4.

quick sympathy for the trials and aspirations of laboring men, and found "very little in the present industrial *régime* to stimulate the intelligence, excite the ambition, and sweeten the toil of ordinary mortals." Unions and the movement for a national eight-hour law were unpleasant but inevitable forms of worker protest. Strikes were "as good a means as can at present be devised of fixing a rate of wages and the nature of all relations between employer and employed." Ultimately, he hoped, cooperatives and profit-sharing arrangements would replace the "régime of wages." [20]

4

But it is not this Godkin—optimistic, nationalistic, the socioeconomic reformer—that is remembered, or that dominates the pages of *Problems of Modern Democracy.* The book, and Godkin's primary impact on his time, rest on other grounds: a rigid classical Liberalism that was indifferent to or conservative on social and economic issues; a deep antagonism to the party system and the active State; and an increasingly alienated and despairing view of American society.

Why did Godkin in the last thirty years of the nineteenth century move so far from the spirit and the attitudes of the Civil War era? His reply would be that he did not move at all; that from a steady vantage point he observed a decline of national morality and purpose. But there is reason to believe that his work was as much the product of crises of professional role and personal consciousness as it was the objective report of a dispassionate observer.

Professional as well as ideological considerations influenced Godkin from the first days of his *Nation* editorship. Questions of

[20] Godkin, "The Labor Crisis," *North American Review*, 105 (1867); 177–213; "The Labor Crisis," *Nation*, 4 (1867): 334–336; "Co-Operation," *North American Review*, 106 (1868): 150–175.

editorial expediency (which could not be divorced, ultimately, from questions of editorial content) made heavy claims upon him. He worried about competition: from established journals such as the *Atlantic Monthly* and *Harper's*, and from the *Round Table*, which appeared in 1863 (and lasted until 1869) as a magazine aimed at the same audience Godkin sought to capture. It nettled him that the *Round Table* was not bound by the *Nation's* constricting ties to former abolitionists. "I am told," he reported to Norton, "they rely for success against us, on their freedom from any responsibility with regard to the Negro, and on being more 'sprightly.' " The *Nation*, he thought, devoted itself overmuch to the subject of the freedmen: "I receive every day, protests against it. You know our plan was not to *dose* the public with this."

He sought from the start to turn out a sprightly and attractive magazine. The *Nation's* second number "does not satisfy me; it is heavy." At the end of the first month of publication his judgment was that "the paper so far is rather heavy and didactic. I am doing everything I can think of to lighten it up." He considered engaging Harriet Beecher Stowe and James Russell Lowell to exclusive contracts in 1866, not so much for the virtue of their ideas as for the attraction of their names.

Inevitably his dissatisfaction focused on content as well as tone —"the general heaviness of writing, and the great preponderance of writers on 'reconstruction' and nothing else, is amazing." And inevitably his purposes clashed with the reforming intentions of his backers. "I do not care particularly about pleasing Stearns Hallowell & Company," he truculently declared, "but I do not want to have it said that I spent $100,000 trying to establish a paper and failed." He fretted over the danger of the *Nation* "degenerating into a mere canting organ of the 'radical wing,' " and argued that too close identification with a factional or partisan cause was bad journalism as well as bad policy. By the end of 1865 it was a matter of pride to him that "Radicals, conservatives, free traders, protectionists, infidels and evangelists" alike had reason "for finding fault with us."

Nuances of social and personal difference widened the gap between Godkin and many of his initial supporters. He pitched his appeal to the highest level of educated Americans rather than to the more heterogeneous lot that was concerned with the freedman. He boasted to Norton: "the cultivated classes we have with us; but the class next below, do not quite know what to make of us, and are suspicious or hostile." The gaucherie of his supporters sometimes annoyed him; he described one of the magazine's trustees as "very rich, *good*, a rigid blue Presbyterian, wife ditto—Sabbatarians, great haters of 'Romanists' . . . and very narrow in every way." [21]

Most of all, differences developed over policy. The tariff was one source of dissension. Godkin's Boston supporters were inclined to tariff reduction; the Philadelphians were staunch protectionists. He steered a middle course for a while, but his predilections were with the Bostonians, and soon the *Nation's* pages reflected his views.

The touchstone of Godkin's estrangement from many of his original supporters was the question of postwar Negro rights. He quickly qualified his support of freedman voting by proposing an educational test for the suffrage. Former abolitionists themselves were sharply divided over what policy to adopt. William Lloyd Garrison inclined to the view that the movement's raison d'être had been satisfied by the end of slavery and the defeat of the Confederacy. But a faction led by Wendell Phillips (and including *Nation* investors Stearns and Hallowell) wanted to develop the social and political implications of emancipation. Godkin conferred at length with Garrison, and reached agreement "as to . . . the necessity for *moderation*, accuracy, and strict adherence to the truth." He became embroiled in a fierce dispute with Stearns (and, behind Stearns, Wendell Phillips). In May 1866 the Stearns group withdrew its capital from the *Nation*, and the magazine was reorganized with Godkin as its proprietor

[21] The quotations are from Godkin's letters to Norton, July–December 1865, Godkin Mss.

as well as its editor. Now he was free to turn it away from the special concerns of its original supporters and take up in its pages public matters that had more significance for him. By 1870 he was denying to James Miller McKim that "the Nation was started as a 'freedmen's paper,'" and by 1880 he was writing sympathetically of "The White Side of the Southern Question" and describing the South as "the region which is most seriously threatened by barbarism." [22]

As Godkin devoted himself to a new and independent editorial stance, he found the day-to-day tasks of the editor-proprietor to be an increasing burden. Nor did the *Nation* prosper in the 1870's; it did not immediately find an audience attuned to its new course. Norton told James Russell Lowell at the end of the decade that Godkin still was "tried by the condition of the 'Nation'; the subscription list declines, and the paper is still dependent on him so exclusively that he can get no release from constant work."

In 1881 Godkin resolved these problems of finance and management, and at the same time gained access to a wider audience. The *Nation* became the weekly (and primarily literary) edition of the New York *Evening Post*. Godkin relinquished its editorship to Wendell Phillips Garrison, and with Henry White joined the *Evening Post* as an associate editor. In 1883 he replaced Carl Schurz as editor-in-chief, and held that position until his retirement in 1900.[23]

The new arrangement formalized Godkin's departure from the *Nation's* original aims. The man whose money made it possible was Henry Villard, who had taken a very similar ideological

---

[22] McPherson, *Struggle for Equality*, pp. 324–326; Godkin to Norton, Oct. 19, 1865, Godkin Mss; Stearns, *George Luther Stearns*, pp. 335–336; Ogden, ed., *Godkin*, I, 246–247; Godkin to McKim, Nov. 22, 1870, Godkin Mss; *Nation*, 31 (1880): 126–127; "The Role of the Universities," in Godkin, *Reflections and Comments*, pp. 180–181. See also "The South after the War," in *ibid.*, pp.173–191, and Godkin, "The Republican Party and the Negro," *Forum*, 7 (1889): 246–257.

[23] Allan Nevins, *The Evening Post* (New York, 1922), pp. 438f; Norton to Lowell, Feb. 22, 1879, in Norton and Howe, eds., *Letters of Charles Eliot Norton*, II, 86.

journey. Villard had shared the postwar belief in beneficent social control. He played a central part in the creation of the American Social Science Association, which was organized in 1869 to link the scientific study of society to social and political reform. But by 1881 the onetime journalist Villard was in midstream of a new career: he was president and controlling stockholder of the Northern Pacific Railroad. Now he interested himself more in the purification of politics than in its broader application to social problems. Godkin gave him in the *Evening Post* an editorial line that applied the fervor of the Civil War era to the imperfections of a democratic politics and culture rather than to the plight of Negroes and workers, or the rapacity of enterprise.

Godkin nevertheless continued to face special professional difficulties as a journalist. He brought to his career a strong sense of the social importance of the editor's role. He thought that the journalist, as provider of news and as social critic, should be a student of history, of political science, of political economy— should have talents and training commensurate with the complexity and importance of his calling. He confessed that he "never like Horace Greeley . . . and from my point of view thought his equipment for journalism wretched." But he yearned to wield an influence comparable to that time "when no one knew where the Republican party stood or ought to stand without hearing from the New York *Tribune*." This was not to be. His most heartfelt crusades—against the spoils system, against the protective tariff, against imperialism—did not catch the public imagination. As James Bryce observed, Godkin unlike Greeley was "never . . . the exponent of any widespread sentiment or potent movement, but was frequently in opposition to the feeling for the moment dominant." [24]

[24] Charles F. Wingate, comp., *Views and Interviews on Journalism* (New York, 1875), pp. 208–215; Godkin to William Dean Howells, Nov. 29, 1899, Godkin Mss; "The Influence of the Press," *Nation*, 65 (1897): 410–411; Bryce, *Studies in Contemporary Biography*, p. 366.

Godkin was keenly aware of the limit imposed upon his journalistic influence; and it became an important part of his critique
of contemporary American life. He frequently complained of
"the gradual exclusion from public life of intelligent men of
every calling"—particularly of the press. In 1897 he concluded:
"the role of the press in political discussion in America has so
greatly diminished that, in some localities, the newspapers have
ceased to have any part in it at all. What the press says does not
count with political men as it used to count in the anti-slavery
days." [25]

The tone and style of his writing reflected his professional
estrangement. His gentle personal manner coexisted with a growing journalistic asperity. William James once lightly asked
Godkin: "Who would suppose so much public ferocity to cover
so much private sweetness?" and spoke of his "curious blending
of earnestness and humor, pugnacity and affectionateness." He
let the death of his onetime friend Francis A. Walker go un-
noticed in the *Nation* because of a difference of opinion over
currency policy. To his easy and vigorous style he added a growing inventiveness in the tools of invective: the ironic use of
capitalization and quotation marks, the deadly parallel columns
of Blaine quotations in the *Evening Post* during the election of
1884.[26]

Godkin's special perspective on late nineteenth century
America was shaped, finally, by intensely personal considerations. In the 1870's a series of domestic tragedies rent his sense
of achievement and optimism. A daughter died in 1873; his ele-
gant and beautiful wife died too, in 1875. In syntax which

---

[25] "One Law of Politics," *Nation*, 51 (1890): 222; "The Influence of the Press," *ibid.*,
65 (1897): 410–411. Godkin has a Lippmannesque essay on "The Growth and Expression of Public Opinion" in *Unforeseen Tendencies of Democracy*, pp. 183–225.

[26] James to Godkin, Aug. 29, 1901, in James, ed., *Letters of William James*, II, 161;
Rhodes, *Historical Essays*, p. 284; Harry T. Peck, "Mr. Godkin and His Book," *Bookman*,
2 (1896): 480–488; Nevins, *Evening Post*, pp. 460–463; Joseph B. Bishop, *Notes and
Anecdotes of Many Years* (New York, 1925), p. 95.

betrayed his tortured feelings he wrote to Charles Eliot Norton:
"To have at forty-five, in a country which in many essential
things, in spite of all the happiness I have had in it, is a foreign
one, neither home nor family after twenty years' residence, I
feel as an almost fatal blow." [27]

He left New York with his son and took up residence in Cambridge, Massachusetts, for several years, all the while editing the
Nation. During this self-induced exile he came very close to
Charles Eliot Norton. He absorbed deeply the bittersweet sense
of good times past, of virtue gone, of prospects ended, that so
characterized Brahmins of Norton's and James Russell Lowell's
type in the postwar years. Though he returned to New York,
and married again in 1884, he never recovered the élan of his
earlier years.

5

From this professional and personal context Godkin viewed
and commented on the society around him. *Problems of Modern
Democracy* is representative of the body of his work during the
last three decades of the nineteenth century. There is, throughout,
the play of a central tension: between his deep theoretical commitment to freedom, progress, and democracy, and assailing
doubts nurtured by his own disappointments.

The pro-democratic note of "Aristocratic Opinions of
Democracy" persists in later pieces: "Popular Government"
(1886), "The Real Problems of Democracy" (1896). He
staunchly rejected the ideological repudiation of democracy by
the English critics Sir Henry Maine and W. E. H. Lecky. While
he doubted the ability of government to help the unfit escape
"from the battle with the fittest," he could not help but believe
that "any abandonment of the effort to protract their existence

[27] Ogden, ed., *Godkin*, II, 116.

and make it more tolerable would mean the stoppage of civilization itself." [28]

The space that he devotes to these mild refutations suggests their importance to him even in the disillusioned later years of his life. His early ideals never left him; but they remained primarily as evocative reminders of what might have been, and of how far the American reality of his time had fallen short of the democratic ideal. The general trend of *Problems of Modern Democracy,* and even more the bulk of his editorial writing, is clear: away from expectation, toward disillusion and despair.

The most commanding facts of American life in the late nineteenth century were the fundamental changes wrought by industrialization on America's class and social structures. But these developments did not deeply engage Godkin's intelligence or his imagination. The social and economic essays of *Problems of Modern Democracy* are the most casual and unconvincing in the book.

"Idleness and Immorality" and "The Expenditure of Rich Men" are in no sense critiques of wealth *per se.* Rather, they are contrived appeals to the wealthy to take the role of national leadership to which their riches entitle them—and appeals to the society at large to let these natural leaders play the role that is theirs by right. For all his yearning for an older and simpler society, Godkin did not see industrial capitalism as a malign social force. That Americans devoted themselves after the Civil War "to the business of money-making" instead of to the ambitions of radical reformers such as Wendell Phillips had "something very fine" about it. He commented on the rise of "commercial immorality" as early as 1868, but ascribed it to "the decline of habit as a social force, before mental and moral culture has reached a sufficiently advanced stage to take its place." Much

[28] *Below,* p. 86. See also Harold W. Stoke, "Edwin Lawrence Godkin, Defender of Democracy," *South Atlantic Quarterly,* 30 (1931): 339–348.

more disturbing was the declining influence of the traditional votaries of culture. The Beecher-Tilton scandal of 1874 moved him to some widely noted comments on America's "Chromo-Civilization," which he found to be "a kind of mental and moral chaos, in which many of the fundamental rules of living . . . seem in imminent risk of disappearing totally." [29]

When Godkin turned his attention to the economic impact of industrialization, it was again with a sense of tradition outraged. His was the vantage point of a classic Liberalism. He argues in "The Economic Man" that the rules governing the economy are rigid, overwhelming, fixed with all the certainty of natural laws. In this immutability he found a refuge from which to view—and to judge—the political economy of his time. The scientific truth of "Economic Man" led inexorably to the immorality of the active State. Proposals for railroad regulation in the 1870's led him to insist that "the railroad question . . . is not simply a question of dollars and cents. It is a question of morality in its highest and most important phases." Coxeyites demonstrating for public works employment in the nineties were only what might be expected of a political environment that encouraged the protective tariff.[30]

Godkin's onetime sympathy for labor was a conspicuous victim of his commitment to the iron laws of economic behavior: "the labor problem remains very much what it has been since agriculture was substituted for hunting and fishing—a problem which, in the main, every man must solve for himself." The "discontent of the poor" was in fact "discontent with the provision the earth makes for her children." "Who Will Pay the Bills of Socialism?"

---

[29] "A Retrospect," *Nation*, 51 (1890): 4–5; Godkin, "Commercial Immorality and Political Corruption," *North American Review*, 107 (1868): 252–253; "Chromo-Civilization," *Nation*, 19 (1874): 201 (reprinted in *Reflections and Comments*, pp. 192–205). See also the discussion by Edward C. Kirkland, "The Moralist Looks at the Businessman," *Business in the Gilded Age* (Madison, Wis., 1952), pp. 21–40.

[30] "The Latest Device for Fixing Rates of Transportation," *Nation*, 17 (1873): 36–37; "The Coxey 'Problem,'" *ibid.*, 58 (1894): 358.

argues that the laborer "gets now all there is for him," and chillingly enslaves him to the precepts of the Dismal Science: "If wheat costs only ten cents a bushel, the man who has not and cannot get the ten cents is clearly a bit of surplus population." The railroads contesting Debs's American Railway Union in 1894 were "really struggling for civilization against large bands of barbarous men, into whose hands our legislators and officials are all the while trying to deliver us." [31]

Godkin saw in the play of parties, elections, and issues the most profound American failure. In 1870, discussing "The Prospects of the Political Art," he worried about the lag of government behind the rest of the culture; and at the very end of his career he observed: "the progress of the nation in all the arts, except that of government, in science, in literature, in commerce, in invention, is something unprecedented . . . How it is that this splendid progress does not drag on politics with it I do not profess to know." [32] The specifics of this failure constituted the great topic of his days, and are the central concern of *Problems of Modern Democracy*.

His highest postwar expectations were for the polity; and nowhere were his expectations more rudely dashed. In 1867 Godkin thought that the political era just ending "has been such as to bring the moral qualities of public men into very high esteem, and make the intellectual ones seem of very little account." But there was no longer a "strong tendency towards moral legislation"; instead, the time had come for the play of superior, trained intelligence in the political arena. Government now was to "per-

---

[31] *Below*, p. 179; Godkin, "Social Classes in the Republic," *Atlantic Monthly*, 78 (1896): 728; *below*, pp. 234, 242; "The Congressional Remedy for Railroad Strikes," *Nation*, 60 (1895): 120–121. For a contemporary criticism of the rigidity of Godkin's economic doctrines, see Henry S. Green, "Mr. Godkin and the New Political Economy," *Arena*, 20 (1898): 27–38.

[32] Godkin, "The Prospects of the Political Art," *North American Review*, 110 (1870): 404; Bryce, *Historical Essays*, p. 296.

form that nice adjustment and readjustment of men's legal relations which the peculiar nature of modern civilization constantly
calls for"; it was to "place man's relations to society where they
never yet have been placed, under the control of trained human
reason." [33]

In the event the politics of the late nineteenth century turned
out to embody neither the informed moral fervor of the anti-
slavery crusade nor the informed expertise of his imaginings.
Godkin responded with a detailed, passionate critique of the
political order that had so badly failed him. The venture of
politics became the subject of a commentary that had all the
trappings of objective and disinterested consideration, but was in
fact an extension of his own problems of social role and social
adaptation. The political development of the time served him like
the accumulated notebooks of a novelist: as the raw material out
of which he fashioned a personal testament.

Two principles governed Godkin's political responses. The
first of these was his insistence on judging political issues and per-
formances by a yardstick of moral rather than utilitarian standards. Once he had wanted politics to eschew morality for
expertise—the expertise of Godkin and his circle. When the
political system failed to respond he fell back on morality and
character as standards of judgment—or, better, of censure. There
was something compulsive in his emphasis on these guidelines.
Henry Adams recalled "the elevated plateau of the New Jerusalem occupied by Godkin and the *Nation*," and Charles Dudley
Warner labeled his magazine "The Weekly Day of Judgment." [34]
Politics was for Godkin not so much an instrument for accom-
plishing the business of society as a stage on which was enacted
an unending morality play.

To his reliance on moral standards he joined a rigid version of

---

[33] "The Political Value of Good Intentions," *Nation*, 5 (1867): 91–93; "Prospects of
Political Art," pp. 415–417.
[34] Henry Adams, *The Education of Henry Adams* (Boston, 1918), p. 244.

English Liberal laissez-faire. Again, by insisting that the State could not be a constructive force he rejected his immediate political past. These vantage points of political observation— morality and laissez-faire—often conflicted with each other as well; and later critics have made much of the inconsistencies that mar his work.[35] But these are of minor significance when his standards of political judgment are viewed as cathartic rather than descriptive devices.

Godkin found in party politics abundant instances of morality betrayed and intelligence ignored. He feared in 1868 that "the tendency to put party claims about everything else is rapidly increasing," at a time "when we are adding to our voting population a vast body of persons on whom the great laws of morality sit only very lightly, and for whom party discipline has . . . the attraction it has everywhere and always for those who have little other discipline to guide them." His own identification with the Republican party steadily weakened. He participated in the Liberal Republican movement of the early 1870's, but his dislike of Greeley prevented him from supporting the party's candidate in 1872. He explained to Carl Schurz: "What I seek, is not a sham break up of parties, such as the Greeley movement promises, but a real break up, involving something more than the construction of a new party machine, out of the pieces of the old ones." [36]

He found what he was looking for in the Mugwump movement: the bolt of genteel Republicans from Blaine to Cleveland in 1884. Cleveland's campaign seemed to meet his standard of a presidential candidacy committed to "the idea that public servants must be competent, honest, and faithful business men, and must stand for the national morality in its highest aspects." And by nominating Blaine, the ultimate politico, the Republican Party deserted its prime constituency, that portion of the population

[35] See especially Armstrong, *Godkin and Foreign Policy.*
[36] "The Result of the Trial," *Nation,* 6 (1868): 405; Godkin to Schurz, June 28, 1872 (draft), Godkin Mss.

"which possesses the larger share of the intelligence, public spirit, thrift, industry, foresight, and accumulated property of the country." [37]

Godkin of course regarded the Bryan campaign of 1896 with horror and repugnance. But it was a measure of his increasing isolation from the political mainstream that he looked on McKinley with an almost equal distaste. The election of 1896 had for him little of the resonance of the contest of 1884, for between Bryan's free silver and McKinley's high tariff he saw little to choose.[38]

The bulk of Godkin's political writing dealt with issues, not personalities. Themes such as municipal reform, civil service reform, tariff reduction, the gold standard, and anti-imperialism engaged most of his attention: but as questions of political morality more than as devices of public policy.

The most palpable measure of the nation's fall from grace was the city around him—the theme of his essay "Criminal Politics." Men of education and responsibility once held the principal offices in New York, and set the tone of its political life. But universal suffrage and the influx of immigrants had changed the city's political face. In the wake of Tweed he observed: "We must openly acknowledge that a very large proportion of our voters are ignorant and grossly corrupt persons, to whom the rule of a Boss is entirely acceptable, and who are led into setting it up both by their inability to comprehend any other, and by their overpowering anxiety about their daily bread." Those who had "any really lawful occupation outside politics, or any genuine connection with the respectable business or social world" could find no place in the new political order.[39]

---

[37] "The Press and the Nominations," *Nation*, 38 (1884): 480; "What is 'The Republican Party'?", *ibid.*, 39 (1884): 368–369.

[38] "The Political Situation in 1896," *below*, pp. 249–274; Armstrong, *Godkin and Foreign Policy*, pp. 32–33.

[39] Godkin, "A Key to Municipal Reform," *North American Review*, 151 (1890): 430–431; "The Government of Great Cities," *Nation*, 3 (1866): 312–313; *ibid.*, 21 (1875): 289; *below*, p. 140.

He devoted himself more to describing the evil than to the frustrating process of curing it. Thus he could dissect Tammany with a cold precision, as he does in *Problems of Modern Democracy*. Astutely he questioned whether reform would come from charter revision, Committees of 100, or respectable mayors such as Seth Low: "What Tammany offers to the ignorant and poor is always more palpable and succulent than enlightenment, or free reading rooms, or cheap coffee." But when he came to alternatives, his insight failed. Educated respectables were the proper governors of the city, but he could propose no more precise method of electing them than a "union among the honest, industrious, and intelligent." His model of governance was the hardly popular—or politically feasible—one of the business corporation. "The objects of a municipal corporation," he observed, "are nearly as definable as those of a railroad company. They consist simply in supplying the inhabitants of a certain locality with certain conditions of physical health and comfort, plus the education of their children. The work is paid for by an annual subscription, and the executive officers are elected by a general vote." [40]

The first national postwar issue to engage Godkin's attention was civil service reform. He committed the *Nation* to the cause in its earliest days, when the issue "was, to most people, a European whimsey." He later recalled: "The newspapers all began to look about for a cause. The *Nation* was, of course, in as much need of a cause as any of them, and in thinking over what the United States seemed to need most in this new emergency, I bethought myself of a reform in the civil service." [41]

But the attractions of civil service reform went beyond its English origins or its journalistic usages. More than any other issue of the time, it embodied Godkin's belief in what he called

[40] *Below*, pp. 133–146; "The Future of Tammany," *Nation*, 59 (1894): 356–357; *below*, p. 150. See also Godkin's essay "Peculiarities of American Municipal Government" in *Unforeseen Tendencies of Democracy*, pp. 145–182.
[41] Ogden, ed., *Godkin*, II, 40.

"The Duty of Educated Men in a Democracy." Civil service reform was the means by which the educated would be restored to their rightful place in the political order, and the spoils system of professional politicians and professional politics overthrown. He expected that such government would mean "the disappearance from legislation of nearly all acts and resolutions which are passed for what is called 'politics'; that is, for the purpose of pleasing certain bodies of voters, without any reference to their real value as contributions to the work of government." [42]

The evolution of late nineteenth century American politics deepened Godkin's sense of the need for government by an educated elite. Civil service reform at first was an institutional adjustment that would assure the educated a place in politics. Toward the century's end it became a defensive, almost a last-ditch device to preserve "our form of government, and our social organization intact." In 1894 Godkin considered "in what a condition of mental flux we are just now upon nearly everything that holds civilized man together—our political economy and morality and religion,—what a very large population we have which is American only in name, what a very large body of Americans we have who care nothing about either law or political purity as long as it stands in the way of their getting rich." He concluded that "we cannot be in too great haste to give permanence, and the efficiency which comes with permanence, to the machinery of government." [43]

Even more passionate—and hence more suggestive—was Godkin's belief in the iniquity of the protective tariff. His commitment to free trade had deep roots in his English Liberal origins, and he was close to informed critics of protection such as David Ames Wells and Edward Atkinson. But he did not dwell

[42] *Below*, p. 200.
[43] Ogden, ed., *Godkin*, II, 184–185. See also Godkin, "Public Opinion and the Civil Service," *Forum*, 8 (1889): 237–247, and "The Danger of an Office-Holding Aristocracy," *Century*, 24 (1882): 287–292.

on the tariff's deleterious economic effects. Rather, the issue had
for him a fundamental moral significance reminiscent of nothing
so much as the anti-gold zealotry of the advocates of free silver.
Godkin worried about "not the tariff as an economic agency" but
"the venality in politics which the tariff steadily promotes." He
found in protection the source of the unwholesome tone of the
entire political—indeed, the social—order. As he put it in "Some
Political and Social Aspects of the Tariff": "Of all the novelties
which the last twenty-five years have introduced into American
politics and society, decidedly the most dangerous is the practice
of telling large bodies of ignorant and excitable voters at every
election that their daily bread depends not on their own capacity
or industry or ingenuity of their employers, but on the good-will
of the Administration. In other words, the 'tariff issue' . . . is an
issue filled with the seeds of social trouble and perplexity."[44]

Ultimately, the tariff stood for the loss of those qualities in
American life that once had drawn him and won his allegiance.
The United States had been the "first field ever offered for seeing
what the freedom of the individual could accomplish . . . That
opportunity has, under the protective system, been temporarily
allowed to slip away. The old European path has been entered
on."[45] Protection thus joined the political spoils system as a
measure of the nation's fall from the grace of his youth.

The issue of the currency had a meaning for Godkin closely
analogous to that of the tariff. The superior morality of a gold-
based monetary system always was an article of his political faith.
The Greenback movement of the 1870's and the silverite movement of the 1890's heightened his concern for the sanctity of
fiscal values, but he did not view the matter as one appropriate
for public consideration. That the monetary standard should be
"in politics" at all, and not in the hands of the apolitical experts

---

[44] "The Greatest Political Necessity," *Nation*, 55 (1892): 252; *below*, p. 117.

[45] *Below*, p. 118. See also Godkin, "Money Interests in Political Affairs," *Forum*, 10 (1890): 1–10.

to whom it belonged, was an intolerable state of affairs. Supporters of the gold standard really sought "the absolute abandonment of the currency question as a political issue." [46] For—again
—the issue had meaning for him insofar as it was a moral rather
than a political question.

American imperialism was the last national issue to engage
Godkin's attention in a large way; and in it his private anxieties
found their greatest public confirmation. His concern did not
stem from policy specifics: from considerations of strategy or
realpolitik, or the well-being of the native peoples involved.
Rather, the issue served him as the final, the most dramatic cor-
roboration of his growing fear for the future of the Republic, and
of democracy itself.

He read inner, implicit, suggestive meanings into the whole
sweep of American expansion through the nineties. The annexa-
tion of Hawaii, he insisted, must be viewed in terms of its effect
"on our domestic institutions." The Cleveland administration's
handling of the Venezuela crisis of 1895 was a "betrayal of the
nation," a "mad appeal to the basest passions of the mob."
Dewey's victory at Manila was "A Great Moral Catastrophe,"
the "shameless abandonment of the noble faith under which we
have lived for a century." The victory over Spain "seals the fate
of the American Republic." By his acquiescence in an overseas
empire "McKinley has excited my hatred and contempt more
than any man I have ever known." The "fine frenzy" of imperialism made the United States "the great failure of modern
civilization." [47]

Godkin's rhetoric is more revealing of the man than of the

---

[46] Godkin, "The Debtor Class," in *Reflections and Comments*, pp. 227–234; W. A.
Russ, Jr., "Godkin Looks at Western Agrarianism," *Journal of Agricultural History*, 19
(1945): 233–242; "Politics and Currency," *Nation*, 55 (1892): 405–406; *below*, p. 260.

[47] "Naval Politics," *Nation*, 56 (1893): 173–174; Armstrong, *Godkin and Foreign
Policy*, p. 182; "A Great Moral Catastrophe," *Nation*, 68 (1899): 158–159; Godkin to
F. Sheldon, July 5, 1898, and to Wendell P. Garrison, Sept. 28, 1900, Godkin Mss;
"Americanism," *Nation*, 56 (1893): 136–137.

issue. Imperialism came in the last years of his life, and it was easy for him to respond with the imagery of apocalypse, to tell Norton: "We all expected too much of the human race. What stuff we used to talk." There was a special bite, too, in the fact that a new generation of journalists (Hearst, Pulitzer) and educated politicians (Lodge, Roosevelt) came into their own on the wings of imperialism and war. Here, finally, was the change in the complexion of American politics that Godkin for so long had sought; but through such an alien issue, and by such alien men! Bitterly he predicted: "the government will shortly undergo great changes which will be presided over, not by men of light and learning, but by capitalists and adroit politicians . . . the military spirit has taken possession of the masses, to whom power has passed."[48]

6

There were other, more personal measures of Godkin's deepened alienation from American life by the century's end. In 1889 he returned to England after an absence of almost forty years. He received a welcome commensurate with his stature as a journalist and social commentator. The society from which he had fled years before now charmed and attracted him. He wrote home to his wife: "The people here are so polite, and there are so many well dressed, educated men, and life is so well ordered, I am thinking I am not worth a cent as a 'good American.' *This is confidential.*" Soon it was not confidential: he was telling his readers that English mores, English politics, English society were superior to those of his adopted country. He frequently returned to England in the nineties, and his preference for the older country increased. On his departure in November 1897, in the wake of

---

[48] Godkin to Norton, Nov. 29, 1898, quoted in Kirkland, *Business in the Gilded Age*, p. 40; Ogden, ed., *Godkin*, II, 242–243. He was indignant that Hearst, "a blackguard boy with several millions of dollars at his disposal, has more influence on the use a great nation may make of its credit, of its army and navy, of its name and traditions, than all the statesmen and philosophers and professors in the country." "The New Political Force," *Nation*, 66 (1898): 336–337.

Tammany's return to municipal power, he told a friend: "I have seen my last Mayoral election and wish them God-speed. I am tired of having to be continually hopeful; what I long for now is a little comfortable private gloom in despair. It seems in America as if man was made for government, not government for man." [49]

If the turn of the century did not in fact see the end of the Republic, it marked the termination of Godkin's career. A cerebral hemorrhage in September 1899 forced him to resign the editorship of the *Evening Post* by the end of the year. He took up residence in England, and thus formalized his detachment from his adopted land. He had come to the United States fifty years before "with high and fine ideals about America." But "they are now all shattered, and I have apparently to look elsewhere to keep even moderate hopes about the human race alive." [50] On May 21, 1902, Godkin died at his Devonshire home, and was buried in a nearby churchyard. The *Nation* elegiacally took note of his final state:

> He grew old in an age he condemned,
> Felt the dissolving throes
> Of a social order he loved,
> And, like the Theban seer,
> Died in his enemies' day.[51]

There was a widespread sense that with Godkin's death a generation—or a certain part of it—had lost its truest voice. Admirers set themselves to perpetuate his memory. William James and the Boston banker Henry Lee Higginson took the lead in establishing the fund that endowed the Godkin Lectures at Harvard. In 1904 James Bryce gave the first of that distinguished series of disquisitions on the form and art of government.

But younger men of affairs—men who came into their own with the new century—were not impressed by Godkin. Lincoln

---

[49] Ogden, ed., *Godkin*, II, 143; "Politics and Society in England," *Nation*, 57 (1893): 223–224; Ogden, ed., *Godkin*, II, 25.

[50] Ogden, ed., *Godkin*, II, 237.

[51] *Nation*, 61 (1902): 105.

Steffens was a staffer on the *Evening Post* in the early nineties, and found his editor's writing "shallow; clever, forceful, ripping, but personal and not very thoughtful." Theodore Roosevelt, put off by Godkin's Mugwumpery and by his anti-imperialism, considered him "maliciously untruthful and . . . utterly untrustworthy." [52]

It is striking that Godkin's social vision—so deeply personal, in many ways so alien, so suddenly out of date—should have carried such weight with what he called "the busy, active, intelligent portion of the community." (William James told him: "You have the most curious way of always being *right*"; William Dean Howells spoke of Godkin's *Nation* as "the exponent of those who wished our political life to throw off its unprincipled boyishness, and assume the responsibilities and ideals of maturity.")[53]

The common grievance—for it was ultimately this—that united Godkin and his Mugwump readers was political. By dwelling on the problems of modern democracy, he reminded his audience that they were the observers—and the victims—of a profound transformation in the American political institution. Frequently he attempted to sum up that transformation: "No change has been so marked as the transfer to wealth of the political and social influence which was formerly shared, if not absorbed, by literary, oratorical, or professional distinction"; "in nothing do the Northern states of today differ more from the Northern states of 1860 than in this great supremacy in politics of purely material interests." [54] But the object of his critique was not the industrial capitalism that he saw to be the motive force behind the change. Rather, he focused his attention on the new

---

[52] James, ed., *Letters of William James*, II, 181–182; Lincoln Steffens, *Autobiography* (New York, 1931), pp. 179–180; Elting E. Morison, ed., *The Letters of Theodore Roosevelt* (Cambridge, Mass., 1951), II, 1101.

[53] *Unforeseen Tendencies of Democracy*, p. 72; James to Godkin, April 15, 1889, in James, ed., *Letters of William James*, II, 284; Howells, "A Great New York Journalist," *North American Review*, 185 (1907): 45.

[54] "A Restrospect," *Nation*, 51 (1890): 5.

political order that had come into being—one that he found to be uniquely gross, incompetent, irrelevant, and corrupt. His bêtes noires were Ben Butler and boss Tweed, Blaine and Hill, Bryan and McKinley, not Carnegie and Rockefeller. Thus he spoke for a generation that was, above all, harassed by a political revolution.

By social origins or upbringing, most of all by the shared experience of antislavery and the Civil War, Godkin and his audience had been conditioned to look on politics as a moralistic, purposive, ideological social process. It was because of this view of the nature of politics that they strove so mightily to find in civil service reform, free trade, gold monometallism, and anti-imperialism something of the moral, ideological quality of the antislavery movement. "All over the nation," he told Moorfield Storey in 1891, "there are tens of thousands waiting as the anti-slavery men waited for some organization to deliver them." William James, praising Godkin for his fight against imperialism, declared: "I swear it brings back the days of '61 again." [55]

Godkin appealed powerfully not only to his audience's desire for a politics of purpose, but also to their more particular (and not disinterested) desire for a politics of educated intelligence. "The trained men, other things being equal," Godkin declared, "are pretty sure in the long run to be the masters of the world." The theme is conspicuous in several of the essays in *Problems of Modern Democracy:* "The Expenditure of Rich Men," "The Duty of Educated Men in a Democracy," "Idleness and Immorality." He spoke for his audience as well as himself when he declared: "Official life, as our Government is now organized, has no field for a really high ambition," or when he observed: "With matters of a quasi-scientific kind, like the tariff . . . or the currency, on which the opinions of theorists are extremely important and 'practical men' very likely to be wrong, this habit of

[55] Godkin to Storey, May 23, 1891, Godkin Mss; James to Godkin, Dec. 24, 1895, in James, ed., *Letters of William James,* II, 28–29.

excluding science from all say in the political arena, is undoubtedly very unfortunate." [56]

But in the event the political culture of the late nineteenth
century served very different social ends, and called for the
services of very different social types. The deep national weari-
ness at the end of the Civil War and headlong industrial capitalism together created a new political style: emotive more than
purposive; organizational and associational rather than ideological. The parties came to serve not as devices for attaining
ideological goals, but rather as broad voluntaristic bodies commanding men's loyalties and affording them a form of organizational identification. Political leaders such as Blaine, Conkling,
Logan, Sherman, Tilden—even Cleveland—were most concerned with the development of structures of party organization.
Ideological objectives had a subordinate place in their scale of
political values. Voters defined their party loyalties on regional
or ethnic grounds, and remained unresponsive to the appeals of
more purposeful political groups such as the Greenbackers, the
Prohibitionists, or the Liberal Republicans.

Godkin and his Mugwump readers could not adapt to this
public environment. They became irate spectators of a political
process whose style and function were alien to them. Their
relationship to American politics was intellectual and ideological,
and they had little in common with the rude—if skilled—
technicians who dominated the late nineteenth century American
political scene.

Isolation from public power defined the political attitudes of
the Mugwumps. It is the source of the viewpoint, and the passion,
of *Problems of Modern Democracy*. A sympathetic reviewer of
the book caught its author's animus: "Under other conditions
than those which have existed for a generation, Mr. Godkin
would have perhaps been conspicuously engaged in public life."

[56] Godkin, "Culture and War," in *Reflections and Comments*, p. 18; *below*, pp. 198, 92–93.

But since the Civil War, "the gulf between politics . . . and the moral and intellectual forces which determine the development of the country has deepened and widened."[57]

Godkin's situation sometimes made him captious and narrow, but *Problems of Modern Democracy* is considerably more than a record of social displacement. Its discussions of the frontier's effect on American life and the nature of Tammany Hall are first-rate pieces of social analysis.[58] As much as anyone, Godkin established a tradition of sustained, ironic, vigorous criticism of American public life that lived on in the *Nation*, and indeed in modern American liberalism. His insistence on honesty and expertise in government took on added meaning as the State became more complex and socially important. And most of all, his belief that the educated citizen had a role to play in the political process bore fruit in the twentieth century. Gradually there came a restoration of the interplay between intellectuals' ideas and politicians' techniques that was so tragically lost in the decades after the Civil War.

[57] "Mr. Godkin's Political Writings," *Atlantic Monthly*, 79 (1897): 121.
[58] *Below*, 26–57, 133–146.

A NOTE ON THE TEXT

The text has been reproduced photographically from the edition published in 1896 by Charles Scribner's Sons. The starred footnotes are Godkin's; the editor's notes, which follow the text, are numbered consecutively chapter by chapter.

PROBLEMS OF MODERN DEMOCRACY

ARISTOCRATIC OPINIONS OF DEMOCRACY[1]

THE controversy between the supporters of oligarchy and those of democracy, which has raged with greater or less heat ever since the middle of the last century, has drawn fresh vigor from the spectacle of the American war. Both sides have found in this great struggle, not only, to use the pulpit phrase, " an occasion to improve," but an endless supply of illustrations for the enforcement or elevation of their respective theories. The one sees, both in the causes of the struggle and in the manner in which it has been conducted, a series of conclusive proofs of the failure of popular government; the other finds in the incidents of each hour some new justification of its confidence in popular fortitude, honesty, and sagacity.

And the discussion has been exacerbated by the fact, that neither party has been a disinterested spectator of the contest. By the friends of democracy abroad, the convulsion through which the American commonwealth is passing is felt to be a crucial test of the soundness of those political opinions of which they have long been the champions, and with which their political fortunes are inseparably linked. To its friends in America it has come home as a personal calamity. It has either wasted their substance, or made their hearths desolate, or, which is often as hard to bear as either, it has inflicted lasting wounds on their pride. In the eyes of the party of aristocracy, too, it is not simply the political unity of the North American continent which is debated on Southern battle-fields, but the stability of their own order, the continuance of that form of social organization in which they have been bred, and with the security and perpetuation of which all that they hold precious in life is indissolubly connected. To them the defeat of the South signifies the triumph of that "principle of equality" from the spread of which they look not only for their own degradation, but, often honestly enough, for great danger to national liberty, and even to civilization itself.

And to appreciate thoroughly the intensity of the interest which this conflict of ours excites, we must keep in mind the width of the area over which its material consequences have been felt. There is no shore so distant that the waves of this great tempest have not broken on it. The term *orbis terrarum perturbatio*, which, as applied by

Cicero to the great civil war of his day, was but a rhetorical exaggeration, may be bestowed on this one with literal accuracy. The course of the great tides of commerce has been turned by it; the industry of whole nations has been revolutionized by it. From John O'Groat's to the base of the Great Snowy Range, there is no country to which its probable results, and probable duration, are not questions of tremendous moment.

One result, for which students of political philosophy will be thankful, has flowed from the increased sharpness which the events of the day have lent to the discussion, and that is the clearness and frankness with which the opposing parties have been led to enunciate their views. We doubt if the enemies of democracy ever before revealed their objections to it, and their anticipations as to its effects, with as much candor as since our war broke out. We now know, with a tolerable approach to exactness, what we did not know before, the kind of thing they believe it to be, and the kind and amount of evil they expect to proceed from its unchecked working. Excitement caused by the vicissitudes of the armed struggle has loosened the tongues of a great many men who were previously kept silent by caution or indolence, or from never having taken the trouble to put their conclusions into shape. When democracy was prosperous, many only shook their heads when it was mentioned who now make a clean breast of it, and tell the world in good set phrases what they have been thinking about it for years.

And, on the other hand, its friends have been roused by the same causes into more vigorous defence of it than they ever ventured on before. There are many persons in America to-day who five years ago looked grave over universal suffrage, or expressed private doubts of its success, but who are now to be found in the ranks of its most enthusiastic defenders, breathing defiance of aristocrats and aristocracy from every pore, and consigning every form of political organization in which power does not flow directly from the people, in yearly or biennial driblets, to unutterable failure and confusion.

There has, however, in our opinion, been one great mistake made by some advocates of the democratic cause in their manner of conducting the controversy. It consists in ascribing *all* the attacks which have been recently made on democratic institutions to aristocratic malignity, to a blind, perverse pride of caste, or to stupid, over-reasoning prejudice against our political and social organization simply because it is different from something else. There is no doubt, in England especially, a vast amount of ignorant depreciation

of democracy by persons who have no better reasons for objecting to it than a vague notion that
it is vulgar, and a vast deal by others who hate it
from the purely selfish consideration of the probable effect of its spread on their own social position
or that of their families, or from the apprehension
that it would introduce changes in manners which
their temperament and education lead them to regard as obnoxious.

But, in addition to these, democracy has had in
this controversy a number of opponents—a small
number, we admit — against whom we must employ better weapons than railing, whose character
and arguments are both unquestionably respectable, and whose hostility to it is based on conclusions carefully formed, which are enunciated,
not certainly without feeling, but without rancor
or irritation. They are thinkers who look on
politics—ours as well as their own—in the clear
white light of reason, and who, while differing
from us as to the means of promoting it, share
all our solicitude for the welfare of the human
race. Nobody who has been familiar with the
political literature of Europe for some years back,
can have failed to perceive the struggle between
their hopes and fears which shows itself whenever
these men speak of democracy, the ill-disguised
apprehension with which they concede that its

march is now irresistible, and the nervous industry
with which they occupy themselves in providing
breaks and buffers to restrain or direct its course.[2]

The opinions of this class of persons about democracy may, we think, be fairly summed up as
follows.   They think the spread of democracy
(meaning thereby the ascendancy of " the principle
of equality," to use M. de Tocqueville's phrase,
both in politics and in society) over every Christian country, at least, to be certain at no very distant day.   They believe that no precaution can be
taken and no barrier created which will do
more than postpone this result, and then for a
very brief period.   They think that this seems to
be the remedy decreed by Providence for the removal of the great blot on our civilization, the
physical misery and moral degradation of the lower
classes.   And they admit that the establishment of
democracy, whether it take the shape of a republic
or of a Cæsarean despotism, would doubtless be
largely instrumental in securing for the bulk of the
population a certain amount of coarse enjoyments,
such as good shelter, good food, and good clothing,
and a limited amount of education.   But they hold
that every democracy, however free at the period
of its establishment, gravitates strongly toward
subjection to a single absolute ruler, after a period
of great corruption and disorder, and that it derives

this tendency from certain inherent defects; and what these defects are, they fancy they are able to point out by an examination of what they see, or think they see, in the United States.

What they believe they learn about democracy from what they see here is, that it is fatal in the long run to any high degree of excellence in the arts, science, literature, or statesmanship; that it is hostile to every form of distinction, and thus tends to extinguish the nobler kinds of ambition, to create and perpetuate mediocrity, to offer a serious bar to progress, and even to threaten civilization with stagnation; that, by making .equality of conditions the highest political good, it makes civil liberty appear valuable only so long or so far as its existence is compatible with equality; that it converts the ideal of the worst trained and most unthinking portion of the community into the national standard of capacity, and thus drives the ablest men out of public life; that it sets up mere success in the accumulation of money as the proof and test of national prosperity, and elevates material luxury into the great end of social progress; that it takes from manners all their grace and polish and dignity, makes literature feeble and tawdry, and oratory bombastic and violent; that it infuses bitterness into party struggles, while removing the barriers which in aristocratic societies soften and restrain its expression; and, finally, that, by the pains it takes to preserve the equality of conditions, it forces every member of the community to engage as soon as he reaches manhood in an eager scramble for wealth, thus rendering impossible the existence of a class with sufficient leisure to devote themselves to the cultivation of the arts and sciences, or to speculative inquiry in any field of knowledge.

We do not mean to say that all of the foregoing charges are brought against democracy by any one of its enemies, but the whole of them may be found in a very small number of the speeches, articles, and treatises of one sort or other, which the political movements of the last fifteen years have called forth both in England and on the Continent; and it will be confessed by any candid American observer, that there are various phenomena, both social and political, to be witnessed in the United States which do give color to a large proportion of them. There is hardly one of them for which some foundation, or something like foundation, may not be found in some phase or other of American society or government.

If we asked an American of conservative tastes and opinions to say frankly what he thought of this picture, he would probably take exception to a very large portion of it; he would accuse it of

gross exaggeration at least ; and if asked to sketch
the changes for the worse which, in his opinion,
had taken place in American society within the
last fifty or sixty years, he would present us with
something different, but different rather in degree
than in kind. He would say that there had been
since the beginning of the century a great deterioration in the character, attainments, and social
standing of the men sent by the Free States to fill
the various offices of government. (For the purpose of this discussion, we leave the Slave States
out of the argument, and for obvious reasons.)
The men who now occupy the judicial bench, fill
the national and State legislatures, and sit at the
council boards and in the mayoral chairs of the
great cities, are inferior in training, ability, education, and social position to those who filled the
same positions fifty or sixty years ago. Forensic
eloquence has, he would say, consequently undergone a corresponding change for the worse. It is
neither so chaste, so simple, nor so forcible as it
was at the time of the foundation of the government, and for many years after. The art of debating has all but died out, for it is an art which
needs acute and ready intellect, saturated with
reading and experience and trained in fence, to
sustain it. Speeches in Congress and in the legislatures on important questions are now, for the

most part, long essays, written out previously,
often full of irrelevancy and commonplace, and repeated altogether, or in a great degree, from memory, to inattentive audiences. If the orator is
forced by circumstances to depart from his prepared course, and defend himself and his opinions
extemporaneously against an extemporaneous attack, his scanty mental resources force him in the
great majority of cases to fall back on personal
vituperation. And the small amount of previous
thought or culture which is revealed in the legislative discussions is, he would add, very remarkable. Hardly any subject seems important enough
or exciting enough to call out anything much better than the philosophy of hotel parlors or the
logic of newspaper articles. What is worse than
all this, legislation is confessedly more hasty,
more reckless, and more ill-digested than formerly.
None of these things can be ascribed to any diminution in the number of men of culture and
ability produced by the country in our day as
compared with a former one. Their number bears,
there is little doubt, a very much larger proportion
to the population than it ever did. But they are
unceremoniously thrust aside from public life, and
are generally found either toiling in commerce or
in the professions, or else killing time and ambition in social trifling or in foreign travel.

Of the present as compared with the former condition of the bar, too, he would say, that not only has etiquette disappeared from it, but in a large number of the States the relations of judge and counsel are marked by a familiarity which, on one side at least, is mingled with a good deal of contempt. Admission to the profession has come to be, not a proof of fitness, but a political right; and the result is, that its ranks are crowded by needy aspirants, not after forensic distinction, but after money, whose want of learning and preparation for their duties, and entire exemption from the once powerful restraints of professional opinion, are fast destroying the reputation for lore, ability, and integrity which a former generation achieved for the American bar.

If you direct his attention to the social condition of the country, he will tell you that, while the habits of the American population are much more luxurious than they were half a century ago, while there is far more money in circulation, and while most of the pleasures of life are placed within the reach of a much larger class than in the earlier days of the Republic, the manners are not only less ceremonious, but less dignified and refined; that there is not only less punctiliousness, but less courtesy and grace in social intercourse; that the family bond is not so strong as it used to be; that there is less respect for authority, not only in the household, but in the state; that both the father and the judge find themselves much less important and less respected personages than they once were; that dress and manners have less weight and importance than formerly, and that there has grown up within thirty years a sort of affectation of carelessness in attire, in demeanor, and even in language; that the English of the bulk of the population is not so pure, nor their accent so refined, as those of the fathers; that more is now read, but less is digested, than in the last generation; and that in short, on the whole, there is both in externals and in mental characteristics less *finish* to be found amongst Americans of the present day than amongst those of half a century ago.

It matters not for our present purpose which of these pictures of American society is the more faithful. We are content to accept either of them as true, since the explanation which we propose to offer for the phenomena which they bring before us will, if it be of any value whatever, be as applicable to the first as to the last. But the moment we address inquiries as to the cause of these phenomena to any of the political sects of the present day, who are fairly entitled to the credit of either observing or thinking, we find ourselves launched on a sea of contradiction. If we apply to a " conservative," he will, if advanced in years, probably acknowledge the occurrence of the changes we have enumerated above, and will, in nine cases out of ten, assure us that it is foreign immigration that has done it all; that, if no Irish or Germans had ever come to the country, no changes for the worse, either in government or society, would ever have taken place. If we ask an Englishman of any but the radical school, or any of those native political philosophers who import their opinions with their gloves and pomatum, and study science in Sir Archibald Alison and the *Quarterly Review*, they will tell us that whatever of decay or deterioration is visible in anything American is the direct and palpable consequence of universal suffrage; that democracy has ruined the country, and that the only road to improvement lies through revolution.[3]

When we come to inquire to what extent the social or political condition of the Northern States has been influenced or modified by foreign immigration, we find ourselves dealing with a subject on which all those writers whose opinions are largely affected by their taste are agreed; and most of those who in America venture on political speculation belong to this class. If we take up the hundred laments over the degeneracy of our political condition, which issue from them every year in books, newspapers, speeches, and sermons, we shall find that in nine cases out of ten it is ascribed to the great influx of ignorant foreigners which has been going on for the last thirty years. In many, perhaps most, of the controversies which are carried on with European critics touching the state and prospects of the republic, this argument is put very prominently forward. Any coarseness, corruption, or recklessness, either of conduct or language, which shows itself in the management of our public affairs, and attracts the attention of foreign critics, is apt to be ascribed by the native advocate to the malign influence of the human drift, which the convulsions and misfortunes of European society have cast on our shores.

We suspect that much of the prevalence of this theory is due to the fact, that those who most frequently put it forward in print live in the great cities, where foreigners are most numerous, where they are in the habit of acting in masses, and where their influence is most easily seen and felt. It is there that the evils which flow from their presence are most palpable; and those who have under their eyes its effects on the local government are apt to draw from the spectacle the most lugubrious inferences as to the condition of the rest of the country. But the estimate of the weight and extent of foreign influence upon politics and society, based on the impressions thus formed, is not confirmed by a careful consideration of the facts.

The whole number of foreigners who have entered the country between 1790 and 1860 is 5,296,414; and of these, 5,062,000 entered since the year 1820, or an average of 126,500 a year during forty years, being of course a mere driblet when compared to the native population. The immigration since 1860 has been very large; and the number actually resident in the whole of the United States in that year was about 4,000,000, or less than one-seventh of the entire population. But it is not since 1860 that the political or social deterioration which we are discussing has shown itself. One might imagine, on listening to some of the accounts one hears of the extent to which foreigners are responsible for the vices of American politics, that at least half the inhabitants of the Free States had for many years been persons of European birth, and that the intelligent and educated natives of the country had had a severe struggle, under universal suffrage, to retain any share in the government, and had been long threatened with seeing the management of a political system, which requires a large amount of virtue and knowledge on the part of those who live under it to enable it to work successfully, pass into the hands of a class of men bred in ignorance and degraded by oppression. But when it is taken into account that the foreign immigration has flowed slowly during a great number of years, that a large proportion of it has, of course, been composed of women and children, and that the small number of voters which it in any one year has contributed to the electoral body, have been scattered over the Union from Maine to California, and have been divided into different camps by difference of language, religion, and nationality, and have been generally too ignorant and helpless to devise or pursue a common policy, it is easy to see that the current notion of the extent of their influence on national politics and on political life, has been greatly exaggerated.

The only instance, we believe, in which the foreigners can be said to have combined to make their influence felt at the elections, occurred during the " Know Nothing" movement ; but this was the result of a direct attack on their own privileges and standing. On all other occasions, we find them serving under American leaders, and assailing or defending purely American ideas ; and so far from seeking position or influence by banding together, their great aim and desire are, as is well known, to efface all marks of their foreign origin, and secure complete absorption in the American population. And how do they accomplish this? Not by imposing their ideas on the natives, or dragging them down to their level, but by adopting native ideas and manners and customs, educating their children in American habits, or, in other words, raising themselves to the American level. In fact, there is nothing they resent so keenly as any attempt to place them in a different category, or ascribe to them different interests or motives, from those of Americans. If they were conscious of the power of making themselves felt as a separate body, this would hardly be the case. So far from seeking to obliterate the distinction between themselves and Americans, they would endeavor to maintain and perpetuate it.

It may be said, however, that, although the foreign element in the population may not influence American politics in a way sufficient to account for the political changes of the last half-century directly by its votes, it does influence them indirectly by the modifications it effects in the national character through intermarriage and social intercourse. The effect upon temperament of intermixture of blood is very much too obscure a subject, in our opinion, to be safely made the basis of any theory of national progress or decline, even by those who attach most importance to it, and profess to know

most about it. But even if we accord it all the
force they claim for it, time enough has not yet
elapsed to enable us to judge of its effects in this
country. This much is certain, that the great features of the American character do not seem to
have undergone any sensible change since the Revolution. The American of to-day, as an individual,
presents very much the same great traits, moral
and intellectual, which his father and grandfather
presented before him ; the main difference between
the three generations being, that the present one
displays its idiosyncrasies on a very much wider
field. A chemical analysis (as it has been termed)
of natural character is, however, something from
which no sound thinker will ever hope to arrive at
conclusions of much value for any purposes not
purely speculative.

As regards the influence exercised on American
life by foreigners through the medium of social intercourse, we doubt very much if anybody has ever
attached much importance to it, who has given the
matter any serious consideration. All that seems
necessary to remove the idea that it has been instrumental in modifying either American opinions
or manners, is to call attention to the class of society from which the immigrants are generally
drawn, and to the social position which they occupy in this country. If we except a few lawyers,

a few doctors, a few professors and teachers, and a few merchants in the large cities, eager to make money enough to enable them to return with fortunes to their native country, it may be said that ninety-nine out of every hundred foreigners who come to the United States with the intention of settling here, are drawn from the ranks of the European peasantry—Germans, entirely ignorant of the English language; and Irish, who, as well as the Germans, are separated from even the poorest of the native population by an entirely different standard of living, and a wide difference of habits and of religion. There is between them and even the lower grades of American society a barrier, which is none the less formidable for not being recognized by law. They fill, all but exclusively, the menial callings, and intermarriage between them and pure-blooded Americans is very rare. And, as we have said, so far from acting as propagators of foreign opinions or manners, the whole energy of the new-comers is spent, for years after their arrival, not in diffusing their own ways of thinking and feeling, but in strenuous and generally successful efforts to get rid of them, and adopt those of their American neighbors.

When we come to consider the European explanation of the defects which show themselves in the political and social system of the United

States—and it is an explanation which large numbers of Americans belonging to the wealthier classes have of late years been disposed to accept as the true one—that they are the direct and all but inevitable result of the spread of democracy, we are met on the threshold by the authority of a great name, of which we desire to speak with all possible respect. That theory of the cause of the decline in the character and ability of public men in America, and the consequent increasing corruption which marks our public life, of the decrease of respect for law and authority, and of the growing absorption in the pursuit of money, which, before the war at least, were so generally observed and deplored, undoubtedly owes to M. de Tocqueville most of its weight and authority. His "Democracy in America" was and is perhaps the most remarkable contribution to the philosophy of politics in modern times. It solves some of the most puzzling problems of a novel condition of society, and one of which the European world, prior to the appearance of his book, knew very little, with an ease and dexterity which it is impossible, even for those who mistrust many of his conclusions, not to admire. And the book is throughout evidently the product of laborious thinking and conscientious and painstaking observation, controlled by a sound philosophic method. Probably no one, and certainly no foreigner, was ever so successful in sketching American character, in catching the spirit of American life, and in revealing the nature and tendency of American ideas.

He has framed a theory of the influences and tendencies of democracy, partly *a priori* by deductions from the principles of human nature, and partly from his observations of social phenomena in France and America ; and this is, we believe, the process now recognized as the only one that is trustworthy in the conduct of inquiries in social science. But the conclusions thus drawn depend inevitably for their soundness on the accuracy of the observations on which they are partly based, and by which alone their accuracy can, at present, be tested. If the peculiar state of opinions, feelings, and manners, and peculiar tone of thought, which M. de Tocqueville found in America, be not really altogether the result of equality of conditions, or of democratic institutions, that portion of his speculations which is dependent on the correctness of this assumption of course falls to the ground ; and a very large portion of them is dependent upon it.

Nevertheless, to assume that those social phenomena which are peculiar to America are solely the result of democracy, is to attempt the solution of social problems by what Mr. Mill calls the "chemical method," the imperfection of which we cannot do better than describe in his own words.

"If so little can be done by the experimental method to determine the conditions of an effect of many combined causes in the case of medical science, still less is this method applicable to a class of phenomena more complicated than even those of physiology—the phenomena of politics and history. There the plurality of causes exists in almost boundless excess, and the effects are for the most part inextricably interwoven with one another. To add to the embarrassment, most of the inquiries in political science relate to the production of effects of the most comprehensive description, such as the public wealth, public security, public morality, and the like—results liable to be affected directly or indirectly, either in *plus* or in *minus*, by nearly every fact which exists or event which occurs in human society. The vulgar notion that the safe methods on political subjects are those of Baconian induction, that the true guide is not generally reasoning but specific experience, will one day be quoted as among the most unequivocal marks of a low state of the speculative faculties in any age in which it is accredited. Nothing can be more ludicrous than the sort of parodies on experimental reasoning which one is accustomed to meet with, not in popular discussions only, but in grave treatises, when affairs of nations are the theme. 'How,' it is asked, 'can an institution be bad, when the country has prospered under it?' 'How can such or such causes have contributed to the prosperity of one country, when another has prospered without them?' Whoever makes use of an argument of this sort, not intending to deceive, should be sent back to learn the elements of some one of the more easy physical sciences. Such reasoners ignore the fact of a plurality of causes in the very case which affords the most signal example of it."—*Logic,* Vol. II., pp. 489, 490, Eng. ed.[4]

To make American society what it is, no one cause has sufficed, and what number or combination of causes has been instrumental in creating the phenomena which attract so much of the attention of political philosophers, it is impossible in the existing state of political science to determine.

It would be very unjust to M. de Tocqueville to leave it to be understood that he himself was not fully aware of all this. In fact, he expressly acknowledges in more than one place the existence of a plurality of causes for all the phenomena of American society, as well as that of other countries. He recognizes the immense influence " which the nature of the country, the origin of its inhabitants, the religion of the early settlers, their acquired knowledge, their previous habits, have exercised and do exercise independently of democracy upon their mode of thought and feeling." (Vol. II., p. iv, Bowen's ed.) And he in various places warns his readers that the phenomena he is discussing are either due to other causes than " the principle of equality," or are rather American than democratic. But he seems frequently to forget this in the course of his reasoning, and on almost every page draws conclusions as to the probable condition of democratic society in general from what he describes as American society, or else draws these conclusions from general principles, and verifies them by an examination of American institutions or manners. The effect of either of these processes on the mind of the ordinary reader is, of course, very similar. We have not space to quote as fully as would be necessary, if we quoted at all, in support of these comments ; but anyone who consults the chapters entitled, respectively, " Why Americans are more addicted to Practical than to Theoretical Science," " The Literary Characteristics of Democratic Times," " Why American Writers and Orators often use an Inflated Style," " Of Parliamentary Eloquence in the United States," "Why the Americans are so Restless in the midst of their Prosperity," as well as most of the subsequent ones, will find the remarks we have made on the author's method of reasoning fully borne out.[5] And the discussions of the nature and tendencies of democratic institutions which have been created in Europe by the war prove, we think, all but conclusively, that, whatever may have been his own state of mind in writing, De Tocqueville's influence on European opinion has been to a certain extent misleading. Hardly one book or article in newspaper or magazine has appeared on American affairs, in which any attempt is made to extract lessons from our condition for English guidance, which does not take it for granted, not only that democracy has produced everything that is considered objectionable in American society, but that democratic institutions transferred to any other country would give rise to precisely the same phenomena. A very large portion of the intense hostility of the upper classes to the United States is due to the prevalence amongst them of this delusion.

We cannot, for our part, help believing that any speculation as to the causes of the peculiar phenomena of American society, in which its outward circumstances during the last eighty years do not occupy the leading position, must lead to conclusions radically erroneous, and calculated to do great injustice not only to the American people, but to democracy itself. At these, nevertheless, M. de Tocqueville has only glanced, and most of those who have followed him in discussing democratic tendencies have overlooked them altogether.

If we inquire what are those phenomena of American society which it is generally agreed distinguish it from that of older countries, we shall find, we are satisfied, that by far the larger number of them may be attributed in a great measure to what, for want of a better name, we shall call "the frontier life" led by a large proportion of the inhabitants, and to the influence of this portion on manners and legislation, rather than to political institutions, or even to the equality of conditions. In fact, we think that these phenomena, and particularly those of them which excite most odium in Europe, instead of being the effect of democracy, are partly its cause, and that it has been to their agency more than to aught else, that the democratic tide in America has owed most of its force and violence.[6]

If we examine closely the history of the Northern Colonies, we shall find that, just as their founders left England in search of religious liberty, but were careful not to suffer it within their jurisdiction, so also, although they were most of them animated by republican sentiments, and although a commonwealth was doubtless their ideal polity, "the principle of equality" never obtained any recognition, either in fact or in theory, amongst them or their descendants, down to the time of the Revolution. The distinction between the gentleman and the common man not only existed in New England till the end of the last century, but it was recognized in forms of address, a mode of making it peculiarly repugnant to democratic feeling. Nor, so far as we can learn, was "the principle of authority" much weaker in the Colonies, at any period of their history, than in England. The civil functionaries in Boston and Plymouth were held in a respect very little, if at all, short of that which was rendered to such dignitaries in London. The clergy exercised an influence over both manners and politics which, it is very certain, they never secured in the mother country. And the family bond, in spite of the very different conditions by which it was surrounded in the New World, was not, we believe, weaker than in the Old. Down to the time of the Revolution the *paterfamilias* was still a power in society, and exercised an amount of control over the life and conduct of his children, and received from them an amount of homage, which are no longer seen. Etiquette, both public and private, was still an object of attention and respect. Members of the Colonial legislatures were really representatives, and not, as now, delegates; and to sit amongst them was an honor to which persons without an established social position did not readily aspire. Legislation, too, though it might be based on erroneous principles, was rarely so reckless or so hasty as at present. And, though last not least, the religious organizations subjected nearly every member of the community to a dis-

cipline so rigid and exacting, that it has left marks
on the New England mind and character which will
probably not be effaced as long as the race lasts.

How was it that this state of things lasted so
long? How was it that the ideas brought by the
Colonists from the Old World retained their force
for a century and a half, in spite of the facts that
communication with the mother country was rare,
slow, and difficult, that she exercised little or no
influence at that time through her literature, for
literature had not then been popularized, that the
life led by the Colonists was such as to bring the
idea of equality into the fullest prominence, that
hereditary wealth was almost unknown amongst
them, and that their social condition necessarily
fostered individualism? How was it that that
democratic tide which, within the last fifty years,
has overwhelmed everything, during the previous
hundred and fifty gave so few signs of its rising?

The *Saturday Review*, in an attempt it made
about a year ago to answer these questions, ascribed the rapid progress of democracy in America
since the Revolution to the stoppage at that
period of the supply of younger sons of gentlemen, which, according to the writer, was then beginning to flow into the country, and would, if the
separation had not taken place, have continued
to flow in ever since.[7] Another explanation fre-

quently offered by speculators of the same school
is, that the change was due to the removal of the
social influence of the monarchy, which, as long as
the connection with the mother country lasted,
prevented the republican form of government,
which in reality already existed, from producing
its natural effect on manners and ideas.

Both of these theories, however, receive a severe
blow from the course of events in Australia. This
colony was established on a thoroughly aristocratic
basis. It received and continues to receive a large
contribution of " younger sons " than has fallen to
the lot of any other, and great numbers of them
went out with sufficient capital to enable them to
maintain their social position. The land-laws, too,
encouraged the appropriation of large tracts of
country to their exclusive use as sheep pastures,
and for a long while rendered capital almost as
essential to success in life there as in England.
The colony had that which we are now taught
to consider the essential basis of aristocratic society, a servile class, in the convicts, and, more
than this, it has remained up to the present in social and political dependence on England; yet in
spite of all these things the progress of democracy
there has been steady and rapid. Universal suffrage has been established throughout the island ;
the property qualification for members of the

legislatures has been abolished ; the vote is taken
by ballot, and the press and public life are almost
exact counterparts of those of the United States,
and all this within eighty years of the first settlement of the country.[8]

We are far from asserting that the idea of the
equality of men, which, according to Professor
Maine, was extracted from the Roman juridical
maxim that " men were *born* equal," converted, by
a not uncommon transformation, by the French
literary men of the eighteenth century into a political dogma, and by them transmitted to the Vir-
ginian lawyers, had nothing to do, after its ma-
nipulation by the Jeffersonian school, with the
spread of democracy in the United States. But
it could, after all, amongst a people so intensely
practical as the Americans, and so averse from
speculation in politics, have effected very little, if
the field had not been prepared for it by other
causes. It could never have embodied itself either
in political or social movements of the popular
mind, had it not been made ready for its recep-
tion by influences of vastly more potency than a
foreign dogma can ever have amongst a people of
Anglo-Saxon origin.

The agency which, in our opinion, gave democracy its first great impulse in the United States,
which has promoted its spread ever since, and

has contributed most powerfully to the production of those phenomena in American society which hostile critics set down as peculiarly democratic, was neither the origin of the Colonists, nor the circumstances under which they came to the country, nor their religious belief; but the great change in the distribution of the population, which began soon after the Revolution, and which continues its operation up to the present time.

Population during the first hundred years of Colonial history was kept from spreading widely by its smallness, by the Indians, and by the attraction of the sea-coast, which furnished a ready means of intercommunication. The very feebleness of the Colonists in point of numbers constituted a strong motive for keeping close together. The aborigines, who still held the forests all around them, were a standing menace to their security, and could only be kept in check by constant and watchful co-operation. Moreover, labor was too scarce to make the opening of roads into the interior an easy task; and even when opened they furnished but sorry facilities for traffic. The weight of this consideration can be better appreciated by remembering that until the present century America was completely dependent on Europe, not only for the luxuries, but for most of the comforts and conveniences and many of the necessaries of life. During the Colonial period, and especially during the early part of it, most of the clothing and tools of the inhabitants were brought from England; which fact, of course, in itself furnished a strong reason for not wandering far from the coast. Accordingly we find that, at the outbreak of the Revolution, the Colonists consisted of a string of settlements along the shore, lying a few miles apart, and carrying on most of their intercourse by water. Even the pioneers had rarely penetrated inland more than fifty or a hundred miles, and generally along the rivers only.

Now these obstacles to expansion performed for the Colonists precisely the same office which is performed in older countries by want of space, and exercised much the same influence on their social progress. It produced comparative density of population; and the effects of density of population, wherever it is not accompanied by very great numbers, as in large cities, are well known. It strengthens public opinion, represses individualism, tightens the social relations, and thus gives fixity to old customs and ideas, and stability to authority. It did all this and more for the early settlers. They landed from Europe in companies, with a social organization already formed; and the difficulty of scattering enabled them to preserve it, and preserve the ideas on which it was

based, for over a century, in spite of the fact that
their daily life was one which tended powerfully
to develop the spirit of independence and self-
reliance—more so, in fact, than that of our back-
woodsmen at the present day, for most of the appliances by which modern invention mitigates the
hardships of pioneering were then wanting. The
Church retained its hold on the young and on the
old; the opinion of the community kept even the
strongest natures in subjection, and all the more
readily, because in those days the community to
each of its members was the world. It was difficult to leave it, and there was no appeal from its
judgments.

The history of colonization in all ages and climes
tells much the same story. Wherever the colonists
are prevented by any cause from scattering, and
congregate from the outset in communities, the
colony remains a tolerably faithful reflection of life
and manners in the mother country.

The completeness with which the individual in
the Greek republics was merged in the state or
city, rendered the notion of individual action or
individual existence, apart from the community to
which he belonged, abhorrent to him. He never
thought of himself in any character but that of a
citizen. Consequently, we find that Greek colonization meant simply the production on a foreign

shore of as faithful an image of the metropolis as circumstances would permit. The Colonists, far from scattering in search of fortune, massed themselves together in towns ; and the result was that the Greek ideas and traditions and customs, both political and religious, were preserved with the most extraordinary fidelity ; and this is rendered all the more remarkable from the fact that the elements of which ancient colonies were composed were at least as heterogeneous as those of the colonies of modern times.* The Roman colonies, except the military ones of later days, were founded under the influence of the same feeling, and remained, however far removed from the great city, her living images—"effigies parva, simulacraque populi Romani."

* Seneca's account of the causes which led to emigration in ancient times is curious, from its applicability to the emigration of our own day. "Nec omnibus eadem causa relinquendi, quærendique patriam fuit. Alios excidia urbium suarum, hostilibus armis elapsos, in aliena, spoliatos suis, expulerunt; alios domestica seditio submovit; alios nimia superfluentis populi frequentia, ad exonerandas vires, emisit; alios pestilentia, aut frequens terrarum hiatus, aut aliqua intoleranda infelicis soli vitia ejecerunt; quosdam fertilis oræ et in majus laudatæ, fama corrupit; alios alia causa excivit domibus suis."—*Consol. ad Helviam.*, Cap. 6. War, revolution, over-population, pestilence, earthquakes, poverty of soil, and a vague desire of bettering their condition, are the causes that still send men forth in quest of "fresh fields and pastures new." 9

In those modern colonies which have, for any
reason, been prevented from scattering widely, we
witness much the same phenomena. The South
American, who is gregarious by temperament, and
who is cooped up on the edge of his great rivers
by the impenetrability of tropical forests, remains
to this day simply an indolent Spaniard, as conservative, as hostile to novelties or movement, as
any peasant or shop-keeper in Aragon. And if
we travel through Lower Canada, we find that the
habitans, whose French horror of solitude, as well
as the conquest of the country by the British, has
kept them congregated in the old settlements, have
preserved until very recently the social organization under which the first emigrants left their
country. They continued to be the only faithful
picture of the France which the Revolution destroyed, and even yet any one who wishes to get
an accurate knowledge of the feelings, relations,
and ideas which formed the basis of the old *régime*,
would find them in far better preservation on the
banks of the St. Lawrence than on those of the
Loire or the Garonne.

The Revolutionary struggle in America produced the usual effect of great civil commotions.
It unsettled industry, broke up families, reduced
large numbers to poverty, and diminished production; and, by habituating large bodies of men to

the change and license of camp life, rendered the
even tenor of the way which they had previously
pursued in their homes no longer tolerable. Then
came the usual *sequelæ* of a long war. When peace
was concluded, a spirit of restlessness was diffused
through the country, and an eagerness for adven-
ture, which the *fama fertilis oræ* that then began to be wafted from the West intensified from
day to day. The emigration westward set in with
a vigor which had never before been witnessed;
and thenceforward, for a short period, new States
were rapidly added to the confederation. Ken-
tucky came in in 1792; Tennessee, in 1796; Ohio,
in 1802; but here there was a pause. The movement was checked evidently by the material difficulties which attended any further advance. Either
it had reached a point at which remoteness from
civilization became inconvenient or disagreeable,
or else the drain on the population of the Eastern
States had exhausted all that portion of it which
was fit for pioneering. During the next fourteen
years there was no new State added to the Union,
except Louisiana, which was admitted in 1812;
but in 1816 the stream appears to have again begun
to flow into the wilderness. Indiana was admitted
that year; Mississippi followed in 1817; Illinois,
in 1818; Alabama, in 1819; and Missouri, in
1821. Now, as this increase was contemporaneous

with the spread of steam navigation on the great
rivers, it is fair to presume that it was in a large
degree due to it. There was then another pause of
fifteen years, at the close of which the influence of
the railroads which were then getting into operation began to show itself; and from this time forward, the movement of population into the Western wilds has steadily increased from year to year,
being swelled by the affluent from abroad which
has poured into the United States between the
years 1820 and 1860 the enormous number of
5,062,414 persons. Arkansas, Michigan, Texas,
Wisconsin, Iowa, Minnesota, and Kansas have
thus been added to the Union in rapid succession.
We omit from consideration the Pacific States,
California, Oregon, and Nevada.

It must be constantly borne in mind that
this wonderful diffusion of population over the
wilderness which seventy years ago lay between
the seaboard States and the Mississippi Valley,
could not have taken place without the application
of steam to locomotion. In the absence of this
invention, the number of new settlements must
always have borne a small proportion to the old
ones. The portion of the community in which
habits and modes of thought were tolerably fixed,
in which experience was highly valued, traditions
were held in reverence, and on which the past had

left traces of greater or less depth, would have so
largely exceeded the portion engaged in the work
of actually reclaiming the wilderness, that it would
either have held the latter in political and moral
subjection, and have imposed its ideas and manners on it, or would, at all events, have remained
impervious to its influence. The West, instead of
creating, as it has done, a social type in many respects distinct, would have remained completely
under Eastern influence, and have simply reproduced the society from which it had sprung, its
manners, ideas, and aspirations.

But with the assistance of steamboats and rail-
ways, and of immigration from Europe, the pioneering element in the population, the class devoted to the task of creating new political and social
organizations as distinguished from that engaged
in perfecting old ones, assumed a great preponderance. It spread itself thinly over a vast area
of soil, of such extraordinary fertility that a very
slight amount of toil expended on it affords returns
that might have satisfied even the dreams of Spanish avarice. The result has been very much what
we might have concluded, a priori, that it would
be. A society composed at the period of its formation mainly of young men, coming from all parts
of the world in quest of fortune, released from the
ordinary restraints of family, church, and public

opinion, even of the civil law, naturally and inevitably acquires a certain contempt for authority and impatience of it, and individualism among them develops itself very rapidly. If you place this society, thus constituted, in the midst of a wilderness, where each member of it has to contend, tools in hand, with Nature herself for wealth, or even subsistence, the ties which bind him to his fellows will for a while at least be rarely anything stronger than that of simple contiguity. The only mutual obligation which this relation suggests strongly is that of rendering assistance occasionally in overcoming material difficulties—in other words, the simplest bond which can unite human beings. Each person is, from the necessity of the case, so absorbed in his own struggle for existence, that he has seldom occasion or time for the consideration and cultivation of his social relations. He knows nothing of the antecedents of his neighbors, nor they of his. They are not drawn together, in all probability, by a single memory or association. They have drifted into the same locality, it is true, under the guidance of a common impulse, and this a selfish one. So that the settler gets into the habit of looking at himself as an individual, of contemplating himself and his career separate and apart from the social organization. We do not say that this breeds selfishness—far from it; but it breeds individualism.

If the members of such a society are compelled
to work hard for the gratification of their desires,
to meet and overcome great difficulties and hardships and dangers, the result is naturally the production of great energy, of great audacity, and of a
self-confidence that rises into conceit. In this
self-confidence is almost always contained a prodigious contempt for experience and for theory.
The ends which such men have had in view having
all been attained without the aid of either, they
cannot see the use of them. They have found
their own wits sufficient for the solution of every
problem that has presented itself to them, so that
deference to the authority of general maxims
framed by persons who never found themselves
placed in similar circumstances, wears an air of
weakness or absurdity.

The devotion to material pursuits, which is
necessary at the outset, is made absorbing in a
country like the West, by the richness of the
prizes which are offered to shrewd speculation and
successful industry. Where probable or even possible gains are so great, the whole community gives
itself up to the chase of them with an eagerness
which is not democratic, but human. It would not,
we think, be difficult to show that the existence in
old countries of an idle class, content with moderate and secured fortunes, and devoted solely to

amusement and the cultivation of art or literature, is largely due to the immense difficulty of making profitable investments. In those countries the capital accumulated by past generations is so great, and every field of industry is so thronged, that a very large number of those who find themselves possessed of a sum of money are forced to relinquish all hope of increasing it. For we know that whenever, as during "the railway mania" in England, or Law's Mississippi scheme in France, the chance, real or imaginary, is offered of drawing such prizes as every day fall to the lot of hundreds in America, men of every grade and calling rush after them with an ardor which no training or tastes or antecedents seem sufficient to restrain. The desire for wealth is one of the constant forces of human society, and if it seems to assert its sway more imperiously here than in Europe, it is not because it is fostered by the equality of conditions, but because its gratification is surrounded by fewer obstacles.

If to strong individualism, contempt for experience, and eagerness in pursuit of material gain, we add want of respect for training, and profound faith in natural qualities, great indifference as to the future, the absence of a strong sense of social or national continuity, and of taste in art and literature and oratory, we have, we believe, enumerated the leading defects which European writers consider inherent in democratic society. But these, too, are marked peculiarities of all societies newly organized in a new country. We know them to be so by actual observation, for which modern colonization has afforded us abundant facilities ; while it is safe to say that trustworthy illustrations of them have never been discovered in any society which was simply democratic and not new. There is no feature of life in new States in America more marked than the general belief of the people in their own originality, and their respect for this quality. The kind of man they most admire is one who has evolved rules for the conduct of life out of his own brain by the help of his own observation ; and they entertain a strong distrust of men who have learned what they know by a fixed course of study, mainly because persons who have passed the early part of their lives in learning out of books or from teachers are generally found less fitted to grapple with the kind of difficulties which usually present themselves in Western life, than those who were compelled to learn to conquer them by actual contact with them. So that the " self-made man," as he is called, meaning the man who has surmounted, with little or no aid from education, those obstacles by which the larger portion of the community find themselves hampered and harassed, is looked on as a sort of type of merit and ability.

The process by which the ideas that govern private life are transferred to the conduct of public affairs, is not difficult to understand. In a new community, in which there is not much time for either study or reflection, it would be difficult always to convince the public, even if any other kind of man were to be had, that the kind of man who displays most ability in the conduct of his own business is not the fittest to take charge of that of the public. That other qualities than those necessary for success in the career in which everybody else is running should be needed for legislation, is an idea which meets with no acceptance until enforced by experience. And in a really frontier village, in which no disturbing influences are in operation, it will probably be found that the prosperous management of a dry-goods store will be taken as strong indication of ability to fill the post of Secretary of the Treasury, and deal with the most intricate problems of national finance. But the successful politician in a new country, where deference for experience or culture has not yet grown up, is, after all, the man who has most facility in expressing the ideas which are filling the heads of his neighbors.

It may be taken as a general rule, that those

who cannot look very far back do not look very far forward. Experience is the nurse of forethought. Youth is rarely troubled about to-morrow. Age is far-seeing, because it remembers so much. And communities made of the materials we are describing, as they have no past, are apt to be very careless about the future. The sense of political continuity, of the identity, for political purposes, of each generation with the one which has preceded it and the one which is to follow it, and of the consequent responsibility of each for the acts and promises of the other, is rarely deeply rooted in a state which has no past to dwell on. We are therefore not surprised to find that the doctrine of the absence of all right on the part of one generation to enter into any obligations that would bind its successor—a doctrine utterly subversive of what is called "public faith," and which, if carried out to its full extent, would reduce the intercourse of civilized nations to the mere interchange of compliments or abuse—was first openly preached and acted on in Mississippi, the person who now represents Southern statesmanship to the world being its author. But it is a doctrine which grows naturally in a new society. The reverse of it conflicts strongly with the notions of the proper limits of accountability, which are derived from the relations of individuals. There is little in the analo-

gies presented by the relations of a man either
with his family or his fellows, in such a society, to suggest the expediency or propriety of
his helping, as a citizen, to repay money which
was borrowed before he was born. We think
it will generally be found that, when a state formed
by colonization, as carried on in modern times,
displays a proper disposition with regard to the
public liabilities, it is rather owing to the feeling
of local pride than to a deep sense of responsibility. When a loan contracted by the government of California, a few years ago, was declared
unconstitutional by the Supreme Court, the people, when the question was submitted to them, at
once shouldered the debt. But it was spoken of
in their newspapers as a very remarkable display
of virtue, as something of which the State might
fairly be proud. There was evidently at the bot-
tom of these congratulations an opinion that, in
the absence of any legal obligation, the moral one
was not sufficiently strong to be imperative.

The belief that the production of an inflated,
bombastic style of speaking and writing is one of
the necessary results of democracy is very widespread, and is supported by M. de Tocqueville
with more than usual confidence. He says :

" I have frequently remarked that the Americans, who
generally treat of business in clear, plain language, devoid

of all ornament, and so extremely simple as to be often coarse, are apt to become inflated as soon as they attempt a more poetical diction. They then vent their pomposity from one end of a harangue to the other; and to hear them lavish imagery on every occasion, one might fancy that they never spoke of anything with simplicity.

"The English less frequently commit a similar fault. The cause of this may be pointed out without much difficulty. In democratic communities, each citizen is habitually engaged in the contemplation of a very puny object, namely, himself. If he ever raises his looks higher, he perceives only the immense form of society at large, or the still more imposing aspect of mankind. His ideas are all either extremely minute and clear, or extremely general and vague ; what lies between is a void. When he has been drawn out of his own sphere, therefore, he always expects that some amazing object will be offered to his attention ; and it is on these terms alone that he consents to tear himself for a moment from the petty, complicated cares which form the charm and the excitement of his life."—Vol. II., p. 94.

But democracy produces this effect only in so far as it deprives writers and speakers of a high order of education, or draws them from a class which cannot or do not receive it. The uneducated or half-educated in all countries, and under every form of government, and in every condition of society, fall into an exaggerated and inflated style whenever they attempt to treat on paper or in public of any question not purely personal in its nature.

The uncultivated Englishman or Frenchman is guilty of precisely the same rhetorical faults as the uncultivated American; and the only reason why American bombast makes more impression on European observers than that of their own countrymen is that there is more of it, as a class of persons who in Europe are hardly ever called on to address the public, are in America tempted or obliged to do so very frequently. Rhetorical exaggeration is, in fact, an indication, not of a certain political or social state, but of a certain state of mental culture. How it is that taste is not a natural gift, and what kind of training is necessary for its acquisition, it is not necessary to discuss here. It is enough to know that, without training, no people, except perhaps the Greeks, has ever exhibited it. America itself furnishes a very striking illustration of the unsoundness of M. de Tocqueville's theory. A pure written and spoken style is found only in the democratic States of the Northeast, because there the writers and speakers are often either drawn from a cultivated class, or are under their influence. The literature and oratory of the aristocratic States of the South, on the contrary, are marked by an exaggeration, violence, and affectation so barbarous, that it may safely be said that no orators or writers who have ever figured in history have fallen to the same level. It is a

striking proof of the extent to which the European
public has been led astray on these subjects, that
an English legal periodical of high standing, com-
menting a few months ago on the absurdity of the
harangue delivered by Muller's counsel in New
York, assigned as one of the excuses for Southern
secession the natural disgust felt by "cultivated
gentlemen" at the grotesqueness, absurdity, and
inflation which democracy infused into writing
and public speaking at the North.   An assertion
displaying greater ignorance of the peculiar characteristics of the North and of the South, it would
be hard to meet with.

It may be said, however, that if democracy either
deprives the highly educated class of all influence,
and thus prevents their establishing an authorita-
tive standard of taste, or if it places the half-educated in all the prominent positions in public life,
so that it is they who give the oratory of the country its peculiar character, it is really as much responsible for the national tendency to bombast as
if it produced it by its direct action.   But the answer to this is, that nearly all the extravagance and
inflation of speech or composition which are now
to be met with in America are contributed either
by the South or West, both of which are just in
that stage of mental culture in which inflation of
language is produced as naturally as weeds on a

rank soil. The intense and necessary absorption
of the West in the work of developing the material
resources of the country puts high cultivation out
of the question, but it does not do away with the
necessity of government. Members of Congress
have still to be elected; State Legislatures have
still to meet; and weighty questions have to be
discussed by somebody—and, in default of people
of taste, they have to be discussed by people who
have no taste, by men who labor under the usual
weakness and delusion of the uneducated, that
simple and straightforward language is not fit for
use in dealing with great public affairs. If it be
asked how it is that this class so largely prepon-
derates in Congress, and in public life generally, as
to present itself to the world as a fair specimen of
the highest culture that democracy can produce,
we reply that the new States have now for many
years acquired a great preponderance over the
older ones in population and wealth and resources,
and consequently political preponderance also.
Upon this great mass of powerful, energetic rus-
ticity—we do not use the word as a term of re-
proach—the cultivation of the East has so far been
able to make but very little impression. And this
preponderance has been so overwhelming, that the
West has succeeded to a certain extent in propa-
gating in the East its ideas and manners, both

political and social. It has succeeded in diffusing
to some degree, even in New England, its contempt for and indifference to refinement or culture,
its mistrust of men who have made politics a
study, and its faith in the infallibility of majorities,
not simply as a necessary political assumption, but
as an ethical fact. Its influence in Congress is of
course paramount, and its influence on the government every year increases. It now supplies our
Presidents, a large body of our legislators, and a
large portion of our army. It gives its tone to the
national thought, and its direction to the national
policy. As might be expected, it has, with its
rude, wild energy, its excess of animal life, completely overwhelmed the thinkers of the older
States, and driven most of them into private life,
and taken upon itself to represent American
democracy to the world. American democracy is
thus made answerable by superficial observers for
faults which flow not from its own nature, but from
the outward circumstances of some of those who
live under it.

We need hardly say, that we are very far from
asserting that the state of society which we have
been describing as " Western " can be predicated
literally either of the whole West or of any part of
it. There is probably not a village in it of which
our picture is true in every particular. There are

doubtless to be found in every district many departures from the general type which we have
sketched, many modifications effected by the presence of cultivated people, or by the extraordinary
intelligence and unusually favorable antecedents
of the inhabitants. What we have endeavored to
portray is the general features of society in new
countries which have been subjected to the ordinary agencies of frontier life, and exempted from
the disturbing influences of older and more finished organizations. In so far as our sketch
is inaccurate as applied to the new States of the
Union, to the same extent will our description of
their influence on the East require modification.
The study of society is not one of the exact
sciences; and the utmost that the most careful inquirer can hope for is an approximation to the
truth. This is all that we pretend to have achieved
in the present instance, but it is sufficient for our
purpose.

In so far as the influence exercised by that portion of the population which is immersed in the
cares and toils of frontier life on the national character, or manners, or politics, or literature, or oratory, has been deteriorating or obstructive, it is, of
course, fair matter for regret to all friends of rational progress. But those who are most dis-
heartened by the contemplation of its effects may

find abundant consolation in the consideration that
its action is but temporary, and that every day
that passes weakens its force and hastens its disappearance. The greatest fault of new countries
is their newness, and for this the great remedy is
time. As soon as the population gets settled in its
seat, and its attention has ceased to be distracted
by a multiplicity of prizes, and its energies to be
absorbed in the mere struggle for shelter and food,
the polishing process begins. This struggle, if it
have hardened the hands, and tanned the foreheads,
and roughened the manners of those engaged in it,
has also most certainly developed qualities which,
if they do not themselves constitute national great-
ness, are its only sure and lasting foundation. No
friend of democracy who has watched the course of
the West in this war can help feeling his blood
stirred and his hopes strengthened by the vigor
with which it has thrown itself into the strife, and
the great richness of the blood and brain which it
has sent into the arena. All the great generals of
the war are Western men. No higher capacity for
organization, for conceiving great enterprises, and
conducting them with courage and fortitude, accuracy and punctuality, has been displayed than
in those mushroom communities which yesterday
were not. And if we turn from the military to the
political field, we find everywhere the most strik-

ing proofs of the sagacity, foresight, patriotism, and tenacity of their population. We wish we could say there had been exhibited in the East so general, profound, and just an appreciation of the remoter bearings of this great contest, of its possible influence on society and government, as has been exhibited in the West.

There are no fundamental characteristics of "an imperial race," which the people of the new States have not revealed ; and those who know them best see in the progress they are now making every reason to feel satisfied that the great material strength which they are developing will be, erelong, controlled and directed by a very high order of cultivation, both intellectual and æsthetic, and perhaps richer, more varied, and more original in many of its manifestations than any that has been seen in modern times. If the West should in future answer all the demands made on it by civilization with the alacrity and success with which it has answered those made on it by the political crisis through which we are now passing, the human race would, in a very short time, be even more indebted to it than the nation is already.

If, indeed, the defects which foreign observers see, and many of which Americans acknowledge and deplore, in the politics and society of the United States were fairly chargeable to democracy

—if "the principle of equality" were necessarily
fatal to excellence in the arts, to finish in literature, to simplicity and force in oratory, to fruitful
exploration in the fields of science, to statesmanship in the government, to discipline in the army,
to grace and dignity in social intercourse, to sub-
ordination to lawful authority, and to self-restraint in the various relations of life—the future
of the world would be such as no friend of the race
would wish to contemplate : for the spread of democracy is on all sides acknowledged to be irresistible.   Even those who watch its advance with
most fear and foreboding confess that most civilized nations must erelong succumb to its sway.
Its progress in some countries may be slower than
in others, but it is constant in all ; and it is accel-
erated by two powerful agencies—the Christian
religion and the study of political economy.

The Christian doctrine that men, however unequal in their condition or in their gifts on earth,
are of equal value in the eyes of their Creator, and
are entitled to respect and consideration, if for no
other reason, for the simple one that they are
human souls, long as it has been preached, has,
strange to say, only very lately begun to exercise
any perceptible influence on politics.   It led a
troubled and precarious life for nearly eighteen
hundred years in conventicles and debating clubs,

in the romance of poets, in the dreams of philosophers and the schemes of philanthropists. But it is now found in the cabinets of kings and statesmen, on the floor of parliament-houses, and in the most secret of diplomatic conferences. It gives shape and foundation to nearly every great social reform, and its voice is heard above the roar of every revolution.

And it derives invaluable aid in keeping its place and extending its influence in national councils from the rapid spread of the study of political economy, a science which is based on the assumption that men are free and independent. There is hardly one of its principles which is applicable to any state of society in which each individual is not master of his own actions and sole guardian of his own welfare. In a community in which the relations of its members are regulated by status and not by contract, it has no place and no value. The natural result of the study and discussion which the ablest thinkers have expended on it during the last eighty years has been to place before the civilized world in the strongest light the prodigious impulse which is given to human energy and forethought and industry, and the great gain to society at large, by the recognition in legislation of the capacity, as well as of the right, of each human being to seek his own happiness in his own way. Of course no political system in which this principle has a place can long avoid conceding to all who live under it equality before the law; and from equality before the law to the possession of an equal share in the making of the laws, there is, as everybody must see who is familiar with modern history, but a very short step.

If this spread of democracy, however, was sure, as its enemies maintain, to render great attainments and great excellence impossible or rare, to make literary men slovenly and inaccurate and tasteless, artists mediocre, professors of science dull and unenterprising, and statesmen conscienceless and ignorant, it would threaten civilization with such danger that no friend of progress could wish to see it. But it is difficult to discover on what it is, either in history or human nature, that this apprehension is founded. M. de Tocqueville and all his followers take it for granted that the great incentive to excellence, in all countries in which excellence is found, is the patronage and encouragement of an aristocracy; that democracy is generally content with mediocrity. But where is the proof of this? The incentive to exertion which is widest, most constant, and most powerful in its operation in all civilized countries, is the desire of distinction; and this may be composed either of love of fame or love of wealth, or of both. In literary and artistic and scientific pursuits, sometimes the strongest influence is exerted by a love of the subject. But it may be safely said that no man has ever yet labored in any of the higher callings to whom the applause and appreciation of his fellows was not one of the sweetest rewards of his exertions. There is probably not a masterpiece in existence, either in literature or in art, probably few discoveries in science have ever been made, which we do not owe in a large measure to the love of distinction. Who paints pictures, or has ever painted them, that they may delight no eye but his own? Who writes books for the mere pleasure of seeing his thoughts on paper? Who discovers or invents, and is willing, provided the world is the better of his discoveries or inventions, that another should enjoy the honor? Fame has, in short, been in all ages and in all countries recognized as one of the strongest springs of human action—

> " The spur that doth the clear spirit raise
> To scorn delight and live laborious days "—[10]

sweetening toil, robbing danger and poverty and even death itself of their terrors.

What is there, we would ask, in the nature of democratic institutions, that should render this great spring of action powerless, that should deprive glory of all radiance, and put ambition to sleep? Is it not notorious, on the contrary, that one of the most marked peculiarities of democratic society, or of a society drifting toward democracy, is the fire of competition which rages in it, the fevered anxiety which possesses all its members to rise above the dead level to which the law is ever seeking to confine them, and by some brilliant stroke become something higher and more remarkable than their fellows? The secret of that great restlessness, which is one of the most disagreeable accompaniments of life in democratic countries, is in fact due to the eagerness of everybody to grasp the prizes of which in aristocratic countries only the few have much chance. And in no other society is success more worshipped, is distinction of any kind more widely flattered and caressed. Where is the successful author, or artist, or discoverer, the subject of greater homage than in France or America? And yet in both the principle of equality reigns supreme; and his advancement in the social scale has gone on *pari passu* in every country with the spread of democratic ideas and manners. Grub Street was the author's retreat in the aristocratic age; in this democratic one, he is welcome at the King's table, and sits at the national council-board. In democratic societies, in fact, excellence is the first title to distinction; in aristocratic ones, there are two or three others which are far stronger, and which must be stronger, or aristocracy could not exist. The moment you acknowledge that the highest social position ought to be the reward of the man who has the most talent, you make aristocratic institutions impossible. But to make the thirst for distinction lose its power over the human heart, you must do something more than establish equality of conditions; you must recast human nature itself.

Nor does the view which M. de Tocqueville takes, and which Mr. Mill in his "Dissertations and Discussions" seems to share, of the character of the literature which democratic societies are likely to call for, or have supplied to them, derive much support from experience. Mr. Mill says, that in a democratic society

"There is a greatly augmented number of moderate successes, fewer great literary and scientific reputations. Elementary and popular treatises are immensely multiplied; superficial information far more widely diffused; but there are fewer who devote themselves to thought for its own sake, and pursue in retirement those profounder researches, the results of which can only be appreciated by a few. Literary productions are seldom highly finished; they are got up to be read by many, and to be read

but once. If the work sells for a day, the author's time
and pains will be better laid out in writing a second, than
in improving the first." [11]

There could scarcely be a better answer to this
than the immense sale which the works of both
Mr. Mill himself and M. de Tocqueville meet with
here and in England. They are both philosophical and highly finished, and yet they are read and
studied by thousands in the two countries in
which democracy is either triumphant or rapidly
spreading. Illustrations of the same kind might,
if we had space, be indefinitely multiplied. We
will mention only one other. If we take that
branch of literature, history, in which more than
most others accuracy and research are essential,
in which painstaking and industry and careful attention to details are absolutely necessary to give
the result any real value, what do we find ? Why,
that it is a field of inquiry which, until democratic times, was barely scratched over, and that it
is for the gratification and instruction of this much
despised democratic " many " that it has been for
the first time deeply ploughed and carefully cultivated. There is, we believe, hardly a single historical work composed prior to the end of the last
century, except perhaps Gibbon's, which, judged
by the standard that the criticism of our day has
set up, would not, though written for the "few,"

be pronounced careless, slipshod, or superficial. Grote, Hallam, Motley, Prescott, Martin, Niebuhr, Mommsen, the most laborious, accurate, and critical historical inquirers the world has yet seen, have been produced by a democratic age, and have written for a democratic public. Compare them as to thoroughness and completeness with any of their predecessors of any age, and you are astonished by the contrast; and yet millions read and admire them. So also the first attempt to apply the historical method to the study of the philosophy of law has been made within two or three years, and the result is a work of extraordinary profundity, which is in everybody's hands.[12] We might, by looking into other branches of knowledge, produce innumerable examples of the same kind, all going to show, in our opinion, that although there is, and will always be in every democratic community, an immense mass of slipshod, careless writing and speaking, the demand for accuracy, for finish, perhaps not in form, but certainly in substance, for completeness in all efforts to discover truth or enlighten mankind, so far from diminishing, grows with the spread of knowledge and the multiplication of readers.

There are some, however, who, while acknowledging that the love of distinction will retain its force under every form of social or political organization, yet maintain that to excel in the arts, science, or literature requires leisure, and the possession of leisure implies the possession of fortune. This men in a democratic society cannot have, because the absence of great hereditary wealth is necessary to the perpetuation of democracy. Every man, or nearly every man, must toil for a living; and therefore it becomes impossible for him to gratify the thirst for distinction, let him feel it ever so strongly. The attention he can give to literature or art or science must be too desultory and hasty, his mental training too defective, to allow him to work out valuable results, or conduct important researches. To achieve great things in these fields, it is said and insinuated, men must be elevated, by the possession of fortune, above the vulgar, petty cares of life; their material wants must be provided for before they can concentrate their thoughts with the requisite intensity on the task before them. Therefore it is to aristocracy we must look for any great advance in these pursuits.

The history of literature and art and philosophy is, however, very far from lending confirmation to this opinion. If it teaches us anything, it teaches us that the possession of leisure, far from having helped men in the pursuit of knowledge, seems to have impeded them. Those who have pursued it most successfully are all but invariably those who

have pursued it under difficulties.   The possession
of great wealth no doubt gives facilities for study
and cultivation which the mass of mankind do not
possess ; but it at the same time exerts an influence on the character which, in a vast majority of
cases, renders the owner unwilling to avail himself
of them.   We owe to the Roman aristocracy the
great fabric of Roman jurisprudence ; but, since
their time, what has any aristocracy done for art
and literature, or law?   They have for over a thousand years been in possession of nearly the whole
resources of every country in Europe.   They have
had its wealth, its libraries, its archives, its teachers,
at their disposal ; and yet was there ever a more
pitiful record than the list of "Royal and Noble
Authors."   One can hardly help being astonished,
too, at the smallness and paltriness of the legacies
which the aristocracy of the aristocratic age has
bequeathed to this democratic age which is suc-
ceeding it.   It has, indeed, handed down to us
many glorious traditions, many noble and inspiring examples of courage and fortitude and gener-
osity.   The democratic world would certainly be
worse off than it is if it never heard of the Cid, or
Bayard, or Du Guesclin, of Montrose, or Hampden,
or Russell.   But what has it left behind it for which
the lover of art may be thankful, by which literature has been made richer, philosophy more potent

or more fruitful? The painting and sculpture of modern Europe owe not only their glory, but their very existence, to the labors of poor and obscure men. The great architectural monuments by which its soil is covered were hardly any of them the product of aristocratic feeling or liberality. If we accept a few palaces and a few fortresses, we owe nearly all of them to the labor or the genius or the piety of the democratic cities which grew up in the midst of feudalism. If we take away from the sum total of the monuments of Continental art all that was created by the Italian republics, the commercial towns of Germany and Flanders, and the communes of France, and by the unaided efforts of the illustrious obscure, the remainder would form a result poor and pitiful indeed. We may say much the same thing of every great work in literature, and every great discovery in science. Few of them have been produced by men of leisure, nearly all by those whose life was a long struggle to escape from the vulgarest and most sordid cares. And what is perhaps most remarkable of all is, that the Catholic Church, the greatest triumph of organizing genius, the most impressive example of the power of combination and of discipline which the world has ever seen, was built up and has been maintained by the labors of men drawn from the humblest ranks of society.

Aristocracy applied itself exclusively for ages to the profession of arms. If there was anything at which it might have seemed hopeless for democracy to compete with it, it was in the raising, framing, and handling of armies. But the very first time that a democratic society found itself compelled to wage war in defence of its own ideas, it displayed a force, an originality, a vigor and rapidity of conception, in this, to it, new pursuit, which speedily laid Europe at its feet. And the great master of the art of war, be it ever remembered, was born in obscurity and bred in poverty.

Nor, long as men of leisure have devoted themselves to the art of government, have they made any contributions worth mentioning to political science. They have displayed, indeed, consummate skill and tenacity in pursuing any line of policy on which they have once deliberately fixed ; but all the great political reforms have been, though often carried into effect by aristocracies, conceived, agitated, and forced on the acceptance of the government by the middle and lower classes. The idea of equality before the law was originated in France by literary men. In England, the slave-trade was abolished by the labors of the middle classes. The measure met with the most vigorous opposition in the House of Lords. The emancipation of the negroes, Catholic emancipation,

Parliamentary reform, law reform, especially the reform in the criminal law, free trade, and, in fact, nearly every change which has had for its object the increase of national happiness and prosperity, has been conceived by men of low degree, and discussed and forced on the upper classes by men busy about many other things.

We are, however, very far from believing that democratic society has no dangers or defects. What we have been endeavoring to show is, that the inquiry into their nature and number has been greatly impeded by the natural disposition of foreign observers to take the United States as a fair specimen of what democracy is under the most favorable circumstances. The enormous extent of unoccupied land at our disposal, which raises every man in the community above want, by affording a ready outlet for surplus population, is constantly spoken of as a condition wholly favorable to the democratic experiment—more favorable than could possibly offer itself elsewhere. In so far as it contributes to the general happiness and comfort, it no doubt makes the work of government easy; but what we think no political philosopher ought to forget is, that it also offers serious obstacles to the settlement of a new society on a firm basis, and produces a certain appearance of confusion and instability, both in manners and ideas, which unfit it to furnish a basis for any inductions of much value as to the tendencies to defects either of an equality of conditions or of democratic institutions.

POPULAR GOVERNMENT [1]

I HAVE been reading, with the respect due to everything which Sir Henry Maine produces, his last volume, and particularly that most interesting chapter of it on " The Prospects of Popular Government." I confess, however, to having laid it down, after a careful perusal, without getting a very clear idea of the lesson he undertakes to teach. He says in his preface:

> In the essay on the Prospects of Popular Government I have shown that as a matter of fact Popular Government, since its reintroduction into the modern world, has proved itself to be extremely fragile. In the essay on the Nature of Democracy I have given reasons for thinking that, in the extreme form to which it tends, it is of all kinds of government by far the most difficult. . In the Age of Progress I have argued that, in the perpetual change which, as understood in modern times, it appears to demand, it is not in harmony with the normal forces ruling human nature, and is apt, therefore, to lead to cruel disappointment or serious disaster.

Now the phrase " reintroduction into the modern world " implies that Popular Government existed

in the ancient world, and, if so, an account of its
working in the ancient world would certainly be
a very important aid in judging whether it is
really as "fragile" as Sir Henry Maine thinks it,
for the longer the period in which we watch the
working of an institution, the more we know about
its durability. But he disposes of what he calls
"the short-lived Athenian Democracy under
whose shelter Art, Science, and Philosophy shot
so wonderfully upward" by saying that " it was
only an aristocracy which rose on the ruins of still
another." In fact, he lays it down as a general
proposition "that the progress of mankind has
hitherto been effected by the rise and fall of
aristocracies, by the formation of one aristocracy
within another," and that " there have been many
so-called democracies which have rendered services beyond price to civilization, but they were
only peculiar forms of aristocracy." It is fair, I
think, to conclude from this that there was no such
thing as Popular Government in the ancient world
at all, and that its appearance in the modern world
was its first appearance anywhere, and was therefore not a "reintroduction." Consequently all
that Sir Henry Maine, or any one else, knows
about its fragility, he knows from observation of
its working in the modern world. Whether a
thing is durable or not, we can only tell from see-

ing it exposed, over a long period, to destructive
agencies. That this period should in the case of
a government be very long indeed, it is hardly
necessary to say. Nothing is more delusive in
the work of political speculation than short
periods of observation. The most durable government the modern world has seen was that of
the Venetian Republic, but there were in its history several periods of ten, twenty, or even fifty,
years in which its continuance must have seemed
to contemporaries something hardly to be looked
for.

Now what opportunities for observing the durability of Popular Government has Sir Henry Maine
had, on his own showing ? The ancient world has
afforded him none : what has the modern world
afforded him ? In other words, when did Popular
Government first reveal itself to the philosophic
eye ? There is no doubt, he says, that Popular
Government is of purely English origin, and that
it made its first appearance in the triumph of the
doctrine that government is the servant of the
community, over the doctrine that it is the master
of the community. The former, he says, after
" tremendous struggles," was in spirit, if not in
words, " affirmed in 1689." But that triumph was
not complete, for he adds: "It was long before
this doctrine was either fully carried out by the

nation, or fully accepted by its rulers." In fact, he gives us to understand that it has not yet reached its final stage—that is, the stage at which tests of durability can begin to be applied to it. " What we are witnessing," he says, " in West European politics is not so much the establishment of a definite system, as the continuance, at various rates, of a process."

I gather from all this that Popular Government, as now known to us in the modern world, is a process which began about two centuries ago in a change of opinion on the part of the community in England with regard to the relations of the rulers and the ruled ; that it did not, however, really influence English politics until about the beginning of this century. Consequently, Popular Government is, for the purposes of the philosophic observer, about eighty years old, and no more, and anything we desire to know about its durability and its general prospects we must learn from its history during that period. But the history of these eighty years seems to furnish a very small basis for induction on a matter so serious as the nature and prospects of a form of government. Sir Henry Maine, however, makes the most of it. Curiously enough, England furnishes him, apparently, with no materials at all. His reasons for believing Popular Government to be fragile he finds in the experience of the French with it, since 1789 ; of the Spaniards since 1812, and of the South American Republics since 1820. Having given some account of the frequent violent political changes which have occurred in these countries respectively within the above periods, he says :—

> The true reason why the extremely accessible facts which I have noticed are so seldom observed and put together is that the enthusiasts for Popular Government, particularly when it reposes on a wide basis of suffrage, are actuated by much the same spirit as the zealots of Legitimism. They assumed their principle to have a sanction antecedent to fact. It is not thought to be in any way invalidated by practical violations of it, which merely constitute so many more sins against imprescriptible right (p. 20).

Now I am not an enthusiast for Popular Government, or for any other form of government. I believe politics to be an extremely practical kind of business, and that the communities which succeed best in it are those which bring least enthusiasm to the conduct of their affairs. Nevertheless, I think I may so far speak for the enthusiasts as to suggest that the reason why they do not give more attention to Sir Henry Maine's " extremely accessible facts," and are not more troubled by them, is that they soberly and sincerely believe that these facts are irrelevant : that is, that they throw no light whatever on the nature or prospects of Popular Government.

The facts are simply that in two or three countries which have within the present century set up, or attempted to set up, representative institutions, frequent changes in the executive power have been wrought by violence. To make this bear directly on the question of fragility we should have to be sure that the state of mind which Sir Henry makes the first condition of Popular Government—that is, the belief that the rulers are and ought to be the servants of the ruled—prevailed in the countries which he cites as examples ; that, in short, the setting up and casting down of governments which constitute his "extremely accessible facts" were the efforts of a community to carry out a political theory. We cannot judge of the working of any institution, whether monarchy, aristocracy, or democracy, unless it has its roots in popular approval. How monarchy works can only be known by seeing it in a community which believes in kings. How aristocracy works can only be known by seeing it in a community which believes in noblemen. How Popular Government works can, in like manner, only be known by seeing it in a community in which the doctrine on which it is based is fully and intelligently held by the bulk of the people.

To make France and Spain and the Spanish-American Republics good examples of the instability of Popular Government, Sir Henry Maine has to assume that the state of popular opinion and feeling which produced and sustains this form of government in England or America really exists, or has existed during the last half-century, in the Latin countries; and he does assume it tacitly, but very tacitly indeed. He is almost out of sight in his argument before one perceives what a monstrous assumption it is. There is neither in Spain nor in Spanish America any dominating political theory held by the mass of the people; in fact, there is nothing which a political philosopher can call a people. There are great landed proprietors; there is a powerful clergy; there is a standing army; there is an ignorant peasantry. There arise naturally in this state of things frequent disputes over the possession of the sovereignty, but they are disputes like the War of the Roses, or the Seven Years' War, between those who have and those who have not. They illustrate human nature in certain conditions of culture, as do most of the disorders of history, but they do not illustrate any theory of government any more than a fight over a captive's ransom in the cave of Greek brigands. In France, too, it is only since 1870 that the view of relations of the government of the people, on which Sir Henry Maine bases Popular Government, can be said to have really existed among the mass of the people. There have been since 1789 disciples of Rousseau and believers in the social contract—both of them great bugbears to Sir Henry Maine—in Paris and the other great cities, but until the present Republic was set up the peasantry never thought of controlling the government, or of treating its members as their servants. No matter what its form was, whether Constitutional Monarchy, Empire, or Republic, it was, in the eyes of provincials, the master of France, whose edicts, if they came from the proper office, nobody thought of disputing.

Next let me say that in assuming that the instability of government in a given country has and can have only one cause — namely, the view which the ruled take of their relation to the rulers —Sir Henry Maine seems to give countenance to a fallacy which is one of the great difficulties of modern politics, and which Mr. Mill has lucidly exposed as the "Chemical Method" of reasoning about political phenomena. Surely the following has an important bearing on the value of Sir Henry Maine's specific instances, or, as he calls them, "extremely accessible facts : "

In social phenomena the Composition of Causes is the Universal Law. Now, the method of philosophizing which may be termed chemical overlooks this fact, and proceeds as if the nature of man as an individual were not concerned at all, or concerned in a very inferior degree, in the operations of human beings in society. All reasoning in politics or social affairs, grounded on principles of human nature, is objected to by reasoners of this sort, under such names as "abstract theory." For the direction of their opinions and conduct, they profess to demand, in all cases without exception, specific experience. This mode of thinking is not only general with practitioners in politics, and with that very numerous class who (on a subject which no one, however ignorant, thinks himself incompetent to discuss) profess to guide themselves by common sense rather than by science; but is often countenanced by persons with greater pretensions to instruction; persons who, having sufficient acquaintance with books and with the current ideas to have heard that Bacon taught mankind to follow experience, and to ground their conclusions on facts instead of metaphysical dogmas, think that by treating political facts in as directly experimental a method as chemical facts, they are showing themselves true Baconians, and proving their adversaries to be mere syllogizers and schoolmen. As, however, the notion of the applicability of experimental methods to political philosophy cannot coexist with any just conception of these methods themselves, the kind of arguments from experience which the chemical theory brings forth as its fruits (and which form the staple, in this country especially, of Parliamentary and hustings oratory) are such as, at no time since Bacon, would have been admitted to be valid in chemistry itself, or in any other branch of experimental science. They are such as these: that the prohibition of foreign commodities must conduce to national wealth, because

England has flourished under it, or because countries in
general which have adopted it have flourished; that our
laws, or our internal administration, or our constitution,
are excellent for a similar reason : and the eternal arguments from historical examples, from Athens or Rome,
from the fires in Smithfield or the French Revolution. I
will not waste time in contending against modes of argu-
mentation which no person, with the smallest practice in
estimating evidence, could possibly be betrayed into ;
which draw conclusions of general appreciation from a
single unanalyzed instance, or arbitrarily refer an effect to
some one among its antecedents, without any process of
elimination or comparison of instances.—*Logic*, pp. 458–59.[2]

I call this fallacy one of the greatest difficulties
of modern politics because it is the readiest tool
of demagogues, and to the popular eye the most
attractive because the easiest solution of pending
troubles. The most effective argument of the
American protectionists is, that as the United
States have prospered under protection, the tariff
must be the one cause of the prosperity ; that as
Ireland and Turkey are poor under free trade,
their condition shows the danger of throwing open
home markets to foreign producers. So, also, we
are now afflicted with tons of useless silver coin
owing to the popular belief that the slowness of
our recovery from the crisis of 1873 was simply
and solely the demonetization of silver in the same
year. France and Spain and the Spanish-Ameri-

can Republics, says Sir Henry Maine, have popular governments—that is, parliaments elected by a widely extended suffrage. But they have also frequent rebellions; therefore Popular Government is both unstable, and the cause of its instability. It may be that Popular Government in a given country is fragile, but surely we are not justified in assuming that the character, the religion, the culture, the manners, the history, and the material surroundings of the people have nothing to do with the security of their political institutions; or that, in considering whether a new form of government will suit them, we are not called upon to ask how they got on under the old one; whether, for instance, the French were happy and content under absolute monarchy, and the Spanish-Americans peaceful and industrious under the Viceroys and the Bishops.

So completely does Sir Henry Maine commit himself to the Chemical Method that he boldly declares that " the inferences which might be drawn from the stability of the government of the United States are much weakened, if not destroyed, by the remarkable spectacle furnished by the numerous Republics set up from the Mexican border-line to the Straits of Magellan." He notices, it is true, the objection to his theory drawn from the fact that the inhabitants of the Spanish-American Repub-

lics are to a great extent of Indian blood and have
been trained in Roman Catholicism, but he gets
over it by announcing that " such arguments would
be intelligible if they were used by persons who
maintain that a highly special and exceptional
political education is essential to the successful
practice of Popular Government; but they proceed
from those who believe that there is at least a
strong presumption in favor of democratic institutions everywhere."

But why must this argument be used only by
persons who believe that a highly specialized and
exceptional political education is necessary for the
successful practice of Popular Government? Why
is it not good in the mouths of those who believe
simply that Indian blood and Roman Catholic
training are serious obstacles to the practice of
Popular Government? Why may it not be used
by those who believe that the United States Government is largely indebted for its stability, not
to the fact that the American people have had a
highly special and exceptional political education,
but to the fact that they are mainly of Anglo-Saxon blood, and have been trained in Protestantism?
And why, in the name of Aristotle, is an argument
made unintelligible by the fact that some of those
who use it also use other arguments which are
feeble? Surely, if I sometimes reason *à priori*

about politics, that does not make my inductive reasoning worthless.

For my part, I think the example of the United States all important, even from Sir Henry Maine's point of view, for they are the one country in the world in which Popular Government, as he defines it, really exists. They are the one country, that is to say, governed by universal suffrage in which the great mass of the voters have a realizing sense of the fact that the government is their servant and not their master, and that it exists simply to carry out the ideas of the " plain people " who compose the bulk of the community, and not those of a small but more cultivated and more enlightened class ; a government, in short, as Lincoln expressed it, " of the people, by the people, for the people." It may be that their example is sometimes cited by disputants whom consistency or some other obligation forbids to cite it. It may be, too, that inferences drawn from it would not be good against every assailant of Popular Government ; but as against Sir Henry Maine they are, as it seems to me, good in anybody's hands. He is, in fact, estopped by his refusal to take into account anything but the instability of the government in France and Spain and the South American Republics, from taking into account anything but the stability of the government in the case of the United

States. If the Chemical Method be good for one, it is good for the other.

Sir Henry Maine's manner of elucidating the effects of universal suffrage controlled by wire-pullers on social and intellectual progress is even more remarkable than his manner of proving the fragility of Popular Government. He says :

Such a suffrage (a widely extended and universal suffrage) is commonly associated with Radicalism ; no doubt amid its most certain effects would be the extensive destruction of the existing institutions ; but the chances are that in the long run it would produce a mischievous form of Conservatism, and drug society with a potion compared with which Eldonine would be a salutary draught. For to what end, toward what ideal state, is the process of stamping upon law the average opinion of an entire community directed ? The end arrived at is identical with that of the Roman Catholic Church, which attributes a similar sacredness to the average opinion of the Christian world. "Quod semper, quod ubique, quod ab omnibus" was the canon of Vincent of Lerins. "Securus judicat orbis terrarum" were the words which rang in the ears of Newman, and produced such marvellous effects on him. But did any one in his senses ever suppose that these were maxims of progress? The principles of legislation at which they point would put an end to all social and political activities, and arrest everything which has ever been associated with Liberalism. A moment's reflection will satisfy any competently instructed person that this is not too broad a proposition. Let him turn over in his mind the great epochs of scientific invention and social change during the last two centuries,

and consider what would have occurred if universal suffrage had been established at any one of them.   Universal
suffrage which to-day excludes free-trade from the United
States would certainly have prohibited the spinning-jenny
and the power-loom.   It would certainly have forbidden
the thrashing-machine.   It would have forbidden the adoption of the Gregorian Calendar, and would have restored
the Stuarts (p. 36).

A few sentences before this he has acknowledged
that the world has had only a very brief experience
of wide suffrage—that is, about fifty years in the
United States and about twenty in France—but,
brief as it is, it ought to have furnished him with
specific instances in support of this very dark view
of the future of West European society.   He was
able to infer from the example of France and Spain
and the Spanish-American Republics that Popular
Government would be fragile.   It seems to me
that he ought to have been able to infer from the
same source that it would be hostile to civilization.
Strange to say, however, on this point he does not
argue ; he contents himself with prophesying, and
it is one of the commonplaces of rhetoric that you
cannot refute a prophet.   Perhaps it would be
more accurate to say that he guesses, using the
word in its English rather than in its American
sense.   For what other name can we give to an assertion that " the chances are " that, if a certain
thing had happened long before it did happen, a

certain other thing would have happened, which,
as a matter of fact, has never happened at all? In
no place has universal suffrage "put an end to all
social and political activities or arrested everything
which has been associated with Liberalism." In
no place has it ever shown a tendency to do so.
In no place has it ever done anything like prohibiting a spinning-jenny or the power-loom or the
thrashing-machine, or preventing the adoption of
the Gregorian Calendar. Nevertheless, Sir Henry
Maine makes the extremely broad proposition that
it would have done so had it had the opportunity.
I have searched as carefully as I can for the basis
of these very extraordinary deductions. As well
as I can make out, it consists simply in his opinion
that in a democratic community the embodiment
of public opinion in legislation would result in
giving the law the sanctity which in the Catholic
Church is attributed to the consensus of the Christian world on points of doctrine. Admitting it to
be true that the general opinion embodied in a
statute would give the statute in democratic eyes
the sacredness of a Catholic dogma, whence do we
draw the conclusion that it would also have the
permanence of a dogma?

There is, in fact, just enough evidence to show (Sir
Henry Maine says) that even now there is a marked antagonism between democratic opinion and scientific truth ap-

plied to human societies. The central seat in all political
economy was from the first occupied by the Theory of
Population. This theory has now been generalized by Mr.
Darwin and his followers, and, stated as the principle of
the survival of the fittest, it has become the central truth
of all biological science. Yet it is evidently disliked by
the multitude and thrust into the background by those
whom the multitude permits to lead it. It has long been
intensely unpopular in France and on the continent of
Europe, and among ourselves proposals for recognizing it
through the relief of distress by emigration are visibly
being supplanted by schemes founded on the assumption
that, through legislative experiments on society, a given
space of land may always be made to support in comfort
the population which from historical causes has come to be
settled on it (p. 37).

As "just enough evidence" to show that there
is even now " a marked antagonism between democratic opinion and scientific truth as applied to
human societies," the above is very remarkable.
I believe the doctrine of the survival of the fittest
has, as a matter of fact, met with even fiercer opposition from the religious well-to-do middle class
and from the clergy than from the unfortunate
"multitude." But it is a doctrine which must
needs be unpopular—if unpopular means disagreeable—with all but the very successful, that is, with
the great majority of the human race. The survival of the fittest has ever been and must ever be
an odious sight to the unfit or the less fit, who see

that they cannot survive. Sir Henry Maine's re-
proach, that they do not accept it cheerfully re-
minds one of Frederick the Great's savage reproof
to his flying troops, "Hunde, wollte ihr ewig
leben?" In asking the multitude to take to it
kindly, Sir Henry asks something which has
always been beyond human powers. There is no
doctrine with which the race is more familiar in
practice than the doctrine that the strongest must
have the best of it, which is really Darwin's doctrine expressed in terms of politics. The progress
of civilization under all forms of government has
consisted simply in making such changes in the
environment of the multitude as will increase the
number of the fittest. That it has been well to
strive for this end ; that it has been well to try to
make a country like England a place in which
twenty-eight millions can dwell in comfort on soil
which seventy years ago only supported ten millions in comparative misery, has been for ages the
opinion of the wisest and best men under the old
monarchies. Possibly they were wrong. Possibly
it ought to have been the policy of rulers not only
to see that the fittest survived, but that their
number was kept down. But is it not asking too
much of the multitude to ask them to take a totally
new view of the conditions of man's struggle with
nature ?

The great aim of the political art has hitherto been to protect man in some degree from the remorseless working of the laws of the physical universe, to save him from cold, from heat, from savage beasts, from the unwillingness of the earth to yield him her fruits and the sea its fish. All its successes have to some extent increased the number of the fittest. It has filled West Europe with a population which conservative observers like Sir Henry Maine two centuries ago would certainly have declared it incapable of maintaining. Can we possibly expect Democracy to give up the game as soon as it comes into power, and bid the weaklings of the race prepare for extinction? Emigration, which he treats as an acceptance of the Darwinian doctrine, is, of course, in reality simply a transfer of the struggle for survival to another arena. The law of population works everywhere, and with increasing severity, other things being equal, as the population increases. Sending the unfit to New Zealand or Dakota is not a whit more scientific than sending them to till English moors. There is no escape for them anywhere from the battle with the fittest; but any abandonment of the effort to protract their existence and make it more tolerable would mean the stoppage of civilization itself. Democracy may make mistakes in this work, and may attempt more than it can accomplish, but energy in the work and devotion to it is after all what distinguishes a civilized community from a savage one. There is no more reason why the bulk of the race should fold its arms in the presence of the theory of population than in the presence of the great fact of mortality. How many people a given piece of land will maintain and comfort, whether only the number settled on it by "historical causes" or a larger one, is something which can be only ascertained by intelligent experiment. All causes, too, which settle a man on a farm become "historical" after a while; but whether it is well for him to remain there is something only to be learned by experience. The theory of population does not necessarily prescribe emigration when people begin to find it hard to get a living off the land on which they were born, or on which they have settled, but it does prescribe better modes of cultivation and smaller families.

I am not prepared to argue that democratic societies will always accept the conclusions of science with meekness and submission. One sees, I admit, in our own time a good deal to warrant the fear that democratic ignorance will fight unpleasant and inconvenient truths with the pertinacity with which monarchical and aristocratic ignorance has always fought them; and that they will have to owe their triumph in the future, as they have owed it in the past, not to any particular distribution of the political sovereignty, but to the intellectual impulse which has carried the race out of the woods and the caves, and given it its great discoverers and inventors.

But I am very curious to know why Sir Henry Maine should have overlooked the experience of the only really democratic community now existing, that of the Northern States of the American Union, on this point. As a matter of fact, there never has been any society in which new discoveries and inventions and new theories of the art of living have been received with so much readiness as in these States; and they are the countries in which the dominating opinion is most distinctly that of the multitude, in which legislation most distinctly embodies both the prejudices and weakness of the multitude, and in which there is least respect for authority. I think I might safely appeal to American men of science to say whether they do not suffer in reputation and influence with the people, for not making more and greater calls on their faith or credulity ; or, in other words, for their slowness rather than for their haste in making and accepting discoveries. The fertility of Americans in inventions—that is, in the production of new machines and new processes—great as it is, is not so re-

markable as the eagerness with which the people
receive them and use them. The large number of
medical quacks who infest the country, and their
great success in the sale of their nostrums—the
like of which I think can be seen nowhere
else — is undoubtedly due to a sort of impatience with the caution and want of enterprise
of the regular practitioners. The kind of fame
which came to Edison after he had made some
improvements in the electric light and invented
the phonograph, was a very good illustration of
the respect of American people for the novel
and the marvellous. For a good while he was
hailed as a man to whom any problem in physics
would be simple, and he was consulted on a variety
of subjects to which he had given no attention,
such as the means of diminishing the noise of the
trains on the elevated railroads in the streets of this
city. In fact, for a year or two, he held the position — doubtless to his own amusement — of a
"medicine man," to whom any mystery was easy.

Are there, then, no signs in this American
democracy of tendencies in the direction which
Sir Henry Maine predicts or guesses at—that is,
of the emancipation of the people from the control or influence of science, or scientific men, or
of a disposition to go back to the rule of thumb in
the art of living? As I am not posing here as a

champion of Popular Government, or indeed as anything but a humble inquirer into the reasons why Sir Henry Maine wrote his book, I can have no difficulty in answering this question with candor and explicitness.

No observer of American politics can deny that, with regard to matters which can become the subject of legislation, the American voter listens with extreme impatience to anything which has the air of instruction ; but the reason is to be found not in his dislike of instruction so much as his dislike in the political field of anything which savors of superiority. The passion for equality is one of the very strongest influences in American politics. This is so fully recognized now by politicians that self - depreciation, even in the matter of knowledge, has become one of the ways of commending one's self to the multitude, which even the foremost men of both parties do not disdain. In talking on such subjects as the currency, with a view of enlightening the people, skilful orators are very careful to repudiate all pretence of knowing anything more about the matter than their hearers. The speech is made to wear as far as possible the appearance of being simply a reproduction of things with which the audience is just as familiar as the speaker. Nothing is more fatal to a stump orator than an air of superior wisdom on any subject. He has, if he means to persuade, to keep carefully, in outward seeming at all events, on the same intellectual level as those whom he is addressing. Orators of a demagogic turn, of course, push this caution to its extreme, and often affect ignorance, and boast of the small-ness of the educational opportunities enjoyed by them in their youth, and of the extreme difficulty they had in acquiring even the little they know. There is nothing, in fact, people are less willing to tolerate in a man who seeks office at their hands than any sign that he does not consider himself as belonging to the same class as the bulk of the voters—that either birth, or fortune, or education has taken him out of sympathy with them, or caused him, in any sense, to look down on them.

That this has a tendency to make political speaking in this country, especially of late years, remarkably uninstructive, uninteresting, and a poor educational agency, there is no denying. Anyone who judged of the capacity and intelligence of the American voters by the pabulum supplied to them on the stump would certainly be excusable in taking a dark view of the future of American democracy.

The truth seems to be that with regard to all matters within the field of politics the new democracy is extremely sensitive about any doubts of

its competency. It will not suffer any question,
or sign of question, of its full capacity to deal
with any matter which calls for legislation. It is
ready enough to base legislation on investigations
and reports; but the investigations and reports
must be made in its name and by its authority
through what it calls "practical men" as distinguished from scientific or professorial men. By
practical men, it means men engaged in some
industrial or money - making pursuit, like the
bulk of the community, and making no pretence
to book-learning or theoretical knowledge. What
men of this class, who have succeeded in business, say on any subject calling for political action, counts for much more in the United States
with the voters than what specialists or learned
men say. There is, in fact, an inordinate respect for the opinions on all subjects of "successful business men" — that is, men who from
small beginnings have made fortunes by their
own exertions. But this is not more wonderful in
an industrial community than the reverence in a
military community for a great soldier—than the
prolonged belief in England, for instance, in the
political wisdom of the Duke of Wellington for
many years after Waterloo.

　　With matters of a quasi-scientific kind, like the
tariff, for instance, or the currency, on which the

opinions of theorists are extremely important and "practical men" very likely to be wrong, this habit of excluding science from all say in the political arena, is undoubtedly very unfortunate. But it does not have the effect that Sir Henry Maine would expect from it. It sometimes leads to the embodiment in legislation of gross errors and delusions, but it never leads to the conversion of an error or delusion into a sacred dogma. It leads to costly and useless experimentation and to the trial of schemes which have failed a hundred times before in other places and ages. It is rare, indeed, that an economic or other fallacy connected with legislation, which has once taken hold of the popular mind in this country, can be overthrown by the attacks of authority or of historical experience. In fact, the intervention of the professors to expose it, is very apt to hasten its conversion into law, if only for the purpose of showing the literary men that they must not meddle in politics.

But the experiment once tried, there is nothing anywhere like the readiness of the public here to acknowledge failure in the frankest way. The orators and editors go through the process of "owning up," with extraordinary, and some might say cynical, cheerfulness. Some of the most furious newspaper advocates of Bland's Silver Bill

are now its most strenuous opponents. Everything which the theorists predicted of its working
has come to pass, but it would never have done to
allow theorists to suppose that their talk would
turn the people from its purpose, or influence
law-making.[3] In truth, that most marked characteristic of the American commercial character—
its readiness to abandon things which do not pay,
and its unwillingness to spend any time crying
over spilt milk—shows itself just as prominently in
politics as in business. There is not the smallest
sign of the bigoted conservatism which Sir Henry
Maine looks for. The legislative history of every
State in the Union is full of illustrations of the
people's openness to conviction, provided the
conviction be wrought by processes which they
can understand. Nothing is sacred in America,
and nothing elicits so much ridicule as an attempt
to put anything or any person into the category of
the unchangeable or unapproachable.

But, outside of politics, authority occupies a
very different place. The scientific or literary
man who addresses the people without any design
of directly influencing their political action, or
making his opinions felt in legislation, nowhere
receives a more attentive hearing. The success of
instructive lectures in this country, though greater
some years ago than now, is still greater than any-

where else in the world. Scientific men, working
in their own fields, are nowhere so widely known
and respected by the masses. I do not need to
speak of the wide diffusion in the United States
of the reading habit. A large proportion of it—
by far too large a portion of it perhaps—is devoted to newspapers, which have their bad side,
on which I will not dwell here. But they have
one effect which makes any growth of ignorant
conservatism, or any barbarous dislike of novelty,
simply impossible. They fill every corner of the
land with some knowledge of what is going on
everywhere else. They tell the people something
about every famous man in the world, and about
the things which have made him famous. They
familiarize them with every new idea or discovery.
They, in short, prevent mental stagnation. By
keeping people curious about the world outside
their village, they keep them in a state of mental
receptivity.

I might illustrate these things at considerable
length, if I had not taken up so much space. But
I shall, in closing, point out that one of Sir Henry
Maine's examples of popular bigotry—the hostility
of the United States to free trade—shows a sin-
gular ignorance of the exact nature of the tariff
controversy in this country. The tariff is not a
purely fiscal question here, and for that reason the

difficulty of getting Americans to take a scientific view of it is greatly increased.

In the first place, the possession of a continent containing nearly every variety of soil, climate, and product greatly diminishes the force with which the free-trade doctrine, that trade consists in the interchange of the results of special natural advantages, strikes the American mind. No other country can say that it finds within its own borders the means, as far as soil and climate are concerned, of producing nearly everything it buys from foreigners. In the next place, the prohibition of customs duties between the States has given a larger area to free trade here than exists anywhere else, and has thus in a remarkable degree lessened the pinch of protection. Lastly, the enormous immigration—nearly a million a year—of consumers and producers, in the very prime of life, is constantly making new markets, which for many years postponed the glut which is now putting the high tariff in so much peril. The effect of this, in impeding the free-trade agitation, has been very like the effect of opening a small foreign State every year to American goods. In short, anybody who imagines that the free-trade argument presents itself to the American voter in the neat compact shape in which Cobden and Bright were able to offer it to the British public in 1846, or in which

Fawcett was able to offer it in 1880, is greatly mistaken.[4] The American voter, though much deluded about the tariff, is not deluded to the same degree or in the same way as the British fair-trader. He has never had a notion that, as people say here, he could lift himself by his own boot-straps, or make money by swapping jack-knives. His vast reserve of waste lands has always been in his mind, something for a tariff to work on which no other nation possessed.

SOME POLITICAL AND SOCIAL ASPECTS OF THE TARIFF [1]

A TARIFF, in so far as it is intended to be protective, is a tax levied on the community to indemnify a certain number of persons for their losses in carrying on certain kinds of business ; or, rather, if any one likes it better, to furnish them with a fair profit in certain kinds of business. There is, perhaps, no tax which may not be properly submitted to the popular judgment, if it be submitted in its true shape, without disguise. This requires a distinct definition both of its object and of its amount. This rule is rigidly applied to all taxes except the protective tax. It is applied rigidly in all appropriations for the expenses of the Government, such as the salaries of its civil and military servants, the cost of the navy, of fortifications, of the river and harbor improvements, of the public buildings, of subventions to railroads, and of the redemption of the public debt. For none of these things is an appropriation either left indefinite in amount or hidden away in another for

entirely different objects. But in voting funds for
the creation or promotion of certain branches of
industry, the rule is totally disregarded.

In the first place, the money levied on the tax-
payer for this purpose is mixed up with the money
levied for the general expenses of the Government.
How much of the taxes goes for the protection
of native industry is never known or specified,
and no pains are taken to find it out. One may
really approve of a protective tax, and yet be totally
unable to approve of any tax levied in this way
for any purpose whatever. Granting that it is expedient for the Government to spend money in the
maintenance or the promotion of the iron manufacture, for example, it must be expedient, also,
for the public to know the exact amount which it
costs annually ; just as it is expedient that the public should know exactly how much the army and
navy costs, or how much the annual improvement of
rivers and harbors costs. No view, however broad,
of the province of government can furnish an ex-
cuse for concealing the expense of any great
national undertaking. The question " how much,"
is a question which every taxpayer has a right to
ask as regards all branches of the public expenditure, and which every Secretary of the Treasury
ought to be able to answer. There is not a single
good reason for concealing the national expenditure

in protection, any more than for concealing the national expenditure in anything else. But there is no trace of this expenditure in the national accounts. Everybody knows that it must be large, but nobody knows how large. The only sources of information on this subject are the guesses made in free-trade books and pamphlets, which, of course, possess but little authority in the popular eye. The debates between free-traders and protectionists on this point are the most bewildering part of the controversy. Every now and then a free-trader, home or foreign, undertakes to foot up the amount of the contributions which American consumers, and especially the farmers, make to the maintenance of the various branches of domestic industry. Such attempts always excite great indignation among protectionists. A pamphlet containing calculations of this sort, by an Englishman named Montgredien, was published in this country a few years ago, and has been denounced by various protectionist writers with great bitterness, as if it were a sort of impertinent prying into somebody's private affairs.[2] I dare say it was incorrect. I do not, indeed, see how such calculations can come anywhere near correctness. But what a curious state of mind about the national finances that is, which treats as illicit all efforts to discover the exact amount of the national outlay, on what is, admittedly, an object of the highest national importance.

Next, it must be said that any fund of large amount, raised and distributed in this way, must of necessity prove a corruption fund. By this, I do not mean a fund distributed in bribes to individuals or organizations, but a fund the existence of which must be constantly present to the mind of the lazy, the improvident, or incompetent, as something to fall back on if the worst come to the worst. Suppose the national appropriations for the purpose of protecting manufacturing industry were made in the ordinary way by a distinct vote of Congress ; were made, for instance, as the appropriations for the promotion of the carrying trade— the steamship subsidies, as they are called—are made, in the shape of an annual maximum sum. Suppose this sum were paid over to the corporations, or individuals, engaged in each manufacture, on their giving proof that they were carrying on a bonâ-fide business. Suppose that to each were given as much as would meet the loss, as shown by his books, incurred by him in competing with foreigners in the home markets. I am not advocating this. Any one can see its difficulties. I acknowledge how much less troublesome it is to protect by levying duties on foreign goods at the port of entry. But the political objections to the protective system, as now administered, cannot be made so clear in any way as by inquiring how the plan of distributing the money directly by the public Treasury would work.

The measure of each manufacturer's needs would, of course, be the amount lost in his business through foreign competition. It would hardly be possible to restrict the number of participators in the bounty, because one of its great objects would be the multiplication of manufactures. We should have to invite as many people as possible to set up mills and furnaces, and then to come to us for help. But see what an amount of inspection we should need to prevent the distribution of the fund becoming a gross job. It would be impossible, for instance, to pay the subsidy or indemnity on a simple statement of the loss sustained. We should have to inquire *how* the loss was sustained; whether really by foreign competition, or by lax or inefficient or dishonest methods of doing business; whether by simple misfortune, or insufficiency of capital, or want of experience. We would never consent that the Treasury should furnish insurance against loss from any cause whatever; that the same measure should be dealt out to the idle, the improvident, and the slow, as to the industrious, the energetic, and the ingenious. No government would undertake to help in the same degree, through direct subsidies, every one who chose to go into the iron or cotton business. It would investigate and discriminate. It would not treat all men's complaints as equally respectable. Indiscriminate protection, if it were given directly, would speedily be felt to have all the evils of indiscriminate charity. A manufacturer who said, " I am not able to go on with my business and must have more state aid," would be met in the same way as a man who said, " I must have relief, because I have got no money." The latter, before receiving relief, would surely be asked : " Why have you no money ? Is it because you are lazy, or because you are unfortunate ? " In like manner, the manufacturer who demanded more protection, simply because the amount received was not sufficient to save him from bankruptcy, would be asked : " Why is the amount you receive insufficient ? Is it the fault of the market, or your own lack of fitness for the business in which you have engaged? In the former case you are entitled to relief. In the latter it would be a waste of the taxpayers' money, and a waste of your own life, to start you again."

That such a system could long prevail in any country without damage to the moral constitution of those who were benefited by it, all experience of human nature forbids us to expect. The effect

of the possession of money, or of a rich father, on
a young professional man, is well known. It is
only the men of very strong character who make
their mark in spite of it. In all walks in life, indeed, it is generally those who have burnt their
bridges who make the stiffest fight. Manufacturers
would need to be more than human to make the
very best use of their faculties, while knowing
that they had in Congress a protector of boundless
wealth and indulgence, who, when the allowance
was exhausted, asked only one question, namely,
how much more was needed?

Looking at the protective system, as it now exists, from the side of legislation, the political objections to it under our form of government are
still stronger. The only governments fitted to
deal with votes of money of an indefinite amount,
for an ill-defined purpose, if any be fitted, are
governments of the parliamentary type, in which
the finances are managed by a responsible minister,
and all the appropriations collected in a systematic
whole called the budget. Even in such hands, the
support of industry, through indirect taxation, is
open to immense abuse. But such a minister, responsible to the public for the whole financial system, can make some attempt to reconcile the con-
flicting claims of the great industries. Under our
system—the presidential system, as it is called—

nobody in particular is responsible for the financial scheme of the year. There is, in fact, no official scheme, in the strict sense of the term, submitted to Congress. The Secretary of the Treasury puts into his report a mass of multifarious information about the public finances, but the recommendations with which he follows it up are rarely heeded by the Legislature. The real work of what is called in other countries a Minister of Finance, is done by a committee of the House of Representatives, which makes the first draft of the appropriation bills. But these bills, including the tariff bill, never pass the House in the shape in which they are drawn up, or in anything approaching to it. Each member feels himself fully entitled to propose, and, if he can, to carry, modifications in them ; so that when a bill is finally passed it is generally impossible for any one, in or out of the House, to say who its author is. So numerous are the influences which are brought to bear on the framing of it, that the most powerful of them is hardly ever known. The committee is beset by hundreds of manufacturers from all parts of the country, representing every variety of industry, and each claiming to be the final authority on his own subject. Each, too, demands that Congress shall either alter, or shall *not* alter, the duty on some particular article of foreign importation, and supports his demand with an array of figures, the correctness of which nobody attempts to dispute, if for no other reason, for want of time. Failure to influence the committee, too, rarely discourages any tariff lobbyist. He transfers his labors to the House, and attacks the bill through individual members, who, being generally much more ignorant of the subject than the members of the committee, fall an easy prey to him. The general result is apt to be that the bill, as finally passed, has but little, if any, resemblance to the bill as it issued from the committee-room. It is often, when examined, found to be something very different in its operation, not only from what its first projectors intended it to be, but from what everybody else, at the end, thought that it really was. There is hardly a more pitiable spectacle in politics than the vexation and amazement of the country, after a new tariff bill has been passed, over the discovery that nobody can tell what its effect on industry is likely to prove.

There is, however, one other reason of the unfitness of Congress for the proper working of our protective system besides the absence of a responsible ministry charged with the management of the finances. It has been the American policy from the beginning, and a wise policy, to provide, by paying the members, that the legislatures of

the country shall be a fair representation of the
plain people who compose the bulk of the population. The bulk of the population has but little
money, but is keenly alive to the use of money, and
eagerly engaged in the pursuit of it. We send to
the Legislature, both State and Federal, men who
are generally poor and generally honest when they
go there, but not unwilling to be rich if a respectable occasion offers, and are very apt to have their
imagination touched by the history and condition
of millionaires. In plain and simple communities,
such as two or three of the New England States still
remain, in which capital is scarce and great capitalists unknown, the relation of these legislators
to their constituency leaves little to be desired.
But in States in which great accumulations of
wealth have taken place, in which capitalists
frequently have great favors to ask of the State,
and in which legislators are constantly called on
to deal with measures which contain, or are thought
to contain, as Johnson said of the Thrale brew-
ery, " the potentiality of growing rich beyond the
dreams of avarice," these relations leave a great
deal to be desired. The belief of the great capitalists in the venality of legislators in some
States, if not in many, is well known, and is one
of the most unpleasant political phenomena of the
day. In fact, they make hardly an attempt to

conceal it. I have never talked with one who had
ever found himself in the power of a State Legislature, or had to ask anything of it which seriously
affected his interests, who was afraid to avow his
belief that the members were venal, or who did
not pretend to hold proofs of their venality ; who
had not stories to tell, either of his having to
pay in order to get what he sought, or of his having to pay in order to escape a tax on what he
possessed already. In the New York Legislature,
certainly, the practice of introducing bills simply
for the purpose of frightening rich men, or "striking them," as it is called, is by no means uncommon. Nor is the practice unknown of delaying
the passage of measures in which rich men are
interested, until they are forced to inquire what it
is that stops the way. One hears the same stories
for all States in which there are large corporations or great capitalists exposed in any manner
to legislative action. Doubtless there is in all this
much exaggeration, but any one who is determined
to gain his ends with the State government through
corruption, is pretty sure, if he cannot succeed, at
all events to find many ways of spending money
in the attempt.

All this is an illustration of the growth of a
political evil which is both novel and peculiar to
our time. In all past states of society with which

we have any acquaintance, the governing class has
been the wealthy class. The military or feudal
states were ruled by the men who had the most
land. The great commercial republics, like Venice
and Genoa, were ruled by the men who had the
most money. It is in our day and generation, and
in this country, that the Government has for the
first time, both in its legislative and administrative
branches, passed into the hands of the poor, in a
rich community. I say the poor in a rich community, for there have been states before now in
which poor men filled all the offices; but these
were states, such as some of the Swiss cantons, in
which the rulers and ruled were, as regards this
world's goods, pretty much on a level, and in
which the absence of temptation made it easy for
everybody to be virtuous. Here, on the other hand,
we are trying the novel experiment of governing
a commercial community, during a period of
rapidly growing wealth, by the instrumentality of
men without fortunes. This will probably, here-
after, continue, for better, for worse, to be the
democratic way. No other way is possible. The
rule of the many must always be the rule of the
comparatively poor, and, in this age of the world,
the poor have ceased to be content with their poverty. They seek wealth, and, in times when
wealth is accumulating rapidly, they seek it

eagerly. We cannot change this state of things. We must face the problem as it is presented to us. That problem is, I do not hesitate to say, the great problem of government in every civilized country —how to keep wealth in subjection to law; how to prevent its carrying elections, putting its creatures on the judicial bench, or putting fleets and armies in motion in order to push usurious bonds up to par.

There is only one way of meeting this difficulty. We cannot at will put down corruption by a sudden increase of human virtue. In other words, we cannot protect legislators against wealthy speculators, by making them either suddenly purer, or more contented. The way to arm them against temptation is to leave them as little as possible to sell of the things which capitalists are eager to buy.

I do not mean to say that the tariff has produced, or is producing, definite, ascertainable, or provable corruption, in Congress; that is, that manufacturers go down to Washington and pay members for raising the duty on this, or not lowering it on that. But I do say that the state of things is vicious through which Congress has the chance every year of increasing or lessening the incomes of thousands of rich men, of threatening to ruin great industrial enterprises or largely to increase their profits, and this through changes in legislation so slight as not to be perceptible to the great mass of the public, yet so intricate as to be comprehensible only to a small portion of it. Every time the tariff comes under discussion—and it comes under it every year—hundreds of wealthy corporations or individuals either fear a loss or expect a gain. This puts every member of Congress in the position toward them of a possible enemy or a possible benefactor; in the one case to be bought off, in the other to be rewarded. The lobby which looks after the tariff every winter in the protectionists' interest is not composed of speculative economists, occupied with the effect of legislation on the general weal. It is composed of shrewd, practical business men, engaged in procuring or hindering legislation which will increase or diminish their bank account by an amount which they can readily figure out, and which, if called on, they freely submit to the committees.

The protectionist answer to much of what is said with regard to the changeableness of congressional policy about the tariff is, chiefly, that if the tariff were not attacked incessantly by free-traders and their allies, in one disguise or another, these changes would never take place. If, in short, the people who are hostile to the protective system would refrain from criticising the tariff in which it

is embodied, there would be as much stability in
the policy of the Government with regard to import duties as any one could desire. Unfortunately, however, tariffs have to be made for the
community, such as it is, and not as protectionists
would desire to see it. There has always been in
this country a considerable body of persons who
are opposed to any protection at all; there is another body, also considerable, opposed to high
protection. As long as speech is free they
will continue to exert an influence, more or less
pronounced, upon Congress and the voters. If
they do not always have their way in legislation,
they are always able, at every election, to diffuse
among manufacturers the fear that they will have
it. The effect of this fear on business is, manufacturers say, almost as prejudicial as active legislation.

The problem which protectionists have to solve,
therefore, touching the relations of the Government
to industry in this country, would seem to be the
production of a tariff which nobody will attack—a
very difficult task, we must all admit, if it is to be
such a tariff as extreme protectionists really desire.
As long as there exists, about the amount of protection needed, the doubt and mystery which we now
witness; as long as the classes for whose protection the tariff is intended are as numerous and as

clamorous as they now are, it will be impossible
to satisfy them all by any protective tariff whatever. There is only one rule known to us by which
a tariff can really be measured and defended. If
the principle of raising duties for revenue only
were once adopted, every one would know at a
glance how high the tariff ought to be. There
might be disputes about the distribution of its
burdens among different commodities, but there
would be none about the sum it ought to bring in.
If there were in any year a surplus, every one
would agree that the tariff ought to be lowered.
If there were a deficit, every one would agree that
it ought to be raised. We should thus, at least, get
rid of the perennial contention about the weight of
the duties, and we should no longer be dependent
for stability on the wisdom of Congress.

Now, let me consider another, and, from a social
point of view, perhaps the most important, aspect
of the tariff question. Can any one find, in the
work of any American author, or in the speech of
any American orator—I mean, of the free States
—prior to the civil war, any intimation that we
should have, fully developed on American soil,
within the present century, what has long been
known in Europe as "the labor question?" Of
course, we can all recall that sometime famous letter of Lord Macaulay's, in which he predicted the

speedy triumph in this country of poverty over
property, and the periodical division among the
have-nots of the goods and chattels of the haves.[3]
But some of us can remember, too, the mocking
and proud incredulity with which that dismal prediction was received. He was told, in hundreds of
newspaper articles, that European experience furnished no proper materials for forecasting the
economical future of the United States ; that no
such division of classes as he foresaw could take
place here. I do not need to say that his predictions have not been fulfilled, and are never likely
to be. I am one of those, too, who believe firmly
that property will always, in every country, be
able to take care of itself. It will always have the
superiority in physical force, as well as in intelligence on its side. The great bulk of the population
is, in every country, and above all, in this, composed
of those who have property or expect to have it ;
and so it will always be, as long as our civilization
lasts. But certainly, all the answers to Macaulay
have not stood the test of time and experience. In
1860 nobody here was seriously troubled by the
condition or expectations of the working classes.
In fact, Americans were not in the habit of thinking of working-men as a class at all. An American
citizen who wrought with his hands in any calling
was looked on, like other American citizens, as a

man who had his fortunes in his own keeping, and whose judgment alone decided in what manner they could be improved. Nobody thought of him as being in a special degree the protégé of the State. In fact, the idea that he had a special and peculiar claim on State protection was generally treated as a piece of Gallic folly, over which Anglo-Saxons could well afford to smile. There was no mention of the free laborer in political platforms at that day, except as an illustration to Southern slave-holders of the blessings of which their pride and folly deprived their own society.

We have changed all this very much. Under the stimulation of the war tariff, not only has there been an enormous amount of capital invested in industrial enterprises of various sorts ; not only have mills and furnaces and mines and protected interests of all sorts greatly multiplied, but there has appeared in great force, and for the first time on American soil, the dependent, State-managed laborer of Europe, who declines to take care of himself in the old American fashion. When he is out of work, or does not like his work, he looks about, and asks his fellow-citizens sullenly, if not menacingly, what they are going to do about it. He has brought with him, too, what is called " the labor problem," probably the most un-American of all the problems which American society has to work over to-day. The American pulpit and the American press are now hammering away at it steadily. Commissions, both State and Federal, are nearly every year appointed to collect facts bearing on it, and working-men are invited to come before them and explain it. Popular attention to it is stimulated by occasional riots and huge strikes, in which thousands take part, and which every now and then strain to the uttermost the State powers of protecting life and property. Its leading features are, however, well known. The rate of wages paid in the protective industries is seldom as high as working-men think they ought to have, and is often, if not most of the time, greater than their employers think they can afford to pay. And then employment in these industries is somewhat precarious. Every now and then there is a reduction, or a lockout, simply because the protected market is not good enough. In fact, we have to-day before our eyes, at all the great centres of industry, as they are called—at the mills and mines and furnaces— most of the phenomena which " the pauper labor of Europe " now furnishes for the perplexity of European statesmen and philanthropists. Nor must I be told that this is an exceptional state of things, arising out of a brief and transient depression of industry. It has lasted from 1873, with a very brief interval of two years, until the present year.

Now, this labor problem, which so many statesmen and philanthropists and economists are trying their teeth on, is every day made more difficult, every day further removed from solution, by that fatal lesson of government responsibility for the condition of a particular class of a community, which every believer in high tariffs, every manufacturer who depends on the tariff, is compelled to preach. Of all the novelties which the last twenty-five years have introduced into American politics and society, decidedly the most dangerous is the practice of telling large bodies of ignorant and excitable voters at every election that their daily bread depends not on their own capacity or industry or ingenuity, or on the capacity or industry or ingenuity of their employers, but on the good-will of the Legislature, or, worse still, on the good-will of the Administration. In other words, the "tariff issue," as it is called in every canvass, is an issue filled with the seeds of social trouble and perplexity. Anything less American and more imperialist than the regular quadrennial proclamation that if the presidential election results in a certain way the foundations will be knocked from under American industry, the factories closed, and the workers thrown out of employment, could hardly be conceived. And yet, as long as a large number of industries exist through the tariff, and could not exist without it, and men's eyes are turned, whenever there is a depression in business, not to the market of the world or to the resources of their own ingenuity, but to the lobbies of the Capitol, this announcement is inevitable. Every canvass thus becomes a lesson in dependence on the State. It becomes a sort of formal acknowledgment by the leading men of both political parties, that one class of the community, at least, is composed of governmental protégés; for the party which denies that its coming into power will derange industry makes this acknowledgment, just as effectually as the party which brings the charge.

The truth is, that the first field ever offered for seeing what the freedom of the individual could accomplish, in the art of growing rich and of diversifying industry, was offered on this continent. It was blessed with the greatest variety of soil and climate, with the finest ports and harbors, with the greatest extent of inland navigation, with the richest supply of minerals, of any country in the world. The population was singularly daring, hardy, ingenious, and self-reliant, and untrammelled by feudal tradition. That opportunity has, under the protective system, been temporarily allowed to slip away. The old European path has been entered on, under the influence of the old European motives; the be-

lief that gold is the only wealth; that, in trading
with a foreigner, unless you sell him more in specie
value than he sells you, you lose by the transaction; that diversity of industry being necessary to
sound progress, diversity of individual tastes, bent,
and capacity cannot be depended on to produce it;
that manufactures being necessary to make the
nation independent of foreigners in time of war,
individual energy and sagacity cannot be trusted
to create them.

The result is that we have, during the last quarter of a century, deliberately resorted to the policy of forcing capital into channels into which it
did not naturally flow. We thus have supplied
ourselves with manufactures on a large scale, but
in doing so we have brought society in most of
the large towns, in the East, at least, back to the
old European model, divided largely into two
classes, the one great capitalists, the other day-
laborers, living from hand to mouth, and dependent for their bread and butter on the constant
maintenance by the Government of artificial means
of support. Agriculture has in this way been destroyed in some of the Eastern States, and, what
is worse, so has commerce.

Had individuals in America been left to their
own devices in the matter of building up manufactures, it is possible that the gross production of

the country in many branches would have been
less than it is now; but it is very certain that
American society would have been in a healthier
condition, and American industry would have been
" taken out of politics," or, rather would never have
got into it. An agricultural population, such as that
of the Northern States sixty years ago, was sure not
to confine itself to one field of industry exclusively.
Enterprise and activity, love of work and love
of trying all kinds of work, were as marked features of the national character then as they are
now. The American population could boast of
much greater superiority over the European population than it can now. There was sure, therefore,
to have been a constant overflow from the farms
of the most quick-witted, sharp-sighted, and enterprising men of the community, for the creation of
new manufactures. They would have toiled, contrived, invented, copied, until they had brought
into requisition and turned to account—as, in fact,
they did to a considerable extent in colonial days
—one by one, all the resources of the country, all
its advantages over other countries in climate, soil,
water-power, in minerals, or mental or moral force.
Whatever manufactures were thus built up, too,
would have been built up forever. They would
have needed no hothouse legislation to save them.
They would have flourished as naturally and could

have been counted on with as much certainty as the wheat crop or the corn crop. Instead of being a constant source of uncertainty and anxiety and legislative corruption, they would have been one of the main-stays of our social and political system. American manufactures would then, in short, have been the legitimate outgrowth of American agriculture. They would have grown as it grew, in just and true relations to it. They would have absorbed steadily and comfortably its surplus population, and the American ideas of man's capacity, value, and needs would have reigned in the regulation of the new industry.

The present state of things is one which no thinking man can contemplate without concern. If the protectionist policy is persisted in, the process of assimilating American society to that of Europe must go on. The accumulation of capital in the hands of comparatively few individuals and corporations must continue and increase. Larger and larger masses of the population must every day be reduced to the condition of day-laborers, on fixed wages, contracting more and more the habit of looking on their vote simply as a mode of raising or lowering their wages, and, what is worse than all, learning to consider themselves a class apart, with rights and interests opposed to, or different from, those of the rest of the community.

What, then, is to be done by way of remedy? Nothing can be done suddenly; much can be done slowly. We must retrace our steps by degrees, by taking the duties off raw materials, so as to enable those manufactures which are nearly able to go alone to get out of the habit of dependence on legislation, and to go forth into all the markets of the world without fear and with a manly heart. We must deprive those manufactures which are able to go alone already, of the protection which they now receive, as the reward of log-rolling in Congress in aid of those still weaker than themselves. And we must finally, if it be possible, by a persistent progress in the direction of a truly natural state of things, prepare both laborers and employers for that real independence of foreigners, which is the result, simply and solely, of native superiority, either in energy or industry or inventiveness, or in natural advantages.

CRIMINAL POLITICS [1]

THE most serious question which faces the modern world to-day is the question of the government of great cities under universal suffrage. There is hardly any political or social puzzle the solution of which has not to be worked out in the streets of the great towns. The labor problem, for instance, is almost exclusively a city problem. It is in cities the great labor troubles occur. It is in them that population is growing most rapidly.

The following table shows the increase in the population in five great capitals during twenty years, ending in the year of the latest census:

	1861.		1871.		1881.
London...............	2,803,989	....	3,254,260	....	3,814,571
	1861.		1872.		1881.
Paris...................	1,090,741	....	1,851,792	....	2,269,023
	1867.	1871.	1874.		1885.
Berlin	702,437	825,389	949,144	....	1,315,297
	1858.		1870.	1872.	1881.
Rome	180,359	....	216,000	244,484	300,467
	1860.		1870.		1880.
New York...........	805,658	....	942,292	....	1,206,299

Far from being dependent for their increase in numbers, as the country districts are in the main, on the majority of births over deaths, they grow in size through immigration on a great scale. In all the leading countries there is a steady stream of men, women, and children into them. Men who have made their fortunes move into them as the places in which there are the most varied opportunities for such pleasures as wealth brings. Men who have their fortunes still to make crowd into them as the places in which there are the best markets and the best opening for every variety of talent.

But far more important than this is the fact that nearly all the poor, the improvident, the disgraced, the criminals, all the adventurers of both sexes, are consumed with the passion for city life. There is hardly any unsuccessful or unfortunate man in the United States, in England, France, Germany, or Italy, possessed of any mental activity or bodily strength, who does not think his condition would be bettered by getting to some great capital. The laborers are even more eager for the change than the other classes. A disgust with country life has spread, or is spreading, among workingmen in all these countries. Farmers in England and France complain that, in spite of the aid of machinery, farming is becoming increasingly difficult through want of hands. The new generation are unwilling to cultivate the earth any longer, or endure the solitude of farm life, if they can possibly avoid it.

The cities themselves do everything to stimulate this movement. Parks and gardens, cheap concerts, free museums and art galleries, cheap means of conveyance, model lodging-houses, rich charities, such as every city is now offering in abundance to all comers, are so many inducements to country poor to try their luck in the streets. They are the exact equivalents, as an invitation to the lazy and the pleasure-loving, of the Roman circus and free flour which we all use in explanation of the decline and fall of the Empire. They are luxuries which seem to be within every man's reach gratis, and they act with tremendous force on the rural imagination. Nor is there as yet the slightest sign of reaction. The great transmigrations of the world are, in the main, those of the farmers from one farm to another; but there is no sign among the poor of a return to the country of those who have once tasted the sweets of city life. That this aversion from the land among the masses should be contemporaneous with the rapid spread of Henry George's theory, that poverty is due to the difficulty men have in getting hold of ground to cultivate, is surely a very curious social phenomenon. Its success, however, has been mainly in the towns. He has had but few disciples among the agricultural population, and I suspect that even in the towns, if it were possible to analyze the grounds on which his followers have taken up his gospel, it would be found, in nine cases out of ten, that land, in their minds, simply stood for wealth in general, and that they thought of it as something that yielded ground-rent or house-rent, rather than as something that grew crops.

Though last, not least, the opportunities for concealment, for escaping observation, or, in other words, of securing solitude, which great masses of population afford, make the cities very attractive to criminals. They are the chosen homes of everybody inclined to, or actually living, a life of crime or a life bordering on crime. Gamblers, thieves, receivers of stolen goods, brothel-keepers, and the great army of those who shirk regular industry, all throng to the city as the place which affords the best opportunities for the exercise of their peculiar talents. The last-named class forms in every city a very large body of persons who, though not, strictly speaking, part of the criminal population, live on it or through it, and readily descend into its ranks.

This tendency is aggravated in this country by

immigration, especially in the case of New York, which is the great receiving port for such additions to our population as come from Europe. In spite of frequent assertions to the contrary, and in spite of appearances to the contrary created by such excesses as those of the Anarchists in Chicago and elsewhere, the bulk of the European immigrants to this country are orderly, industrious people who have contributed much to its material prosperity, and have made, by the sums of money they bring with them, no less than by their labor, by no means insignificant additions to its capital. They have undoubtedly played a very large part in the opening up and reclamation of the regions beyond the Alleghanies known as the West. Without them the creation of the manufacturing industries which we are now so frantically trying to protect through the tariff, would have been impossible. So it will not do to throw on them all the responsibility of our political disorders and shortcomings. But nobody can deny that they have greatly increased the difficulty of the problem of city government under universal suffrage.

Every ship-load of immigrants which lands in New York contains a certain proportion of what may, for political purposes, be called sediment— that is, of persons with no fixed trade or calling or any kind of industrial training, who started with but little money beyond what was necessary to pay their passage at sea. To some of these New York is as far as they want to go; to most of them it is as far as they can go, and they at once recruit the legion of what the French call "*déclassés*"—that is, of social adventurers who are compelled to live either by manual labor or by their wits; and there is, of course, no one who has any wits who does not prefer the latter. That they furnish constant re-enforcements to the vicious and criminal elements of the population it is hardly necessary to say. More than this, they furnish the puzzle of philosophers and the despair of statesmen.

It is impossible to discuss this subject, as far as New York is concerned, without distinguishing between the influence on politics of the different nationalities which are represented in the voting population of the city. The two which play the leading part are the Germans and the Irish. At the last census their numbers were about equal. But there is a great difference in their political activity, partly owing to difference of temperament, partly to difference of training. The Germans are a slow, plodding, somewhat phlegmatic, and very serious people, who, as Dr. Von Holst, in a review of Mr. Bryce's book, truly says, in a feverish intensity of American activity, with their moderate and sober ideals, quiet and steady energy, and modest self-confidence, act as a wholesome leaven.

The Irish are quick, passionate, impetuous, impressionable, easily influenced, and with a hereditary disposition to personal loyalty to a leader of some sort. Their immigration is a more ignorant one than the German—indeed, I might say less civilized. They have for the most part but little, if any, industrial training, while the Germans have a great deal. There are probably ten Germans who come here with a trade of some sort, for one Irishman, and their trades are apt to be skilled ones which no man can successfully follow without having some sort of mental discipline and steadiness of character. The Germans, too, come with more or less affection for the government they have left behind, and pride in its success. The Irish come with hatred for their home government bred in their very bones. What is, perhaps, as serious a difference as any is that all classes of Germans, except the military aristocracy, are represented in the German immigration. It has always a mixture of educated men and successful business men who are on excellent terms with their humbler countrymen, and united to them by all the usual social and political ties. It is the misfortune of the Irish that their educated class and successful business class have to a great extent been separated from the bulk of the population at home by differences of race and religion, which continue under the new skies ; and the religious differences occasionally treat Americans to the, to them, astonishing phenomena known as " Orange riots."[2] Consequently, the bulk of the poor Irish who drop down into the New York streets as a deposit from each successive wave of immigration, find themselves without respectable natural leaders, and a ready prey to sharp-witted political adventurers. They are separated from Americans, too, not only by difference of habits, traditions, and ideals, but by difference of religion—perhaps the most formidable barrier of all. They have to contend against that dread of Catholicism which has now become among all classes of Anglo-Saxons, whether religious or sceptical, an integral part of their mental and moral make-up. And the Irish soon learn to regard the Americans, as they have learned through sorrowful experience to regard the well-to-do class in their own country, as in some sort lawful political prey, whom it is not improper to tax, if they get a chance, without mercy or compunction.

What makes this all the more formidable is that they have familiarity with political machinery, without having any political experience ; that is, they know all about voting and agitating and canvassing, but they have never yet elected legislators who were responsible for the government under which they lived, whom they could fairly call to account if their affairs were mismanaged, or of whose misconduct they felt the direct effects. In other words, they have never had the only political training which develops public spirit or a sense of public morality—the strongest argument of all, to my mind, for Irish home rule. Irish parliamentary elections are, in fact, as a means of political training, complete shams. Nor have the Irish had any educating experience in the conduct of their local affairs. The consequence is that a large body of the Irish voters in our large cities enter on the game of politics in what may be called a predatory state of mind, without any sense of public duty, or of community of interest with the rest of the taxpayers. When we add to all this the fact that they are the only large body of immigrants who land in this country with a knowledge of the English language, and therefore can at once become acquainted with the ins and outs of the spoils system as practised by the natives, and with the whole system of "pulls" by which justice is denied or perverted, the public money converted into "boodle," and places won by the incompetent, the part they play in aggravating the puzzle of city government is not surprising. As voters simply, the Bohemians and Poles are just as manageable as they are. In what

is called "the banner Republican district " in this
city, the Eighth, in which the late Johnny O'Brien
held sway, there are but few Irish.[3] The bulk of
the voters are Slavs of one denomination or another, and follow a leader with just such fidelity as
the Irish, but they do not know enough to get hold
of offices.   They do not secure any of the prizes of
corruption ; and the reason is that they are ignorant of the language and unfamiliar with the machinery by which a share in the electoral plunder
can be obtained.

Though last, not least, the temptation to immigrants who have no skilled trade and are averse to
manual labor, and yet have a little more push and
intelligence than the mass of their compatriots, to
go into the liquor business in New York, owing to
the ease with which licenses are obtained, is very
strong, and the Irish fall victims to it in larger
numbers than any other class of new-comers.   But
very little capital is required ; in fact, hardly any,
as credit for liquor is readily obtained from the
distillers and brewers by pushing fellows, and the
furniture and fixtures of a " rum-hole " involve but
little outlay.   With a barrel of cheap whiskey,
which can be easily increased by adulteration,
and a few kegs of beer on hand, an energetic new-
comer in New York not only obtains at once the
means of livelihood, but finds himself speedily a

prominent social and political figure in his ward, whom men that he thinks highly placed consider it worth their while to flatter, or cajole, or encourage. The ease with which he can enter the liquor business,—an ease the like of which is not to be found in any other civilized city,—and his joy at finding that in a rum-shop he has made the first step in what seems to him a public career, naturally affect profoundly the imagination of hundreds of his countrymen, both here and at home, who know something about him and watch his progress, and form their estimate of American politics and morals from his example.

It was unfortunate that the change in the constitution of this State in 1846, establishing universal suffrage, occurred simultaneously with the beginning of the great tide of emigration which followed the Irish famine.[4] Its result was that the city was soon flooded with a large body of ignorant voters, who at once furnished political speculators with a new field for their peculiar talents. Within six years they produced a kind of demagogue, previously unknown to the American public, in the person of Fernando Wood, who, by their aid, got into the mayoralty in 1854—the first of his kind who had ever done so, for he was to all intents and purposes an adventurer, with no standing in the business community. It was really he

who organized New York city politics on what
may be called a criminal basis ; that is, he discovered the use which might be made in politics of
the newly arrived foreigner, and the part which
the liquor-dealers and all keepers of criminal or
semi-criminal drinking-places might be made to
play in maintaining party discipline and organization. In controlling a body of ignorant voters,
who did not read, no agents could be so useful
as the keepers of " resorts " in which men congregated in the evening, and at which they got credit
for both food and drink.

Consequently the liquor-dealer, whether as a
keeper of a bar, or of a " dive," or of a brothel, or
of a cheap hotel, rapidly rose into the political
prominence which he has ever since enjoyed. He
became a captain of ten, or of fifty, or of a hundred, according to the size of his rum-shop and
his own capacity for leadership. He rapidly took
the place in politics which in the early part of the
century was held by the foremen of the volunteer
fire companies, as a centre of political influence
and as the transmitter to the various wards of the
will of the gods of the Tammany Society. Wood
was succeeded as a boss by Tweed, and Tweed, of
course, brought the Wood system to perfection.
He gave the liquor - dealers increased political
weight, and made his way to the hearts of the ten-

ement-house population by lavish charities, such as the distribution of free coal in winter, which Wood had never thought of. His success may be estimated from the fact that he was re-elected to the State Senate by his constituents while the intelligent and well-to-do world above them was ringing with the exposure of his frauds and thefts.

How Tweed passed away everybody knows. He was the victim of his own excess. He might have stolen with perfect impunity for a long period, had he been more moderate. He was ruined by the scale on which he did his work. But his system remained, and in due time produced a successor in the person of John Kelly, who had profited by Tweed's example, practised the great Greek maxim " not too much of anything," simply made every candidate pay handsomely for his nomination, pocketed the money himself, and, whether he rendered any account of it or not, died in possession of a handsome fortune. His policy was the very safe one of making the city money go as far as possible among the workers, by compelling every office-holder to divide his salary and perquisites with a number of other persons. In this way no one person made the gains known under Tweed, but a far greater number were kept in a state of contentment, and the danger of exposures was thus averted or greatly lessened.

The more the Tammany organization had to rely on the liquor-dealers, the more certain and rapid was the transfer of its government to the hands of the criminal class. By criminal class I do not mean simply the class which commits highway robbery or burglary, or receives stolen goods, or keeps gambling-houses or houses of ill-fame. I mean not these only, but all who associate with them in political work, and who share political spoils with them ; who help to shield them from judicial pursuit either by their influence with the district attorney or with the police justices, or with the police ; in other words, both the actual perpetrators of crimes and those who are not repelled by them and are willing to profit in politics by their activity.

As I have said before, each of the numerous small sets, or " gangs," of which this world is made up has its " head-quarters " at some liquor store, or bar, or club, the keeper of which is its political guide and friend in times of trouble ; and he is under a constant impulse to push the political fortunes of his clients and demand recognition for them so as to justify their reliance on him and respect for him. As long as Democratic victories in this city have to be won by his exertions, it is, of course, difficult or impossible to gainsay him. Men of all other trades and callings occasionally retire from "politics" altogether, for a long or short period. But the liquor-dealer never retires. He remains an agitator, organizer, and counsellor by virtue of his calling. His "place" is the centre of political gossip. He knows more of what is going on in the ward or district than anybody else—who hates whom; who is going to "get even" with whom; what Billy has been promised, or why he did not get it; from whom Jake borrowed his assessment, and how much he owes Barney, and what "deals" are in progress or have been contemplated. Consequently, every organization which counts on him tends more and more to pass into his hands and those of his customers.

This tendency has been strong in Tammany for many years. It has ended in excluding nearly all men of good character and respectable associations from its management. The public, which remembers that it used to have prominent lawyers and business men among its sachems and on its Executive Committee, is habitually startled at finding it in charge of liquor-dealers and "toughs." The remedy so often proposed, of taking away the charter which the Tammany Society obtained in its early and better days as a semi-charitable organization, is puerile on its face. The only use of the charter of the organization, as at present constituted, is to enable it to own real estate. But it does not need to own real estate in order to exist and flourish. It could get on just as well with a hired hall as with a hall in fee-simple. Its strength, I repeat, lies in the control it exerts over the ignorant, criminal, and vicious classes through its liquor-dealers, who never concern themselves in the least about the charter, and do not need to do so. It can exert all its present strength without any legal organization whatever, like any other political club. Its original construction and design and history are important in only one way.

No organization such as it now is could be started in our day ; that is, the vicious and criminal class could not in any large city get up a club or association which would have the coherence, prestige, and authority that Tammany has. The attempt would be a failure from the outset, even if the organization did not succumb to the attacks of the police. No civilized community would witness with calm or indifference the deliberate formation of a combination which was plainly hostile to public prosperity and order, or the efficient administration of justice. Steps would soon be taken to break it up, or discredit it in some manner, so as to destroy its attractiveness to its supporters. Membership in it would bring such disrepute that men seeking any foothold in the respectable business or professional class would be unwilling to belong to it; politicians would be afraid to have it known that they relied on it, and it would rapidly go to pieces or be reduced to insignificance, even if it for a short period managed to show power.

The reason why the Tammany Society manages to stand its ground is that it is nearly a century old, and for fully half that time was a real political club, engaged in the maintenance and diffusion of certain political ideas which were, during all that period, making a considerable noise in the world, and effecting great governmental changes in many civilized countries. The leading men of the party which was the exponent of these ideas in this State, belonged to it, and a share in its management was one of the rewards of some kind of prominence in the world outside, either political or professional or commercial. Of course this gave it, in process of time, great political weight. Any organization which has managed to exist and flourish for half a century acquires great prestige in a society as changeful as ours, in which organizations of all sorts rise, flourish, and fade with so much rapidity, and in which even the most brilliant local reputations so soon pass out of men's memories. With the aureole thus acquired Tammany came down almost to 1850. Soon after that the vicious element began gradually to enter it and secure control of it, and drive politics, in the best sense of the term, out of it, but with so little outward sign of what was going on that the change, when suddenly revealed in Tweed's day, gave the public a shock of surprise.

Old New-Yorkers learned then that what had seemed to their youthful imagination a sort of temple of liberty, of which the worst that could be said was that it was too much given up to Southern worship of negro slavery, had really been taken possession of by a lot of tramps and converted into a " boozing ken." But they got over this shock somewhat after Tweed's day and the establishment of Tilden's supremacy in Democratic councils, and an air of respectability once more began to surround the ancient edifice. It did not, however, last for very long. The process of degeneration set in once more. The criminal classes renewed their activity, and they were in full possession before Tilden's death; but once more, and in spite of everything, the age of the edifice, the traditions which surrounded it, prevented the public from realizing what was passing within. It consequently almost astounded good people the other day to learn how few members of the Executive Committee could be said to have any really lawful occupation outside politics, or any genuine connection with the respectable business or social world.

Nothing is more surprising in the attempt to deal with the problems of urban life than the way in which religious and philanthropic people ignore the close connection between municipal politics and the various evils about which they are most concerned. All the churches occupy themselves, in a greater or less degree, with the moral condition of the poor. Charitable associations spend hundreds of thousands every year in trying to improve their physical condition. A conference of Protestant ministers met in this city two years ago to consider the best means of reviving religious interest among the working classes and inducing a larger number of them to attend church on Sundays. Of course these gentlemen did not seek an increase in the number of church-goers as an end in itself. The Protestant churches do not, as the Catholic Church does, ascribe any serious spiritual efficacy to mere bodily presence at religious worship. Protestant ministers ask people to go to church in the hope that the words which they will hear " with their outward ears may be so grafted inwardly in their hearts that they may bring forth the fruit of good living." What was remarkable in the debates of this conference, therefore, was the absence of any mention of the very successful rivalry with the religion which, as an influence on the poor and ignorant foreign population, politics in this city carries on. The same thing may be said, *mutatis mutandis,* of the charitable associations. No one would get from their speeches or reports an inkling of the solemn fact that the newly arrived immigrant who settles in New York gets tenfold more of his notions of American right and wrong from city politics than he gets from the city missionaries, or the schools, or the mission chapels ; and yet such is the case. I believe it is quite within the truth to say that, as a moral influence on the poor and ignorant, the clergyman and philanthropist are hopelessly distanced by the politician.

It must be remembered that the poor immigrant who drops down in New York generally comes from a country in which the idea that the public functionaries are the servants of the people, or the product of popular selection, has not as yet penetrated the popular mind. He is apt to hold on still, in a blind, unreflective way, to the old doctrine that the powers that be are of God, and that what a man in authority says or does is, in some sense, the expression of the national morality. He has not as yet learned to criticise public officers or call them to account. He obeys them ; he seeks to ingratiate himself with them. He accepts their decisions, if unfavorable, as misfortunes ; if favorable, as blessings. He does not dream of appealing against them to public opinion, for he does not know what public opinion is. No sooner has he established himself in a tenement-house or a boarding-house than he finds himself face to face with three functionaries who represent to him the government of his new country—the police justice of the district, the police captain of his precinct, and the political " district leader." These are, to him, the Federal, State, and municipal governments rolled into one. He does not read Story or Bryce. He knows nothing about the limitation of powers, or the division of spheres, or constitutional guarantees.

What he learns very soon is that, if he makes himself obnoxious to the captain of the precinct, he may be visited with so much vexation as to drive him out of the ward ; that if he would avoid the severities of the police justice whenever he has a little scrimmage with one of his neighbors, or gets into "trouble " of any description, he must have a mediator or protector, and this mediator or protector must be "the district leader " or a politician belonging to one party or the other. He then perceives very soon that, as far as he is concerned, ours is not a government of laws, but a government of "pulls." When he goes into the only court of justice of which he has any knowledge, he is told he must have a "pull" with the magistrate or he will fare badly. When he opens a liquor-store, he is told he must have a "pull" with the police in order not to be "raided" or arrested for violation of a mysterious something which he hears called "law." He learns from those of his countrymen who have been here longer than he that, in order to come into possession of this "pull," he must secure the friendship of the district leader. These three men are to him America. Everything else in the national institutions in which Americans pride themselves, he only sees through a glass darkly, if he sees it at all.

If he is a man of parts and energy, or rises above the condition of a manual laborer into that of a liquor-dealer or small contractor, he finds himself impeded or helped at every step by "pulls." If he wants a small place in the public service, he must have a "pull." If he wants a government contract, he must have a "pull." Whether he wants to get his just rights under it, or to escape punishment for fraud or bad work in the execution of it, he must have a "pull." In the ward in which he lives he never comes across any sign of moral right or moral wrong, human or divine justice. All that he learns of the ways of Providence in the government of the city is that the man with the most "pulls" gets what he wants, and that the man with no "pulls" goes to the wall. Every experience of the municipality satisfies him that he is living in a world of favor and not of law. He hears that large sums of money are voted every year for the cleaning of the streets, but he sees that they are not cleaned. He hears that it is forbidden to throw out dirt and ashes into the highway, but he sees that all his neighbors do it with impunity. He hears that gambling-houses and houses of prostitution are forbidden, but he sees them doing a roaring trade all around him. He hears that it is a crime to keep a liquor-saloon open on Sunday, but he finds the one he frequents is as accessible on Sunday as on any other day. He hears that licenses to sell liquor should be granted only to persons of good character, but he sees that the greatest scoundrels in his neighborhood get them and keep them as readily as anyone else. He has come over the sea with the notion that magistrates should be grave and discreet persons, learned in the law, but he sees seated on the bench in his own district his own friend, Billy McGrath, who plays poker every night with him and "the boys" in Mike Grogan's saloon, and in court always gives his cronies "a show." Nowhere does he come on any standard of propriety or fitness in the transaction of public business, or on any recognition of such things as duty or honor in dealing with the public interests.

Now, what chance have the city missionaries and philanthropists of making themselves felt in an atmosphere of this sort ? They might as well go to the African heathen, and try to make Christians by dividing their preaching time with the medicine-men, as to try to make an impression on the poor of this city as long as the administration of its affairs is a standing denial of God. What helpless visionaries they must seem to thousands as they wander about the liquor-saloons with their Bibles, and tell their tales of what good Americans think about life and death and judgment, and about the prosperity which waits on the honest man and good citizen. The truth is that anyone who occupies himself with the moral and religious elevation of the poor in this city can no more disregard politics than a doctor, in treating physical disease, can refuse to take notice of bad drains or decaying garbage. He must not only take politics into account in his work, but must take it into account at the very beginning.

What is to be done by reformers generally to introduce a new and better régime into city affairs, it is not easy to describe fully within the limits of an article like this. There are certain things, however, which have been fully tried and have so plainly failed that no more mention should be made of them. One is the denunciation of universal suffrage. There is no doubt that universal suffrage has added to the difficulties of city government, and has lowered the standard of official purity and fitness; but, to use the slang phrase, it has so plainly "come to stay," and is so firmly lodged in the political arrangements of most civilized nations, that it is a mere waste of time to declaim against it. Complaining of it as an obstacle to good government is like complaining of a stormy sea as a reason for giving up navigation.

Another is reliance on the State Legislature for new charters, or for the expulsion of bad men from office by special legislation. This mode of reform was begun in 1857, when the Republican party got possession of the State government, and it has ended in converting the interests of the city into gambling - stakes for Albany politicians to play with. They oust each other from city offices with no more reference to the interests of city taxpayers than butchers on killing-day to the feelings of the oxen. There have been eleven charters enacted since 1846, and we have now got the best of them all, and the best we are in the least likely to get. It is the simplest, and puts more direct power into the hands of the city voters than they have ever had before. Its excellence lies in the fact that it concentrates in the mayor responsibility for appointments to all the leading offices except the comptrollership, and puts the control of taxation in the hands of a small body of conspicuous men elected on a general ticket. We cannot do better than this. It makes every election a direct appeal to the good sense and public spirit of the voter. No community as heterogeneous as ours can manage its affairs successfully through democratic forms without reducing to its lowest possible point the number of executive officers whom it has to watch, and call to account when things go wrong. As soon as responsibility is widely diffused in such a community, " deals " or bargains between politicians for the division of the offices at once begin.

For we have among our other difficulties to deal with the fact—in some of its aspects a tremendous one—that the fifty years of the spoils system have almost destroyed in the popular mind the tradition of trusteeship in connection with public offices. Among active politicians they are now almost universally looked upon, as in France under the old régime, as franchises or privileges authorizing the holder to levy a certain amount of toll on the State for a certain limited period. Until this view has been eradicated, it is reasonable to fear that a large municipal legislature or council, which some are thinking of, would simply be a reproduction on a smaller scale of the Albany Legislature, with whose weaknesses and defects the public by this time is tolerably familiar. It is safe to say that, as things are to-day, we cannot better ourselves by any changes in the framework of the city government which there is the least chance of obtaining from the law-making power, except in one particular, and that is the exaction of higher qualifications for the office of police justice. The police magistrates are, after the mayor, perhaps the most important city officers. They have a more direct relation to municipal health and morals than any other. They ought to be lawyers, of at least seven years' standing at the bar, and men of established character and repute. At present there is no standard of fitness for the office whatever. Any man who can get it through " pulls " is held to be competent to fill it, and it is, as a matter of fact, disposed of as a piece of party spoil to active local politicians. So that it may be said that, with this exception, we have had since 1885, when the absolute power of appointment was put into the mayor's hands, as good a scheme of local government as we have ever had, or are likely to have within any period worth thinking about for practical purposes.

Have we, then, exhausted our resources ? Is

the rule of the criminal classes under which we are living at this moment destined to be permanent? Who or what is to blame for it? Can it not be shaken off, or can its recurrence not be prevented?

The answer to these questions is comparatively easy. There is nothing unnatural or abnormal in our condition. It is the plain and natural effect of causes of the simplest and most obvious kind. In fact, it would be very odd if we were any better off than we are, considering the way in which we manage our municipal business. The objects of a municipal corporation are nearly as definable as those of a railroad company. They consist simply in supplying the inhabitants of a certain locality with certain conditions of physical health and comfort, plus the education of their children. The work is paid for by an annual subscription, and the executive officers are elected by a general vote.

If there be in this world a plain moral obligation, it is the obligation which rests on every inhabitant to use his vote in electing these officers solely in the common interest of himself and his neighbors. To use it in his own individual interest, or in the interest of some other corporation or body of persons not dwelling in the locality or owning property in it, is of exactly the same moral quality as the transaction called " wrecking a railroad," in which the directors of a railroad corporation ruin it either for their own personal gain or in order to contribute to the prosperity of some other railroad.

In other words, it is a breach of trust. The more poor, or ignorant, or helpless the neighbors of an inhabitant of a municipal corporation are, the more solemn is the obligation which rests on him to use his superior intelligence for their benefit. He has no right to let them be swindled by clever sharpers if he can prevent it, simply because they are easily duped. He has no right to say that, as he can take care of himself in any event, he is not going to trouble himself about the plight of those who have neither knowledge enough nor money enough to protect themselves against fraud. He has no right to shut his eyes to dirty streets elsewhere because he can afford to keep his own street clean by private contract, and has a country house where he spends half the year. He has no right to surrender the poor to corrupt or ignorant judges, because he can pay for the best police the country affords. In short, he has no right to live an absolutely selfish life in the city any more than in the country at large. Patriotism has its municipal obligations as well as national obligations, and, in fact, makes duty to the municipality far clearer to the plain man than duty to the nation.

If this be all true,—and I do not think it will

meet with denial from any respectable source,—
we shall have little difficulty in showing that the
responsibility for our local misgovernment by no
means rests on " the ignorant foreigners " : on the
contrary, it rests very distinctly on the intelligent
and well-to-do natives. They have three times
since 1884 deliberately gone through the process
known in railroading as " wrecking "—that is,
have tried to use the municipal administration to
promote schemes in which the city, as a city, has
no special interest whatever. If the minority of
the stockholders of a bank were to endeavor to
put into office a certain board of directors, in order that they might make heavy loans to political
committees, or merely in order to show their own
strength, they would soon stand in the public eye
in the same moral, if not legal, position as the
men who wrecked the Sixth National Bank. And
yet it is difficult, from the moral point of view,
to distinguish between such conduct as this and
the conduct of the Republicans who at every
mayoralty election, when they know they cannot
succeed, persist in running a third candidate in
order to exert influence on the Presidential election or on congressional legislation.

New York is, has been, and probably will remain for an indefinite period, a Democratic city.
In so far as " Democratic " means the votes of the

more ignorant of the population, of course this is to be regretted. I regret it as much as anybody. But it is a fact, and has to be dealt with as a fact. And there is another fact of the situation still more important than this—a fact which I think may be called unique as a political phenomenon ; namely, that the ignorance and vice of the city have been organized in an association mainly for the purpose of plundering the municipal treasury and quartering a large body of shiftless people on the public service. But, fortunately for the city, this association does not contain a majority of the municipal voters, though it does contain a majority of Democratic voters.

But the minority of Democrats who are hostile to it and to its works and ways, and are willing to act against it, is considerable — considerable enough to put the association in a minority at city elections. These dissentient Democrats cannot be got to accept Republican nominations, no matter how good they are : this, too, is very regrettable. It would not be true if all Democrats were as intelligent and public-spirited as we should wish to see them. But it is a fact, and has to be dealt with as a fact. It has, therefore, to be taken into account by intelligent and honorable men, in providing the city with an administration, just as much as the liability of city houses to take fire. Municipal politics, like all other politics, is a practical art. It deals with men as they are, and not as we wish them to be. There is hardly one of us who, if he had the power of peopling New York anew, would not make an immense number of changes among its present inhabitants. But the problem before the wise and good is simply how to give the present inhabitants, such as they are, with all their imperfections on their heads, the best attainable government. The lesson of experience on this point is that we should vote for the best candidate whom either Democratic faction puts up, and try to extract a good nomination from it by the promise or offer of this support. In nine cases out of ten this would give us as good a city government as we are, in the present condition of human nature, entitled to.

It would have given Mayors Grace and Hewitt overwhelming majorities in 1884 and 1888.[5] They were elected, it is true, in its absence, and they began a process of filling city offices which, but for the Republican mistake in running a candidate in aid of General Harrison in 1888, would, in spite of some haltings, have gradually revolutionized the municipal service and established sound and probably permanent administrative traditions. As it was, this process put first-rate men at the head of the Board of Public Works and of the Health Board. It partially rescued the Excise Board from the liquor-dealers and considerably improved the Park Board; and had the large number of vacancies which have fallen into the hands of Tammany during the term of Mayor Grant been placed at the disposal of Mayor Hewitt, or of a man like him, we should have entered on the year 1891 with brighter municipal prospects than New York has known for fifty years.

But there can be no hope of permanent improvement in municipal business, any more than in any other business, until city elections are conducted for the sake of the city. Any business which is administered in the interest of some other business soon ends in bankruptcy. A dry-goods business managed with a view not to the sale of the dry goods, but the establishment of a newspaper, would not last very long. New York is too rich to be brought to insolvency. Great cities, when badly administered, cannot be sold and abolished; they simply become dirty, unhealthy, unsafe, disgraceful, and expensive. It is high time that this great municipal shame disappeared from among us, and deliverance ought not to be difficult, for we believe there is not a city in the Union in which the honest, well-meaning, orderly, and industrious voters are not in a large majority.

"THE ECONOMIC MAN"[1]

WE have been hearing during the past twenty years, and with greatly increased emphasis during the past ten, of the utter discredit which has overtaken the older political economy of Adam Smith, and Ricardo, and Mill, and Cairnes, and Say, and Cobden, and Bastiat. Their system, we have been told, is largely a deductive system, in which the premises are furnished by hypotheses which have no basis in the actual facts of industrial life, and are not verified either by experiment or observation. Not only are these premises not true of the world at large, but they are not true of any particular country in the world. They assume that the civilized world lives under the régime of competition, whereas there are only two or three countries which can be said, with any approach to accuracy, to do so. The "Economic Man" of Ricardo always buys in the cheapest markets, and always waits patiently until he can sell in the dearest, and he assumes that in so doing he renders the best service in his power to the community.

Moral considerations do not, in any degree, affect his business transactions. There is no place in his system for brotherly kindness or charity. It is inexpedient for the state to attempt to regulate him in any way, either by keeping him out of the cheapest market or impeding his access to the dearest. All he asks of it is to be left alone to deal with his fellow-men in such manner as his own natural acuteness or his command of capital may permit. His one desire is to make all the money he can by every means not illegal. *Laissez faire, laissez passer*, comprises the sole and whole duty of the state toward him.

Ricardo, who is the scapegoat who has to bear the burden of most of the sins of the old school, or who, at all events, figures most prominently in this discussion, has, it is said, built up his political economy on the desires and fears of an entirely mythical personage. For his " Economic Man " is not a real man. This man does not represent the human race in general or any particular part of it. He is a creature of the economist's imagination. The facts of human life have not entered into his composition. The old political economy—the " Smithianismus," as the Germans call it—has been based on the assumption that this economic man exists. It must be discarded when it is shown that he does not exist ; that his assumed motives and activities are

not the law of industrial communities. A new inductive political economy must, therefore, take the
place of this old deductive one, and must be based
on the observation and careful accumulation of the
facts of industrial life in civilized countries, either
as they now exist or as they are historically re-
corded. As the economic history of every country differs in some degree from that of every other
country, it follows that every country must have
its own political economy and its own staff of ex-
pounders of the local science.

This is, accordingly, what has happened. There
have arisen a German school, an Austrian school,
an English school, a Russian school, and an American school, which all differ in the matter of
"method," but all agree in repudiating Adam
Smith and his economic followers, in denouncing
laissez faire, laissez passer, as an economic rule, in
being intensely "historical," and in endeavoring to
supply morality to trade through some sort of government interference, not as yet clearly defined.
The scorn of the new schools for Smith and Mill
and Ricardo is indeed almost bitter, but their differences about "method"—that is, about the exact
nature of the mental processes by which they reach
their conclusions—are already nearly as numerous
as those of the metaphysicians, and are apparently
likely to prove as barren. If Comte, who first

flouted the pretensions of political economy to be considered a science, were now living, these differences would please him hugely as illustrations of the soundness of his position. A little volume on "The Scope and Method of Political Economy," recently published by Mr. Keynes, the Lecturer on Moral Science in Cambridge University (England), should be read by any one who wishes to get an adequate idea not so much of economical methodology as of the methodological confusion which reigns among the economists. He remarks truly:

"Economic science deals with phenomena which are more complex and less uniform than those with which the natural sciences are concerned; and its conclusions, except in their most abstract form, lack both the certainty and precision that pertain to physical laws. There is a corresponding difficulty in regard to the proper method of economic study, and the problem of defining the conditions and limits of the validity of economic reasoning becomes one of exceptional complexity. It is, moreover, impossible to establish the right of any one method to hold the field to the exclusion of others. Different methods are appropriate according to the materials available, the stage of investigation reached, and the object in view; hence arises the special task of assigning to each its legitimate place and relative importance." (P. 6.)

Still more pertinent is the following:

"The sharp distinctions drawn by opposing schools, and their narrow dogmatism, have unnecessarily complicated the whole problem. The subject has become involved in heated controversies that have not only made it wearisome to unprejudiced persons, but have also done injury to the credit of political economy itself. Outsiders are naturally suspicious of a science in the treatment of which a new departure is so often and so loudly proclaimed essential." (P. 8.)[2]

This contempt for the "Economic Man" is the more remarkable because the members of the historic school themselves perforce make use of him. Roscher, who may be called the chief of it, relies on him fully as much as Ricardo. Such phrases as these abound in him :

" The systematic effort of *every* rational individual in his household management is directed towards the obtaining by a minimum of sacrifice of pleasure and energy a maximum satisfaction of his wants." (Vol. I, pp. 60–66.) "The incentive to ameliorate one's condition is common to *all* men, no matter how varied the form, or how different the intensity of its imagination. It follows us *all* from the cradle to the grave. It may be restricted within certain limits, but is never *entirely* extinguished." *All* normal economy aims at securing a maximum of personal advantage with a minimum of cost or outlay." (P. 73.) "Self-interest causes *every one* to choose the course in life in which he shall meet with least competition and the most abundant patronage." (P. 75.) "The abstraction according to which *all* men are by nature the same, different only in consequence of a difference of education, position in life, etc., *all* equally well equipped, skilful, and free in the matter of

economic production and consumption, is one which, as
Ricardo and Von Thunen have shown, must pass as an *indispensable stage* in the preparatory labors of political economists." (P. 105.) "The mathematical laws of motion
operate in a hypothetical vacuum, and when applied are subject to important modifications in consequence of atmospheric resistances. Something similar is true of most of
the laws of our science ; as, for instance, those in accord-
ance with which the price of a commodity is fixed by the
buyer and seller. It also *always* supposes the parties to the
contract to be guided *only* by a sense of their own best interest, and not to be influenced by secondary considerations." (P. 103.)*

The comparison of Ricardo's Economic Man to
the first law of motion is an old one, but it is as
good to-day as when it was first made. It is quite
true, as far as human knowledge goes, that no body
actually continues for an indefinite period in rec-
tilinear and uniform motion. But it is also true
that no real progress would ever have been made
in astronomy or mechanics without the assumption
that if a body were set in motion in a vacuum this
is the way in which it would move. It is no less
true that political economy, no matter how defined,
cannot be taught without assuming the existence
of an Economic Man who desires above all things,
and without reference to ethical considerations, to
get as much of the world's goods as he can with

* These quotations are all made from Lalor's translation.[3]

the least possible expenditure of effort or energy on his own part. The fact that he is not humane or God-fearing no more affects his usefulness for scientific purposes than the fact that the first law of motion would carry a cannon-ball through a poor man's cottage. The theory of production, of value, and of exchange, rests on his assumed existence. He supplies the *raison d'être* of the whole criminal law and of a large part of the civil law of all civilized countries. Ethics, and religion in so far as it furnishes a sanction for ethics, exist for the purpose of deflecting him from his normal course. The well-known " Gresham's Law," which declares that the less valuable of two kinds of legal-tender money will drive the more valuable out of circulation, has been understood by some of our more ignorant bimetallists as meaning that one will exert some kind of mechanical pressure or chemical repulsion on the other. But " Gresham's Law " is simply a deduction from observation of the working of the Economic Man's mind when brought into contact with two kinds of currency of unequal value, and through our knowledge of the Economic Man we can predict its operation with almost as much certainty as the operation of a law of chemistry or physics.

Ethics and religion, in fact, constitute the disturbing forces which make possible the organiza-

tion and prosperous existence of civilized states.
They have to be calculated and allowed for and
their working observed, just as the disturbing force
of gravity, or atmospheric or other resistance, has
to be calculated, allowed for, and its working observed, in astronomy or mechanics. But this cal-
culation would be impossible if the constant
tendency were not known. If the Economic Man
were blotted out of existence, nearly all the discussions of the economists would be as empty
logomachy as the attempts to reconcile fixed fate
and free will. That I am not here fighting a shadow
is shown by the fact that General Francis A.
Walker, himself an economist of eminence, in a recent address before the American Economic Association, on "The Tide of Economic Thought," gives
the following as one of the reasons for the currency
at this juncture of "the vaguest and wildest
schemes for human regeneration upon an economic
basis":

"First. The economists themselves are largely responsible for this state of things, on account of the arbitrary
and unreal character of their assumptions and the haughty
and contemptuous spirit in which they have too often
chosen to deliver their precepts. Especially are our American economists sinners above the rest in these respects.
Long after even the English economists, who have been
lordly enough, Heaven knows! had *importantly modified the
traditional premises of the science to meet the facts of human*

nature, and had, with a wider outlook, admitted many extensive qualifications of the doctrine of *laissez faire*, the professors of political economy in the leading American colleges continued to write about the economic man of Ricardo and James Mill as if he was worth all the real men who ever lived ; and the editors of the journals and reviews which especially affected to exercise authority in economics, greeted with contumely every suggestion of an exception to the rule of individualism, from whatever source proceeding, for whatever reason proposed. Even the complete establishment of such an exception in the policy of half a dozen nations, and its triumphant vindication in practical working to the satisfaction of all publicists, all men of affairs, and even of those who had once been selfishly interested to oppose it, constituted no reason why these high priests of economic orthodoxy should accept it." [4]

I might, if I had space, take serious exception to these allegations about the teachings of professors in American colleges, on the score of exaggeration, and also to the proposition touching the satisfaction of " *all* publicists and *all* men of affairs," on the score of accuracy. But I am not concerned about this so much as about the statement that the English and other economists have " importantly modified the traditional premises of the science." I am sure that were General Walker debating any topic but political economy, in discussing which no man ever gets fully outside of his subject, he would at once recognize the fact

that the premises of "a science" cannot be altered
to suit any one's fancy or convenience. Science
means the law which regulates the succession of
phenomena. Scientific investigation means an
attempt by observation or experiment, or both, to
get at this law. But it is only in theology or
metaphysics that the scientific investigator creates
his own premises, and makes hypotheses which
account for nothing. In all other fields, political
economy included—if it be a science—the premises are not furnished by the logician, but by the
phenomena of nature. Human society furnishes
the economist with his phenomena, and therefore
with his premises. He can, if he be a scientific
man, no more modify them "importantly" or
otherwise than he can by taking thought add a
cubit to his stature. He can, of course, as in any
line of investigation, frame hypotheses, but the
hypotheses have to be verifiable by observation or
experiment. But under all circumstances, and for
all purposes, there is no getting away from the
phenomena. You may dislike them, or wish they
were otherwise, but accept them you must. You
may approach them inductively by collecting
them for your premises, or you may approach them
deductively by concocting a hypothesis or theory
to explain them, but you must still apply them
promptly to your conclusion to see whether they

fit. I venture to assert that there is not a single economist of the old school, beginning with Adam Smith, who, as a scientific man, has not used both these methods with such success as his diligence and skill permitted. But in all economic investigation the first inquiry is, and, so far as it is economical, must forever remain : what will the Economic Man do when brought in contact with certain selected phenomena of the physical or social world ? And the more complicated the facts of the industrial and social world are, the more necessary to the economist the Economic Man is, in order to enable him to steer his way through the maze.

The existing confusion in the economic world, which General Walker's charge, quoted above, well illustrates, is due, apparently, to difficulty in getting the members of the new or historical schools to tell us in what character they appear. One can never tell, in listening to them, whether they are addressing us as scientific men or statesmen. Their air of authority is that of scientists, but the eager philanthropy of their utterances indicates that they are really would-be legislators. Their clothes are economical, but their talk is ethical. To take Roscher again as an example of the best-known and most moderate of them, one finds that what he has added to the work of the older economists, besides the illustrations supplied by an enormous erudition, consists mainly of theology and metaphysics. The new schools profess to know far more about the will of God, and about duty and the moral sources of happiness, and the ethical foundations of the state, than the older economists; but they have not contributed anything of practical importance to our knowledge of the laws of value, of production, or of exchange, as extracted from the mind of the producer and purchaser. The test of science is that it enables one to predict consequences. Until our researches have enabled us to foresee exactly what will happen if something else happens, although we may have discovered valuable and interesting facts, we have not discovered a law. That the historical school has laid before us a large mass of interesting information about the industrial condition of various countries at various periods cannot be denied, but I am unable to see in what its contributions to economical literature differ from the books of intelligent and observant travellers. Its great objection to the policy of *laissez faire*—that it permits a considerable amount of cruelty, oppression, and suffering, and that, in spite of its teachings, poverty exists on a great scale among the laboring classes—is an ethical or political, not a scientific, objection. It is simply saying to the rich what the " Society for the Abolition of Poverty " says—that they are cruel or unjust. It does not suggest any economical mode, in the scientific sense of the term, for improving the condition of the poor.

Take as an example of my meaning General Walker's announcement, in the passage I have just quoted, of "the complete establishment" of "an exception to the rule of individualism" (I presume the regulation of factory labor) "in the policy of half a dozen nations" "to the satisfaction of all publicists, all men of affairs," etc. This exception, let us observe, was first made in the country which has been supposed to be most influenced by the individualists. But no matter what its merits, or what its results, the fact remains that it is not an exception in the economic sense. It is a political or social measure, not an economic one. It is not a conclusion of economic science. It is a dictate of humanity or physiology or religion. It is a police regulation, to which the Economic Man is no more opposed than to the restrictions on the use of public water or the municipal prohibition of the storing of gunpowder. It was opposed in the beginning not by economists, but by manufacturers who happened to be at the time strongly combating the kind of government interference with production which had been the rule in Europe ever since the Middle Ages. There is no foundation for the suggestion that in any "half

dozen " countries in the world the Economic Man
has offered any serious impediment to the kind of
special interference with distribution for the benefit of the race which is known as socialistic legislation. The legislation has, as a matter of fact,
begun earliest in England, where individualism
has been supposed to be most powerful, and has
gone on, *pari passu*, with the spread of the opinions
associated with the names of Smith and Ricardo
and Cobden. The only effect of these opinions
on English legislation has been to abolish the
former hindrances to exchange with foreign countries ; and those who advocated this have certainly
not been brought to shame by the resulting effect
on the national industry and on the condition of
the working classes.

In short, the new school of economists are
rather politicians, using the word in its good
sense, than scientific men. What mainly occupies
them is legislation for taking away money from
capitalists and distributing it among laborers.
The earlier school may have paid too much attention to the problem of production. The later
ones can hardly be said to pay any attention at
all to production. With the effect of their plans
on production—that is, on the dividend which the
earth yields every year to the labor of its inhabitants—they hardly seem to concern themselves.

To talk of their championship of the working classes as being in any sense scientific would be an abuse of language.

I cannot help thinking that General Walker's ascription of the existing currency "of the vaguest and wildest schemes for human regeneration on an economic basis" to the economists —meaning by that the followers of Ricardo and Mill — is a curious misapprehension. It reads very like the criticism of the wolf on the lamb's pollution of the water. If dates throw any light on the matter, "the wild and vague schemes for human regeneration upon an economic basis" did not begin to spread or take hold of any civilized community with marked force or effect until after the convention of the "Katheder Socialisten" in Germany in 1877, and the appearance of the historical school in Germany, England, and America. Professor Ingram's attack on political economy in general in the "Encyclopædia Britannica" undoubtedly gave somewhat of a blow to "Smithianismus," but he only repeated what Comte had already said of the absurdity of supposing that there could be any such thing as economical science apart from the general science of sociology.[5] He, however, greatly diminished the apparent value of the Economic Man and helped to start crowds of young professors and labor agitators and politicians in search of a new economy which would shorten hours of labor, raise wages, humble the employer, give the laborer a fair share in the luxuries of life, and eventually abolish poverty.

The progress of this *quasi* scientific movement toward social regeneration through government interference, of the discredit of the older economists, and of the resulting economic confusion of which General Walker speaks, has been hastened by two other agencies of which he takes no notice. The charge that this confusion has been brought about through the bad manners of the old economists, and the hard-and-fast way in which they presented their theories to the multitude, shows that it is not science but politics which has been expected of them. The fact—if it be a fact—that the multitude refuses to listen to them any longer, and has gone off to worship new gods, does not prove that they have reasoned wrongly on the facts of society. It simply proves that their conclusions are unpopular. That a certain number of persons have gone into "the vaguest and wildest schemes for human regeneration on an economic basis" does not show that the assumptions of the old economists have been "arbitrary and unreal," although it may show that their precepts have been delivered in a "haughty and con-

temptuous spirit." But judging these economists
as legislators, which is really what the new school
does, it is impossible to decide, on any data now
in our possession, whether the *laissez-faire* system, as it is called, has been, or will be, successful or not.

There is, unhappily, no absolute test of success in economic legislation. All that the wisest
legislator can look for as a sign of his success
in dealing with economic problems is a reduction in the amount of discontent among the
poor. To abolish discontent among the poor completely, in any country, is as hopeless a task as
to abolish poverty, and no statesman attempts
it. Whether he has succeeded in lessening discontent he can only ascertain approximately, by
means of an inference from the increase of consumption as shown in statistics collected from
various sources. He concludes, *à priori*, that the
poor are less discontented when they consume
more of the necessaries and luxuries, because he
has observed that, as a rule, physical comfort
among the great bulk of mankind tends to produce happiness ; but no economist can say with
certainty that any particular kind of economical
legislation is the best possible, or has produced
effects which no other kind would or will produce.
It is here that the complexity of all sociological

problems comes in to baffle the politician, and compels him, in the vast majority of cases, to legislate simply for the Economic Man, with whose needs and tendencies he is, as a rule, far more familiar than he is with the needs of the ethical man. So that if the new schools of political economy enter the field, as they are apparently doing, not as scientists, but as legislators, their attacks on the old one as politicians cannot have any better basis than pride of opinion. It remains to be seen whether their plans for the promotion of human happiness are in any way superior to those of the old school or not.

It seems to be forgotten that the paternal system of government, in which what is called "the state" plays the part of an earthly parent to the individual, has been tried on an extensive scale in various communities and at various periods of the world's history, and with very poor success. I grant that it has not been tried under conditions as favorable as those which now exist. The experiment may now be made with greatly improved administrative machinery, with minute as well as wide knowledge of economic facts and tendencies, and under the watch of a powerful public opinion. But, on the other hand, the state has lost completely, in the eyes of the multitude, the moral and intellectual authority it once possessed. It does

not any longer represent God on earth.   In democratic countries it represents the party which
secured most votes at the last election, and is, in
many cases, administered by men whom no one
would make guardians of his children or trustees
of his property.   When I read the accounts given
by the young lions of the historical school of the
glorious future which awaits us as soon as we get
the proper amount of state interference with our
private concerns for the benefit of the masses, and
remember that in New York " the state " consists
of the Albany Legislature under the guidance of
Governor Hill, and in New York city of the little
Tammany junta known as "the Big Four," I confess I am lost in amazement.[6] I ask myself, How
can anybody who attacks the old school with such
vigor for its indifference to the facts of daily life,
be so completely oblivious of that most patent
fact, that the capacity of the state for interfering
with people profitably, has not grown in anything
like the same ratio as the popular intelligence, and
that there is nothing in which modern democracy
is showing itself so deficient as in the provision of
inspecting machinery—that is, in securing the
faithful execution of its plans for the promotion
of popular comfort ?

The agencies which have really done most to
discredit the older political economy with the

masses, and to produce an efflorescence of wild schemes of social regeneration on an economic basis, are, as I have said, two in number. The first is the extravagant expectations about the powers of the state in the solution of economical problems raised by the historical school since its appearance in 1877. Its promises and denunciations have been flung into democratic communities in which, as in France, Germany, and England, the poorer classes were just becoming aware of the extent of the power over the government which universal suffrage had put into their hands. In no country have " the masses," in the modern sense of that term, ever been greatly concerned about political liberty, as the men of the seventeenth and eighteenth centuries in this country and England understood it and fought for it; that is, about the division of the sovereignty between different bodies so as to prevent the growth of arbitrary power. The greatest political interest of that vast majority of the human race which is in but a small degree removed from want, always has been, and probably always will be, the power of legislation over distribution. A good government always has been to them a government under which trade is brisk, wages are high, and food is cheap. The reason why the older political economy has seemed to them "a dismal science " has been that its teach-

ings, in so far as it attempted to teach, discouraged
reliance on the state for these things, and made the
attainment of them dependent on individual character. I am not now discussing whether this doctrine was or was not pushed too far ; I simply say
that it was the most natural thing in the world for
the working classes of England, for example, which
had been so long familiar with legislation for the
direct benefit of the middle and upper classes, to
receive with anger or suspicion the announcement
that the care of any class by the state was a mistake, and that individual independence was the
true rule of industrial life. When these classes,
therefore, found themselves invested through the
suffrage with political power, it was inevitable that
they should seek at once to improve their condition through legislation, and should receive with
acclamation the news that a new school of political
economy had been founded which taught as "science " that the politicians were the true fathers of
their country, and would, on application, put an
end to unjust distribution. In short, the new departure which the new schools are all calling for is
a new departure in politics, not in political economy. There is hardly a trace of science in their
talk any more than in that of city missionaries.
What they are asking us to do is simply to try a
hazardous experiment in popular government.

The second agency in producing the existing economic confusion, which, as it appears to me, General Walker overlooks, is the substitution in nearly all the churches of the "gospel of social endeavor," as it has been called, for the old theological gospel. There are very few clergymen to-day who venture to expound in their pulpits what was formerly called the "Queen of the Sciences," the science of Christian theology. This used to be their chief business. Of this science they were the acknowledged masters. They were supposed to have the key to the greatest of all earthly problems, and their contentions with each other over the proper solution of it, furnished the chief interest of the intellectual world in all countries. When Dr. Lyman Beecher took the charge of a group of "anxious inquirers" out of the hands of Judge Gould at Litchfield, he did so as a professional man, just as a physician would have taken a case of typhoid fever out of the hands of an apothecary, and the church saw clearly the overwhelming necessity of the judge's deposition.[7] Probably nine out of ten of the members to-day would smile over the good doctor's notion that his skill in dealing with spiritual suffering was, *ex officio*, any greater than the judge's. In fact, authority has departed from the pulpit as a profession. Everybody nowadays acknowledges this, and clergymen feel it.

They feel especially that they have failed in obtaining influence for revealed religion over the great masses of population congregated in modern cities, and yet it is these masses which have raised what is called the "labor problem," and have produced the prodigious economic tumult which the historical school is trying to allay.

That ministers who feel that the old gospel has lost its power to soothe discontent and to account for social evils, should endeavor to get at the point of view of the laboring poor, and should in a large number of cases, through force of sympathy, come to share in their illusions touching the power of government over distribution, is surely very natural. The socialist view of what social arrangements ought to be, is very much like that of the early Christians, and the clergyman's imagination is naturally touched by finding it held by large bodies of his contemporaries. Moreover, was not the world once conquered by an ethical idea, and what is easier than for an ardent preacher to believe that it is not too late to do it over again? It has been maintained in this city in a clerical convention within twenty years, in all seriousness, that the whole world might be, and probably would be, with proper effort, "converted," in the technical sense of that term, within thirty years. What is there very wonderful in the opinion that this conversion might be hastened by a rearrangement, under government superintendence, of the relations of labor and capital.

Moreover, the notion that the economists are to blame for the aberrations of " the benevolent clergymen, ecstatic ladies," and other " prophets and disciples of an industrial millennium," would be more plausible if an industrial millennium were anything new, or if, from the days of Hesiod to our own, the evils of man's condition had not been laid on the greed of the rich, on the pride of the wise and learned, and on the inhumanity of the great, by a long catena of poets, sages, and prophets. That the volume of social discontent is now greater than in former ages is due mainly to the multitude of new problems we have to face, to the immensely improved means of spreading ideas, to the wonderful economic changes effected by science and invention, and, though last not least, to the appearance on the scene of the new schools of political economy to preach the limitlessness of the province of government. But the labor problem remains very much what it has been ever since agriculture was substituted for hunting and fishing—a problem which, in the main, each man must solve for himself.

IDLENESS AND IMMORALITY [1]

ONE of the most curious and interesting political and economical changes of the last hundred years, although it has attracted comparatively little notice, is the transfer of the legislative and administrative branches of government from the rich to the poor. We hear a great deal about the recent transfer of *power* to the people in certain countries, such as France, England, the United States, Germany, Italy, meaning thereby the power of determining at the polls who shall compose the government and what its policy on certain questions shall be. But we hear little about the change in the character of the governing class, which is also a very marked feature of the democratic movement.

Now, the governing class all over Europe was, from the fall of the Roman Empire to the Revolution in France and down to the passage of the Reform Bill in England, and, we may say, down to Andrew Jackson's time in America, the wealthy class; and the wealthy class until the present century were the owners of the soil. Modern Europe was in fact settled, if I may use the expression, on the theory that the landowners were "the country," the "legal country" as the French called it, and that everybody else was in a certain sense a sojourner or interloper. Before the Reform Bill in England, all extension of the suffrage beyond the freeholders, and all admission to Parliament of men who had no property in land, was denounced as committing the public affairs to people who had "no stake in the country." The property qualification for the suffrage which existed in most States of the Union at the Revolution, and confined it to "freeholders," was based on the same assumption, that is, that the nation was made up of those who owned the land in fee simple, and that all others might betray it, or run away from it, or had but a faint interest in its fame or prosperity.

That this notion had good traditional authority there is no denying, for it was the great landed proprietors who evoked some sort of order out of the chaos which followed the invasion of the Barbarians. The man who by force of character and military talent was able to gather a sufficient body of armed followers to protect a certain bit of territory against pillage by marauders, to build a fortified house on it in which his dependents might find temporary shelter for their families and cattle, and guarantee to the cultivators of the soil a fair amount of security while working in the fields, became outwardly the governor of his *protégés*. Far from wishing to share his authority, the great dread of their lives was that he would lay it down or fail to exercise it with sufficient vigor. For similar reasons they were only too glad to have his oldest son assume the same rights and duties on his father's death, and in two or three generations a hereditary landed aristocracy was established, and the reorganized society found it in full possession of all the government there was, and kept it there for a thousand years.

The men who owned the land, too, were during all this period the only wealthy class except the Jews. Land was the only investment which furnished anything that could be called an income. Everybody was more or less afraid to let his property out of his sight, or own property which could be carried away. The name given to land in the nomenclature of the English common law —"real property " or "real estate"—expressed not only the popular notion about it, but described the greatest political and economical fact of the day. The "man of property " was the landed man. He and his followers owned the country, and it seemed for ages perfectly natural and right that they should govern the country.

Now, the peculiarity of landed property which draws its income from rents is that it needs the personal attention of the owner. It used to make him a great man among his tenants, over whose future he exercised much power; and this power was increased in many countries by attaching to it the administration of local justice and the management of the financial affairs of the district or county. The country gentleman for fully twelve hundred years exercised jurisdiction over local affairs and small controversies, besides levying and spending the local taxes. He was, as a rule, consequently an extremely busy man, and became in popular estimation the only real statesman. Even in Burke's day a man of his great political genius was held by the Whigs to be unworthy of a seat in the Cabinet, because he was not connected with the landed gentry. So late as the Peninsular war, that most practical of commanders, Wellington, sent home earnest appeals for officers of "good family," meaning the sons of country gentlemen, as having some special and mysterious superiority in the work of fighting, although he was opposed to an enemy who had overrun Europe with an army led by the sons of butchers, bakers, and tavern-keepers. The necessity for keeping the property together in the hands of the eldest son to enable him to maintain the position of the family in society or politics, compelled the youngest sons to shift for themselves, and in every modern European country they were enabled to shift for themselves by having the public service reserved for them. They officered the army and navy and the diplomatic service, and got all the best places in the civil administration. In fact, John Bright did not exaggerate greatly when, speaking of the period before the introduction of the method of filling subordinate places by competitive examination, he called the public service a " huge system of out-door relief for the younger members of the aristocracy." The French Revolution made the first break in this system in France ; but it has lasted in England almost down to our own day, and is still in existence, in a modified degree, in Germany and Austria.

It will be easily seen that this is a description of a state of things in which, as a rule, the owners of the wealth of the country were both its legislators and administrators, and that both the fathers and the sons were kept busy. They all had their duties and responsibilities, either as managers of their own estates, or as local magistrates, or as legislators, or as officers of the army and navy, or of the civil service, or as ministers of the estab-

lished Church—an organization which in all countries in which it existed, possessed an enormous
mass of property. The economical or political
revolutions which have occurred within the present
century have greatly changed all this. Power has
passed from the owners of the land to people
of every kind of occupation. The work of legislation has been largely given over to poor men,
or the sons of poor men, who in all parliamentary
countries except England, draw pay for it. The
administrative offices have been thrown open to
the same class. The great landowner has been
converted almost everywhere into an annuitant,
drawing a certain income from his estates, but ex-
erting comparatively little influence on the lives or
fortunes of the tenants. In a word, the aristocracy of
all countries except Germany has become our idle
class. It is literally true of the aristocrats now,
that they toil not, neither do they spin. They no
longer render the state the service which the old
feudal tenures exacted of them, and their enjoyment of large incomes drawn from the industry
expended on the soil by others, becomes increasingly difficult to defend in the forum of abstract
justice. The great landholders of the world have,
in fact, more and more to protect themselves by
showing the danger to all property that would
probably result from an attack on their particular

kind of property. One consequence of this is that the accumulated wealth of the world no longer passes into the land. The passion for "broad acres" has died or is rapidly dying out. The number of people who are "land poor" increases. The extraordinary improvement in the means of communication has, for practical purposes, thrown all the agricultural land of the world into one market, and thereby all the farmers, from China to Peru, compete with each other.

As either a consequence or an accompaniment of this, the accumulated capital of each year is now gathered up by corporations who turn it over in all sorts of industrial enterprises, through the instrumentality of hired employees, and pay the owners a moderate but tolerably sure percentage on it. If it is not disposed of in this way, it goes into government loans, on which interest is paid out of the taxes. Now, the amount of these investments from which men may draw a certain income, without any exertion of mind or body on their own part, is something enormous. The capital invested in the railroads of the world is estimated at $30,000,000,000. The total national debts of the world are estimated at $32,000,000,000. A good deal of this, of course, does not yield interest, but if, on the average, it pays one per cent., the income drawn from it is immense, and we leave out of sight the very large number of various industrial enterprises owned by corporations whose shares may be held by anybody, however unused to and unfit for active business.

The interest on this great sum, of course, goes in a considerable degree into the pockets of men and women who are actively engaged in some sort of industry, and represents their savings. A considerable part of it is devoted to the support of helpless people, widows and orphans, and the aged and infirm. Much of it passes into the treasury of charitable and educational institutions and churches. But it affords also to a large and increasing body of persons of both sexes the means of living lives of absolute leisure, of abstaining, that is to say, from all distasteful labor, from doing the things they do not like to do; and what is perhaps fully as important in its moral aspect is, that it breaks their connection with any particular locality. In the old days before the creation of this great mass of stocks and bonds, nearly every man was bound by ties of some sort to a particular place, in which his presence during the greater part of the year was made necessary by some sort of duty, or from which departure was difficult or inconvenient. Of course this is still true of the great bulk of mankind. The majority of the human race are still in a certain sense *adscripti glebæ*, bound by uncontrollable circumstances to pass their lives in some particular spot of earth. But the proportion which can, if they please, lead nomad lives, that is, can pass from place to place at will and settle themselves for longer or shorter periods in any one that takes their fancy, gains very rapidly and is now very large in every country. England and America supply by far the greater number of these " *heim-athlosen*," as the Germans call people who have no fixed domicile, owing doubtless in part to Anglo-Saxon restlessness, but certainly in a very large degree to the large revenue yielded in these countries by various kinds of what we call "interest-bearing securities," or, in other words, to the large number of persons in both countries who have investments which do not call for their personal attention and are made fruitful by other people's management and labor. No doubt a good deal of this migration has serious objects in view—such as health or education. But the proportion of it that is simply aimless wandering in search of new forms of excitement or amusement, is very large and is growing. One of the most marked effects of this migratory habit is a certain volatility which makes it difficult to keep the attention fixed very long on one object or on one species of occupation or amusement, and ends by reducing its victims to a somewhat childish mental condition. Every one who has had any ac-

quaintance with the world of fashion and leisure
which is to be found at any of the European winter and summer resorts, must have observed how
easily people tire of their amusements and com-
panions, how necessary frequent change of place
or pursuit is to their comfort, and how often
they remind one of the perennial childish cry,
" Mamma, what shall I do next ? "

Mr. Gladstone, in discussing Lord Tennyson's
" Locksley Hall Sixty Years After," enumerates
the changes which have come over England within
that period, and mentions as one of the most
marked the great increase of this idle class, and
he throws on them the burden of justifying their
existence.[2] But the increase continues in an accel-
erated ratio. The last thing in the world they
think of is justifying either their existence or the
manner of their existence. No class are less given
to any species of speculative inquiry or less
troubled about the moral aspect of their pursuits.
In so far as the members have become serious, it
is in desiring new forms of amusement or new
places to play in. In fact, they have made amusement a business, and engage in it with an attention
to details, a regard to finish and efficiency, which
in many cases would be sufficient to insure success
in any species of trade or industry. Where they
are weak is in want of persistence, for to nothing

is a life of amusement more fatal, as I have said,
than the power of continuance in any one pursuit.
The will becomes gradually weakened under long
release from strenuous exertion, and the thing "got
up," however successful it may be, soon becomes
tiresome.

There is one distraction, however, of which the
idle class can hardly be said ever to tire, and
which idle people can hardly be considered capable of avoiding, and that is the distraction of love-
making under more or less illicit conditions. This
is what they fall back on when all else fails or
becomes vapid. When men and women are
thrown together in the midst of luxury without
duties or responsibility, and without exposure to
any criticism except what comes from persons
similarly situated, the possibilities of scandal grow
very rapidly, and the air is soon filled with it.
The sexual passion is of all passions the most
wayward, watchful, and readiest for temptations.
Neither law nor religion, nor tradition nor custom, has yet been able to furnish a force capable
of keeping it wholly within the artificial channels
which society has provided for it. Propinquity, as
is well known, is always liable to rouse it into
action even in the most humdrum conditions.
The disposition of the "any man" to fall in love
with the "any woman" whom he sees most fre-

quently is one of the commonplaces of worldly
wisdom. So is the disposition of the "any
woman" to see in the "any man" with whom she
may be thrown into daily or frequent intercourse,
a possible lover. On this very solid anthropologi-
cal fact the code of propriety which in all countries regulates the intercourse of the sexes has
been framed. In semi-barbarous societies it is
framed by men, is rigid in its requirements and
Draconian in its penalties. In highly civilized
societies it is largely framed and enforced by
women, and though its provisions have been
greatly relaxed and its sanctions much mitigated,
nevertheless its basal assumption, as the philosophers say, remains undisturbed. That assumption
is that when young persons of both sexes are
thrown together with nothing to do, they need,
whether married or single, to be closely super-
vised.

This precise situation does not often arise when
people are living in their homes in their own
countries. They have their cares and responsibilities, and perhaps work to do. They are surrounded by relatives or friends, and feel the har-
ness of custom and tradition and public opinion in
nearly every act of their lives. The first step in
the path of vice or folly draws forth warnings
which they have been taught by long habit to

respect. But when removed from the pressure of
these time-honored restraints, as in the large
country-houses in England or on the Continent,
and as in the fashionable resorts, such as Pau or
Monte Carlo, or a score of other places which I
need not enumerate, which in our time are crowded
with the rich and idle both summer and winter, the
air becomes charged with amorous electricity ; men
and women become, consciously or unconsciously,
ready for amorous adventures. There are few
women who are not, under such conditions, more
or less ready for the mild excitement at least of
repelling unlawful advances, and few or no men
who do not believe themselves worthy of a *bonne
fortune*, and likely to fall in for one any day.
Hunting, polo, lawn tennis, gambling, dinner-giv-
ing, all pall in the long run, or are confined to certain seasons, but the *ewige Weib* remains as a
perennial resource. The annual social chronicles
of the Indian *sanitaria* in " the Hills " and of the
pleasure resorts of the European continents, contain illustrations in abundance of the tremendous strain which an idle and luxurious life puts
on the bonds of the old morality. The murders,
the duels, or the elopements which every now and
then occur, impressive as they are, give but a
slight idea of the moral turmoil which goes on below the surface. Every year contributes its list of

catastrophes of which the world never hears, of work made hopelessly repulsive on the very threshold of life, of family peace destroyed beyond recovery, of affections irretrievably diverted from their old and lawful channels, of honest worth covered with ridicule, of high aspirations quenched in a swash of triviality or childish "gayety." The worship of wealth, in its coarsest and most undraped form, too, that is, wealth as a purveyor of meat, drink, clothing, and ornamentation, which goes on in this *milieu*, "makes hay" of all noble standards of individual and social conduct.

Perhaps the very worst influence of the idler, however, is to be found in the effect of the spectacle of their lives on what is called "the labor problem." "The labor problem" is really the problem of making the manual laborers of the world content with their lot. In my judgment this is an insoluble problem. No discoveries nor inventions will ever solve it as long as population continues to press close on the available products of human industry. The causes of the dissatisfaction of the masses with their condition may change from age to age, but the dissatisfaction will continue, and the blame will be always laid on those who have a larger share of the world's goods than others. But there is no question that the existing discontent is, and not unreasonably, aggravated by the spectacle of the enjoyment by the growing idle class, of the benefits of the social and political organizations, without any contribution worth mention to the trouble and cost of maintaining these organizations. The taxes paid by the annuitant or *rentier* class are but a trifling return, in reality, for the security they possess for person and property. The workers of the world provide them with police, with courts of justice, and means of travel—in short, every agency which makes their enjoyment possible, for sums in cash which they would hardly pay to a good club. Reasonably or unreasonably, the masses resent this more and more. It gives mere envy an air of respectability and rationality. They say that even if a good defence may be made for inequality of conditions based on inequality of capacity and services, there ought not in truly democratic communities, to be any people who render no service at all, and who allow others to till, and spin and weave, and police, and fight, and teach, and invent and discover, plough the seas and dig the mines for them, while they look on and draw their quarterly dividends and spend them in childishness ; that we shall never have social peace till every man has a fair share of the social burdens.

The arguments in favor of the existence of the class called "men of leisure" are familiar to every

one. The contributions of this class to civilization
have been very great. There are books of the
greatest value to the community which cannot be
contributed by busy men. It is only the men of
leisure who can look after the artistic side of life,
and the artistic side of life has to be cultivated in
order to keep man above the contented ox or
porker. The services, too, which they render to
the state by being allowed to choose their work
are often of inestimable value. No one can think of
Darwin's, or Grote's, or Cavour's, or Gladstone's, or
Howard's, or Motley's pecuniary competency, without thankfulness.[3] Even the socialists share this
feeling. It is impossible to say which of all men
of leisure will turn their leisure to useful account;
and it would be therefore dangerous, even if it were
possible, to make a rule prohibiting their existence.
The best thing in the world is individual freedom;
and a man who is compelled to work by law when
there is no fear of his becoming dependent on the
labor of others for a livelihood, is to all intents and
purposes a slave. Better that ten men should
"loaf" than that one should lose his liberty.

But the modern democracy must take on itself
part of the blame which it throws on the idlers.
The rich are being gradually and relentlessly ex-
cluded as a rule from public office in all the democratic countries. There are enough well-to-do men

of leisure in New York to give us an excellent city
government without payment, except in the subordinate places, were the poor willing to give up their
chance of the salaries. Venice, in its best days,
secured a large body of good officials by compelling
men of fortune to serve in the offices to which they
were elected. Berlin has to-day a first-rate common council made up in the same way. But there
is very little chance of our seeing this system
spread. The most discouraging phenomena of
government by universal suffrage thus far, is its
strong tendency to treat public offices as "plums"
rather than trusts, to be distributed among poor
men as rewards for winning elections, and to consider indifference to the salary as a positive dis-
qualification.

As long as this tendency lasts, we fear the alienation of the rich and their disposition to make
amusement a serious business will continue, and
the chief cure will be found only in the resolute
resistance of the individual conscience. Nothing
does more in this country to recruit the ranks of
the pleasure-seekers than the tendency of rich
fathers, backed up in this by the public generally,
to treat money-making as the only serious business
of life. A young man bred in this notion naturally says to himself when he inherits a fortune :
" Money-getting, however laudable a pursuit in it-

self, is surely only incumbent on those who have not
got money or want more of it than they have got.
Why should I, who have got all I want, continue
to work for it? No, I must enjoy it." And when
he has given himself up to the child's life, buying
fresh toys every day and throwing them away the
next, the only thing which excites the wonder of
those of his friends and neighbors who do not envy
him, is that he should not have " stayed in business."

The truth is that there has never been an
age of the world in which there were such opportunities for men of fortune to find enjoyment in
contributions to the general welfare. To some
natures philanthropy, pure and simple, is odious,
but there remain art, literature, science, agriculture,
education. By this last I do not mean simply the
instruction of youth either at schools or colleges,
but also the work of persuasion through voice and
pen. There never has been in the history of the
world such a field for orators and writers as a
democratic country now offers. There is no nobler
nor more fascinating game than the work of chang-
ing the opinions of great bodies of men, by inducing them to discard old beliefs and take on new
ones, or arresting their rush after strange gods.
But very few indeed ever take up any such work
late in life. The taste for it must be formed and

the equipment provided in youth. Though last, not least, the delusion must be got rid of that there is no use in trying to act on the minds of one's fellow-men unless one can thereby get an office. It is this which makes a great many useful young men wash their hands of politics and go in for polo and tennis and flirtations instead. Official life, as our Government is now organized, has no field for a really high ambition. Public functionaries are becoming more and more the puppets of the managers outside, and the managers are whatever public opinion lets them be or insists on their being. The coming rulers of men are those who mould the thoughts or sway the passions of the multitude.

THE DUTY OF EDUCATED MEN IN A DEMOCRACY [1]

PERHAPS I ought not to say it, but college graduates are not, as a rule, remarkable for the amount of knowledge, properly so called, which they bring away from the universities. Everything they learn there in the way of languages or of science makes a comparatively small impression on the great mass of them. The great use of the college course is the formation of the habit of attention and study at the age when mental and other habits are most easily formed. But a college education has a perceptible general effect on the intellectual outlook. Its most marked effect on men in relation to their duties to the community at large, is in raising their standards. Their notions of how things ought to be done are changed. They expect a good deal more in the character and attainments of public men, and in the order of public business. The municipal government, for instance, which the educated men would set up, if they had their way, would be something consider-

ably different from any municipal government now
in existence.   Congress and the State legislatures,
too, would be, if the suffrage were confined to college graduates, composed of another class of men
than that which now fills them.   A very large portion of our present legislation would never be enacted, and the probabilities are that the ceremonial
side of the government would be much enlarged.
I remember that two or three years ago President
Eliot wrote in *The Forum*,* pointing out that our
municipal government would never be what it
ought to be until all our city officials had received
a special training for their work, and he mentioned
the various kinds of training which they needed.
Now this was distinctly the college graduate's
view of the matter.   The popular mind was not
then occupied with the need or the difficulty of
getting trained men for such work.   It would have
been satisfied with men of ordinary honesty.   The
notion that trained men were a possibility, probably never occurred to the bulk of the citizens.

We should probably, in a college-graduate government, witness the disappearance from legislation of nearly all acts and resolutions which are
passed for what is called " politics ; " that is, for
the purpose of pleasing certain bodies of voters,
without any reference to their real value as contri-

* Vol. XII., p. 153, October, 1891. [2]

butions to the work of government. This would
of course effect a very great reduction in the size
of the annual statute-book. For, to the mind of
the ordinary legislator of to-day, the duty of pleasing the voters is even more obligatory than the
duty of furnishing them with good government. In
this duty of pleasing the voters there is no question that a college education as a rule unfits a man.
He cannot discharge it without a fight with his
ideals formed at a susceptible age. James Russell
Lowell furnishes an illustration of my meaning.
He was unquestionably as patriotic an American
as ever lived, and a thorough Democrat. Democracy has never received so fine a tribute as he paid
to it in Birmingham. But, somehow, as an educated man, he was out of tune with the multitude.
The West never quite took to him. The *New York
Tribune* denied him even the right to be considered
" a good American." Senator Sherman and other
Republicans wrote " Ichabod " on him when he supported Mr. Cleveland. The cause of all this really
was that his political standards differed from
theirs. He lived in an earlier republic of the
mind, in which the legislation was done by first-
class men, whom the people elected and followed.
In a republic in which the multitude told the legislators what to do, he never really was at home.[3]

This brings to me the question, what is really

the attitude of educated men toward universal suffrage to-day? As a general rule I think they
really mistrust or regret it, but accept it as the
inevitable. Probably no system of government
was ever so easy to attack and ridicule, but no
government has ever come upon the world from
which there seemed so little prospect of escape.
It has, in spite of its imperfections and oddities,
something of the majesty of doom, and nobody
now pretends that any people can avoid it. There
has been, however, a notable change within forty
years, in the opinion of the educated class, as to
its value, owing to its numerous mistakes; but,
curiously enough, these mistakes seem often to be
due to the difficulty experienced in finding out
what its mind is. Its mass in countries in which
it exists, is so large that the process of interrogat-
ing it is one of extraordinary difficulty even for
the most expert. Politicians, of all varieties, think
they know what the people think upon any given
question of the day, but most of them are always
wrong. There could not be a better illustration of
this than the mistake made by Senator Hill, Governor Flower, and other politicians in this State
about Maynard's nomination. They had the deepest interest in knowing what the popular judgment
on this nomination would be, but fell into an immense error about it.[4]

This difficulty is not likely to decrease, and is likely to produce a great many legislative follies ; because, unhappily, it seems to be the way of most politicians in all countries, when puzzled or uncertain about the drift of public sentiment, to choose the course which seems the least wise or most childish, meaning by that the course which seems to promise most immediate gratification, or to display most indifference to remoter results. One consequence of this is that universal suffrage has taken the blame of a great many mistakes for which it is not responsible, and which have come to pass simply owing to want of skill in questioning it on the part of law-makers. But, after all allowances and excuses have been made, its errors are sure to be frequent and on a considerable scale. We may expect, for instance, such mistakes as our silver policy, with increasing frequency, because the politics of the world are becoming more and more a controversy between rich and poor. The influential and the rich men are taking the place of the feudal baron and the absolute monarch as objects of popular attack, and moderate physical comforts for all, or a "living wage," have taken the place of political liberty. But the rich man cannot and will not be openly robbed. He runs no risk of having his head cut off, or his property confiscated. He will probably

be got at through experiments in taxation, or in
currency, which unfortunately rarely reach the
precise objects at which they are aimed, and
sooner or later, like the silver purchases, involve
the whole community in great distress.

The idea that *distribution* must be, in some manner, reformed, is taking greater and greater hold
of the world, and the popular mind is so much impressed with what seems to be the injustice of the
present system, that hardly any attention is paid
to the size of the earth's dividend. And yet, to
divide among the people of every country all the
accumulated wealth there is in it, or to divide
among them the annual yield of its land and labor,
is one of the simplest of arithmetical problems. In
no case would any such dividend make any material
change in the condition of the great bulk of the
population. There is no deduction from the operation of nature more certain than that the earth is
not meant to afford much more than a fair subsistence to the dwellers on it. The mass of mankind
have been poor from the earliest ages, simply because they multiply close up to the provision which
the earth normally makes for them. They have
always done so, and probably will always do so, in
every country. It is true that their condition has
improved since the introduction of steam into the
work of production ; but their content has not in-

creased, and the contrast between their mode of
life and that of the very rich remains about the
same. There is no wider interval now between the
house of the modern rich man and the laborer's cottage than there was between the castle and the hut
of the Middle Ages. If all that needed to be done
to make everybody comfortable and contented was
to pull down the rich man's palace, and decree that
no more should be built, the problem of modern
politics would be easy. But the truth is that there
is no cure for the evils of our present condition
but a great increase in the produce of the earth,
without any corresponding increase in population,
and without any abatement in the industry, enterprise, and energy of the existing workers. When
we think of the enormous resources of the globe
which are still untouched, we are apt to forget that,
in order to get at them, we have to go on breeding
an increased number of men and women, who will
keep alive, generation after generation, the old
story of unequal and unjust distribution.

But to divide the earth's products equally, or
anywhere near equally, among the people, would
be to ignore the claims of superior talent, industry,
or frugality upon the larger share, or, in other
words, to ignore differences of character. I think
most educated men will agree that in the long run
our civilization could not stand this. All progress

has been made hitherto on the competitive principle, which means giving the prize to the best
man ; and we can hardly conceive of its being made
in any other way. To prescribe that no one shall
do better than any one else, is to reproduce China.

Now, in the presence of all this, the rôle of the
educated man is really a very difficult one. No intelligent man can or ought to ignore the part which
hope of better things plays in our present social
system. It has largely, among the working classes,
taken the place of religious belief. They have
brought their heaven down to earth; and are literally looking forward to a sort of New Jerusalem, in
which all comforts and many of the luxuries of
life, will be within easy reach of all. The great
success of Utopian works like Bellamy's shows
the hold which these ideas have taken of the popular mind. The world has to have a religion of some
kind, and the hope of better food and clothing,
more leisure, and a greater variety of amusements,
has become the religion of the working classes.
Hope makes them peaceful, industrious, and re-
signed under present suffering. A Frenchman
saw a ragged pauper spend his last few cents on a
lottery ticket, and asked him how he could commit such a folly. "In order to have something to
hope for," he said. And from this point of view
the outlay was undoubtedly excusable. It is liter-

ally hope which makes the world go round, and one of the hardest things an educated man who opens his mouth about public affairs has to do, is to say one word or anything to dampen or destroy it. Yet his highest duty is to speak the truth.

Luckily, there is one truth which can always be spoken without offence, and that is that on the whole the race advances through the increase of intelligence and the improvement of character, and has not advanced in any other way. The great amelioration in the condition of the working classes in Europe within this century, including the increasing power of the trades-unions, is the result not of any increase of benevolence in the upper classes, but of the growth of knowledge and self-reliance and foresight among the working classes themselves. The changes in legislation which have improved their condition are changes which they have demanded. When a workingman becomes a capitalist, and raises himself in any way above his early condition, it is rarely the result of miracle or accident. It is due to his superior intelligence and thrift. Nothing, on the whole, can be more delusive than official and other inquiries into the labor problem, through commissions and legislative committees. They all assume that there is some secret in the relations of labor and capital which can be found out by taking testimony. But they never find anything out. Their reports during the last fifty years would make a small library, but they never tell us anything new. They are meant to pacify and amuse the laborer, and they do so; but to their constant failure to do anything more we owe some of the Socialist movement. The Socialists believe this failure due to want of will, and that Karl Marx has discovered the great truth of the situation, which is, that labor is entitled to the whole product. The great law which Nature seems to have prescribed for the government of the world, and the only law of human society which we are able to extract from history, is that the more intelligent and thoughtful of the race shall inherit the earth and have the best time, and that all others shall find life on the whole dull and unprofitable. Socialism is an attempt to contravene this law and ensure a good time to everybody independently of character and talents; but Nature will see that she is not frustrated or brought to nought, and I do not think educated men should ever cease to call attention to this fact, that is, ever cease to preach hopefulness, not to everybody, but to good people. This is no bar to benevolence to bad people or any people, but our first duty is loyalty to the great qualities of our kind, to the great human virtues, which raise the civilized man above the savage.

There is probably no government in the world to-day as stable as that of the United States. The chief advantage of democratic government is, in a country like this, the enormous force it can command on an emergency. By " emergency " I mean the suppression of an insurrection or the conduct of a foreign war. But it is not equally strong in the ordinary work of administration. A good many governments, by far inferior to it in strength, fill the offices, collect the taxes, administer justice, and do the work of legislation with much greater efficiency. One cause of this inefficiency is that the popular standard in such matters is low, and that it resents dissatisfaction as an assumption of superiority. When a man says these and those things ought not to be, his neighbors, who find no fault with them, naturally accuse him of giving himself airs. It seems as if he thought he knew more than they did, and was trying to impose his plans on them. The consequence is, that, in a land of pure equality, as this is, critics are always an unpopular class, and criticism is, in some sense, an odious work. The only condemnation passed on the governmental acts or systems is apt to come from the opposite party in the form of what is called "arraignment," which generally consists in wholesale abuse of the party in power, treating all their acts, small or great, as due to folly or depravity, and all their public men as either fools or knaves. Of course this makes but small impression on the public mind. It is taken to indicate not so much a desire to improve the public service as to get hold of the offices, and has, as a general rule, but little effect. Parties lose their hold on power through some conspicuously obnoxious acts or failures; never, or very rarely, through the judgments passed on them by hostile writers or orators. And yet nothing is more necessary to successful government than abundant criticism from sources not open to the suspicion of particular interest. There is nothing which bad governments so much dislike and resent as criticism, and have in past ages taken so much pains to put down. In fact, a history of the civil liberty would consist, largely, of an account of the resistance to criticism on the part of rulers. One of the first acts of a successful tyranny or despotism is always the silencing of the press or the establishment of a censorship.

Popular objection to criticism is, however, senseless, because it is through criticism—that is, through discrimination between two things, customs or courses—that the race has managed to come out of the woods and lead a civilized life. The first man who objected to the general nakedness, and advised his fellows to put on clothes, was the first critic. Criticism of a high tariff recommends a low tariff; criticism of monarchy recommends a republic; criticism of vice recommends virtue. In fact almost every act of life in the practice of a profession or the conduct of a business, condemns one course and suggests another. The word means *judging*, and judgment is the highest of the human faculties, the one which most distinguishes us from the animals.

There is, probably, nothing from which the public service of the country suffers more to-day than the silence of its educated class; that is, the small amount of criticism which comes from the disinterested and competent sources. It is a very rare thing for an educated man to say anything publicly about the questions of the day. He is absorbed in science, or art, or literature, in the practice of his profession, or in the conduct of his business; and if he has any interest at all in public affairs, it is a languid one. He is silent because he does not much care, or because he does not wish to embarrass the administration or " hurt the party," or because he does not feel that anything he could say would make much difference. So that, on the whole, it is very rarely that the instructed opinion of the country is ever heard on any subject. The report of the Bar Association on the nomination of Maynard in New York was a remarkable exception to this rule. Some improve-

ment in this direction has been made by the appearance of the set of people known as the
"Mugwumps," who are, in the main, men of cultivation. They have been defined in various ways.
They are known to the masses mainly as "kickers ;"
that is, dissatisfied, querulous people, who complain of everybody and cannot submit to party
discipline. But they are the only critics who do
not criticise in the interest of party, but simply in
that of good government. They are a kind of
personage whom the bulk of the voters know nothing about, and find it difficult to understand, and
consequently load with ridicule and abuse. But
their movement, though its visible recognizable
effects on elections may be small, has done inestimable service in slackening the bonds of party
discipline, in making the expression of open dissent
from party programmes respectable and common,
and in increasing the unreliable vote in large States
like New York. It is of the last importance that
this unreliable vote—that is, the vote which party
leaders cannot count on with certainty—should be
large in such States. The mere fear of it prevents
a great many excesses.

But in criticism one always has hard work in
steering a straight course between optimism and
pessimism. These are the Scylla and Charybdis
of the critic's career. Almost every man who

thinks or speaks about public affairs is either an
optimist or a pessimist; which he is, depends a
good deal on temperament, but often on character.
The political jobber or corruptionist is almost always an optimist. So is the prosperous business
man. So is nearly every politician, because the
optimist is nearly always the more popular of the
two. As a general rule, people like cheerful men
and the promise of good times. The kill-joy and
the bearer of bad news has always been an odious
character. But for the cultivated man there is no
virtue in either optimism or pessimism. Some
people think it a duty to be optimistic, and for
some people it may be a duty; but one of the
great uses of education is to teach us to be neither
one nor the other. In the management of our personal affairs, we try to be neither one nor the other.
In business, a persistent and uproarious optimist
would certainly have poor credit. And why? Because in business the trustworthy man, as everybody knows, is the man who sees things as they
are; and to see things as they are, without glamour
or illusion, is the first condition of worldly success.
It is absolutely essential in war, in finance, in law,
in every field of human activity in which the future
has to be thought of and provided for. It is just
as essential in politics. The only reason why it is
not thought as essential in politics is, the punish-

ment for failure or neglect comes in politics more slowly.

The pessimist has generally a bad name, but there is a good deal to be said for him. To take a recent illustration, the man who took pessimistic views of the silver movement was for nearly twenty years under a cloud. This gloomy anticipation of 1873 was not realized until 1893. For a thousand years after Marcus Aurelius, the pessimist, if I may use the expression, was "cock of the walk." He certainly has no reason to be ashamed of his rôle in the Eastern world for a thousand years after the Mohammedan Hegira. In Italy and Spain he has not needed to hang his head since the Renaissance. In fact, if we take various nations and long reaches of time, we shall find that the gloomy man has been nearly as often justified by the course of events as the cheerful one. Neither of them has any special claim to a hearing on public affairs. A persistent optimist, although he may be a most agreeable man in family life, is likely, in business or politics, to be just as foolish and unbearable as a persistent pessimist. He is as much out of harmony with the order of nature. The universe is not governed on optimistic any more than on pessimistic principles. The best and wisest of men make their mistakes and have their share of sorrow and sickness and losses. So, also, the most happily situated nations must suffer from internal discord, the blunders of statesmen, and the madness of the people. What Cato said in the Senate of the conditions of success, "*vigilando, agendo, bene consulendo, prospere omnia cedunt,*" is as true to-day as it was two thousand years ago. We must remember that, though the optimist may be the pleasantest man to have about us, he is the least likely to take precautions; that is, the least likely to watch and work for success. We owe a great deal of our slovenly legislation to his presence in large numbers in Congress and the legislatures. The great suffering through which we are now passing, in consequence of the persistence in our silver purchases, is the direct result of unreasoning optimism. Its promoters disregarded the warnings of economists and financiers because they believed that—somehow, they did not know how—the thing would come out right in the end. This silver collapse, together with the Civil War over slavery, are striking illustrations to occur in one century, of the fact that, if things come out right in the end, it is often after periods of great suffering and disaster. Could people have foreseen how the slavery controversy would end, what frantic efforts would have been made for peaceful abolition! Could people have foreseen the panic of last year, with its widespread disaster, what

haste would have been made to stop the silver purchases ! And yet the experience of mankind afforded abundant reason for anticipating both results.

This leads me to say that the reason why educated men should try and keep a fair mental balance between both pessimism and optimism is that
there has come over the world in the last twenty-
five or thirty years a very great change of opinion
touching the relations of the government to the community. When Europe settled down to peaceful
work after the great wars of the French Revolution, it was possessed with the idea that the freedom of the individual was all that was needed for
public prosperity and private happiness. The
old government interference with people's movements and doings was supposed to be the reason
why nations had not been happy in the past.
This became the creed, in this country, of the
Democratic party which came into existence after
the foundation of the Federal government. At
the same time there grew up here the popular idea
of the American character, in which individualism was the most marked trait. If you are not familiar with it in your own time, you may remember
it in the literature of the earlier half of the century. The typical American was always the architect of his own fortunes. He sailed the seas and
penetrated the forest, and built cities and lynched

the horse-thieves, and fought the Indians and dug the mines, without anybody's help or support. He had even an ill-concealed contempt for regular troops, as men under control and discipline. He scorned government for any other purposes than security and the administration of justice. This was the kind of American that Tocqueville found here in 1833. He says : *

"The European often sees in the public functionaries simply force; the American sees nothing but law. One may then say that in America a man never obeys a man, or anything but justice and law. Consequently he has formed of himself an opinion which is often exaggerated, but is always salutary. He trusts without fear to his own strength, which appears to him equal to anything. A private individual conceives some sort of enterprise. Even if this enterprise have some sort of connection with the public welfare, it never occurs to him to address himself to the government in order to obtain its aid. He makes his plan known, offers to carry it out, calls other individuals to his aid, and struggles with all his might against any obstacles there may be in his way. Often, without doubt, he succeeds less well than the State would in his place; but in the long run the general result of individual enterprises far surpasses anything the government could do."

Now there is no doubt that if this type of character has not passed away, it has been greatly modified; and it has been modified by two agencies

* Democracy in America, Vol. I., p. 157.

—the "labor problem," as it is called, and legislative protection to native industry. I am not going to make an argument about the value of this protection in promoting native industry, or about its value from the industrial point of view. We may or we may not owe to it the individual progress and prosperity of the United States. About that I do not propose to say anything. What I want to say is that the doctrine that it is a function of government, not simply to foster industry in general, but to consider the case of every particular industry, and give it the protection that it needs, could not be preached and practised for thirty years in a community like this, without modifying the old American conception of the relation of the government to the individual. It makes the government, in a certain sense, a partner in every industrial enterprise, and makes every Presidential election an affair of the pocket to every miner and manufacturer and to his men ; for the men have for fully thirty years been told that the amount of their wages would depend, to a certain extent, at least, on the way the election went. The notion that the government owes assistance to individuals in carrying on business and making a livelihood has, in fact, largely through the tariff discussions, permeated a very large class of the community, and has materially changed what I may call the American outlook. It has greatly reinforced among the foreign-born population the socialistic ideas which many bring here with them, of the powers and duties of the State toward labor, for it is preached vehemently by the employing class.

What makes this look the more serious is that our political and social manners are not adapted to it. In Europe, the State is possessed of an administrative machine which has a finish, efficacy, and permanence unknown here. Tocqueville comments on its absence among us, and it is, as all the advocates of civil-service reform know, very difficult to supply. All the agencies of the government suffer from the imposition on them of what I may call non-American duties. For instance, a custom-house organized as a political machine was never intended to collect the enormous sum of duties which must pass through its hands under our tariff. A post-office whose master has to be changed every four years to "placate" Tammany, or the anti-Snappers, or any other body of politicians, was never intended to handle the huge mass which American mails have now become.[5] One of the greatest objections to the income tax is the prying into people's affairs which it involves. No man likes to tell what his income is to every stranger, much less to a politician, which our collectors are sure to be. Secrecy on the part of the collector is, in fact, essential to reconcile people to it in England or Germany, where it is firmly established; but our collectors sell their lists to the newspapers in order to make the contributors pay up.

In all these things we are trying to meet the burden and responsibilities of much older societies with the machinery of a much earlier and simpler state of things. It is high time to halt in this progress until our administrative system has been brought up to the level even of our present requirements. It is quite true that, with our system of State and Federal Constitutions laying prohibitions on the Legislature and Congress, any great extension of the sphere of government in our time seems very unlikely. Yet the assumption by Congress, with the support of the Supreme Court, of the power to issue paper money in time of peace, the power to make prolonged purchases of a commodity like silver, the power to impose an income tax, to execute great public works, and to protect native industry, are powers large enough to effect a great change in the constitution of society and in the distribution of wealth, such as, it is safe to say, in the present state of human culture, no government ought to have and exercise.

One hears every day from educated people some addition to the number of things which "govern-

ments " ought to do, but for which any government
we have at present is totally unfit. One listens to
them with amazement, when looking at the material
of which our government is composed, for the matter of that, of which all governments are composed,
for I suppose there is no question that all legislative bodies in the world have in twenty years run
down in quality. The parliamentary system is apparently failing to meet the demands of modern
democratic society, and is falling into some disrepute; but it would seem as if there was at present
just as little chance of a substitute of any kind as
of the dethronement of universal suffrage. It will
probably last indefinitely, and be as good or as bad
as its constituents make it. But this probable
extension of the powers and functions of government make more necessary than ever a free expression of opinion, and especially of educated opinion.
We may rail at "mere talk" as much as we please,
but the probability is that the affairs of nations
and of men will be more and more regulated by
talk. The amount of talk which is now expended
on all subjects of human interest—and in "talk"
I include contributions to periodical literature—
is something of which a previous age has had the
smallest conception. Of course it varies infinitely
in quality. A very large proportion of it does no
good beyond relieving the feelings of the talker.

Political philosophers maintain, and with good reason, that one of its greatest uses is keeping down discontent under popular government. It is undoubtedly true that it is an immense relief to a man with a grievance to express his feelings about it in words, even if he knows that his words will have no immediate effect. Self-love is apt to prevent most men from thinking that anything they say with passion or earnestness will utterly and finally fail. But still it is safe to suppose that one-half of the talk of the world on subjects of general interest is waste. But the other half certainly tells. We know this from the change in ideas from generation to generation. We see that opinions which at one time everybody held became absurd in the course of half a century—opinions about religion and morals and manners and government. Nearly every man of my age can recall old opinions of his own, on subjects of general interest, which he once thought highly respectable, and which he is now almost ashamed of having ever held. He does not remember when he changed them, or why, but somehow they have passed away from him. In communities these changes are often very striking. The transformation, for instance, of the England of Cromwell into the England of Queen Anne, or of the New England of Cotton Mather into the New England of Theodore Parker and

Emerson, was very extraordinary, but it would be very difficult to say in detail what brought it about, or when it began. Lecky has some curious observations, in his "History of Rationalism," on these silent changes in new beliefs *apropos* of the disappearance of the belief in witchcraft. Nobody could say what had swept it away, but it appeared that in a certain year people were ready to burn old women as witches, and a few years later were ready to laugh at or pity any one who thought old women could be witches. "At one period," says he, " we find every one disposed to believe in witches; at a later period we find this predisposition has silently passed away."[6] The belief in witchcraft may perhaps be considered a somewhat violent illustration, like the change in public opinion about slavery in this country. But there can be no doubt that it is talk—somebody's, anybody's, everybody's talk — by which these changes are wrought, by which each generation comes to feel and think differently from its predecessor. No one ever talks freely about anything without contributing something, let it be ever so little, to the unseen forces which carry the race on to its final destiny. Even if he does not make a positive impression, he counteracts or modifies some other impression, or sets in some train of ideas in some one else, which helps to change the face of the world.   So I shall, in disregard of the great laudation of silence which filled the earth in the days of Carlyle, say that one of the functions of an educated man is to talk, and, of course, he should try to talk wisely.

WHO WILL PAY THE BILLS OF SOCIALISM?[1]

IF I were to visit a friend of very moderate means, who was living very simply in a flat, in a remote part of the city, and he were to tell me that he was going to move into a house on Fifth or Madison Avenue; that he was tired, as was his family, of the very restricted life he had been leading; that he meant to give his children better quarters, better clothing, a better education, and more frequent access to the world of fashion and amusements, than they had previously had, I should conclude that he had received, in some way, a considerable addition to his income. But if I found, on inquiry, that not one cent or only a few hundred dollars had been added to it, I should conclude that the poor fellow was insane; that he was laboring under the well-known hallucination called plutomania.

Now I am very much in the same state of mind about the Socialists and ethical economists that I would be about him. I have, during the last two

years, been reading a great deal of socialistic literature, ending the other day with Kidd's "Social
Evolution."[2] The principal thing which I have
learned from it all is that we are on the eve of a
great social transformation. The régime of slavery
has passed away; and the régime of feudalism has
passed away; and the régime of competition is
to pass away, and that before very long. The
process began a few years ago, I am told, with
the overthrow of the Manchester School. That
school taught the doctrine of *laissez faire* as the
best rule of living for the community. It taught
individualism. It taught that the least possible
government was the best. It reasoned about all
social topics from the "economic man," a person
whose main desire was to get money with the
least possible amount of exertion. It was willing
to let the ablest man get the best things in life,
and so on.

I learn that this is all now to be changed, not
because it is not scientific, but because it is
disagreeable or inhuman. Government is to interfere a good deal. It is first of all to take
possession of the gas- and water-works, the railroads and telegraphs of the country. By and by
it is to take possession of all the instruments of
production, and see that nobody ever wants work.
All the very rich men and the idle men are to dis-

appear, and everybody is to be moderately well
off. The differences, whatever they are, between
workingmen and other people are to come to an
end. According to Kidd, the workingmen are to
have the same "social position" as every one else,
because "moderate income is to give as good a
social position as a large one." "The position of
the lower classes is to be raised at the expense of
the wealthier classes." "Education in its highest
forms"—which I suppose means college education
—is to be within the reach of everybody, and not, as
now, the privilege of the well-to-do only. "The
sphere of action of the State is to extend to every
department of our social life." I might quote
indefinitely to this effect from Marshall, from the
Fabian "school" of economists, the "historical
school" in Germany, and the Ely "school" in this
country.[3] In the world which they not only promise us, but which they say is now really near at
hand, there will be no distinction of classes.
Workingmen and their children will have exactly
the same opportunities which professional men
and people of moderate means now have. They
will have their dinners, their balls, their theatres,
their summer trips, their short hours of labor, their
libraries, museums, and so forth. I am told this
great change is coming very fast, though, as far as
I can see, the signs of it are only to be found, as

yet, in authors' studies and in college lecture-
rooms. Mr. Kidd's authorities about it are chiefly
the monthly magazines, Marshall, and an interview
with W. T. Stead.[4] The Fabian School cites no
authorities at all, producing the whole change deductively out of its own head. Professor Ely
bases his beliefs also on his own intuitions. A
very large part of the work is to be wrought
through " ethics," or " the science of ethics," which,
I believe, is the name given by the various schools
to the opinions of some of their members about
the injustices of the competitive or present system.

I do not, as I have said, see any signs of the
new régime in the world outside, except in extension of government interference to some enterprises, " affected," as our courts say, " with a
public use."   But no hard-and-fast line between
government business and private business was
ever drawn, even by the unfortunate Manchester
School. What John Stuart Mill—whom I suppose
I may describe as speaking for them, at all events
to some extent—said, was that the question what
things government should take charge of itself,
and not leave to private enterprise, is to be settled
by judgment, just as the question what things the
head of a family should buy and what make at
home, has to be settled by judgment. Government
is, from the outset, a joint-stock enterprise. To

say that it may run a post-office, but must on no
account carry on a gas-factory or water-works,
would be absurd. But whether, besides running a
post-office, it should also run gas-works and water-
works, depends on time and place and circumstances. To allow the city government of New
York to do things which it is perfectly safe to let
the corporation of Birmingham or Berlin do,
would be extremely foolish. The truth is that the
business of man in this world is to make himself
as happy and comfortable as liability to death and
disease will let him, and not to carry out the
theories of "schools" or doctrinaires.

I make this little digression to get rid of the
supposition that anything the civilized governments of the world are doing—and have done—for
the convenience of their citizens, is to be considered the beginning of any great "movement" or
"evolution." They have done nothing as yet
which interferes seriously with any man's rational
liberty. It makes no difference to me where I get
my gas, or water, or transportation, provided I get
it good and pure, provided I am not forced to take
it if I do not want it, and provided I am not compelled to pay for anybody else's supply. I may
say much the same thing of the education of children. Numerous experiments have shown me in
various countries that if the State does not under-

take the education of children, they will not be educated, and I am so sensible of the value of education to our civilization that I am well satisfied if the State should do it; nay, I insist that the State shall do it. I maintain, therefore, that no beginning of an evolution, or of an organic change in human society, has yet been made by any State. Whatever we are to have in that line is still to come, and it is of what is to come—that is, of what we are promised or threatened with— that I here concern myself.

As I said at the beginning of this article, when a man is about to move into a larger house and change his whole manner of life, he is, if sane, sure to ask himself what the change will cost, that is, what increase in his expenditures it will make necessary. If sane, also, he will follow this question by another, namely, Have I got the money? Now, in reading these stories to which I have referred, of the social evolution through which modern communities are to pass shortly, I find absolutely no allusion to cost. It is quite evident that, when the change comes about, it will make a great increase in the mere living expenses of every civilized population, without any increase of income that I can see or hear of. In this it will differ from all previous evolutions or revolutions. When the world gave up slavery, it substituted for

a very wasteful form of labor a much more pro-
ductive one. When, in the eighteenth century, it
emancipated the peasantry from the kings and
nobles, it gave a great impetus to their industry.
It relieved them of enormous burdens incurred for
the benefit of idle and frivolous men, and it greatly
increased the motives for saving. The French
Revolution gave a powerful stimulus to agriculture, and much enlarged the income of the working farmer. In like manner, in England, the
introduction of the factory régime made large additions to the national income, and, through this,
raised the wages and the standard of living of the
working population. What Sidney Godolphin
Osborne did by sending the Wiltshire farm-labor-
ers to the North tells the whole story. In fact,
the history of all the social and industrial changes
of the civilized world during the past hundred
years is, in the main, the history of great improvements in money-making, the history of additions
both to the national and the individual income.
The Manchester School has been much blamed for
attaching too much importance to this, for thinking too much of additions to wealth without concerning itself as to the manner in which it was distributed. I am not concerned to defend it against
this charge. My point is, that, ever since the fall
of the Roman Empire, changes in the social con-

dition of the civilized world have meant great improvements in the social income. No matter who got the money, more of it came in. Everybody who changed his style of living—barring, of course, spendthrifts and swindlers—did so because he knew his means permitted it.

The peculiarity of the social evolution which the philosophers say is now impending is, that it is to be not a money-making, but a spending evolution. Everybody is to live a great deal better than he has been in the habit of living, and to have far more fun. Poverty is to disappear, and real destitution — what the French call " *la misère* "—to become unknown except as the result of gross misconduct. I was one day last winter in the University Settlement in Delancey Street, New York, and paid a visit to the rooms in the top story of the building occupied by Dr. Stanton Coit and his fellow-laborers.[5] They were very neatly and comfortably furnished, but perfectly simple and plain. Dr. Coit explained to me that the aim of those who furnished them was to show the kind of rooms every workingman would have "if justice were done." I have since inquired what the rent of those rooms would be to-day in that neighborhood, and am told it would be about $750 a year, or about $14.50 per week. But I am also told that $14.50 is about the rent which the better class of laborers now pay for their rooms *per month*. The general run of unskilled laborers do not pay over $10 per month ; so that, to do "justice" to a workingman in this one particular, would cost somebody about $43 a month. Who is this to be? A rent of $58 per month ought, according to the ordinary calculations, to argue an income of $290 per month. What workingman gets this? If he does not get it, and ought to have it, who is keeping him out of it?

What is the real working-class trouble? What is it that makes their condition a "problem?" Why has it become a question of growing importance in the politics of all European countries, as well as in our own? Why are so many books and pamphlets written about it? Why do so many people feel or affect a deep interest in it? Why does it call out so much "ethical" discussion? Why are we threatened with "social evolution" as a means of settling it?

The answer to all these questions is very simple. It is the workingman's want of money which makes him the object of so much pity, and dread, and speculation. If he were better paid—as well paid as a clerk, a clergyman, a lawyer, a doctor, a business man—all the fuss we make about him would be an impertinence. We should bestow no consideration on his food, or clothing, or educa-

tion, or on his " elevation," or on the elevation of
his family.   We should have no " ethical con-
cepts " about him.   So that the labor question is
the question why the workingman does not have
more money.   The answer is that he gets now all
there is for him, and that, if he is to have more, it
must come from some great and sudden increase
of production unattended with a great increase of
population.   The income of this and every other
country in the world, since the plunder of foreign
nations has ceased, is the product of its land and
labor.   Some of this income goes to pay wages,
some goes to repair machinery and buildings, and
some goes to pay profits to capital, or, in other
words, to reward men for saving or for supplying
long-felt wants.   Consequently, to do justice to the
laborer and greatly increase his comforts, so that
he shall be as well off as anybody else, we must cut
down the profits or interest on capital, or seize the
capital, unless some hitherto unknown source of
supply has been discovered.

Now let us see what would be the result of distributing among labor *all* the profit and interest
on capital of the entire country.   It must be observed, however, that, if we took it all, capital
would promptly disappear, and next year, or the
year after, labor would have to depend on its own
resources.   Besides this, the socialistic programme

makes no provision for saving; the money is all to go in furniture, or amusements, and transportation. The capitalistic or saving class—or, in other words, the class which every year keeps back part of the national income for use next year — will vanish from the scene. We believe "the State" is, in the new régime, to play the part of the capitalist, but it could not withhold from labor the means of living with the comfort required by the new creed.

The total wealth of the United States, according to the census of 1890—that is, the total existing product of land, labor, and saving—was $65,037,-091,197 ; the population of the country was at the same date 62,622,250. Evenly divided, this would give $1,039 per caput, or a little more than $5,000 per family on the commonly accepted basis of five persons to a family. If the laborer spent his $5,000 at once in making himself comfortable, of course, he would, as well as the country at large, be worse off than ever. He would, in fact, be plunged at once into a very hopeless kind of poverty. But suppose he invested it; it would not yield him over, say, six per cent. at present rates of interest. This would make his income $300 a year, or about $6 a week. It is evident that he could on this make no material change in his style of living. Six dollars a week does not go far in rent and furniture and dinners and amusements. We have no statistics showing the annual income of the United States, but if we put it down as six per cent. on the total accumulated wealth, we shall certainly not underestimate it. This interest would be $3,902,225,472, which, divided among the population, would give $62.31 a head, or $311.55 per family of five persons — that is, less than a dollar a day.

This does not differ materially from the results obtained in Great Britain. Robert Giffen, the English statistician, in one of his most elaborate articles a few years ago, estimated the total capital of the people of the United Kingdom, or the accumulated wealth of the nation, at £8,500,000,000 sterling, the population at that time being almost exactly 34,000,000, thus giving each individual $1,250 per caput, or about $6,000 per family, counting, as before, five to a family. If this were invested in England, it would hardly give more than four per cent., or $240 a year, which would be a pleasant addition to wages, but would leave no margin for amusements, travel, books, or "swell" clothing. We have no means of getting at the wealth of well-to-do people in the United States, there being as yet no reliable statistics bearing on that subject; but an analysis of the income-tax returns in Great Britain shows that in a year when 456,-680 persons were assessed, 118,830 had incomes over £300 a year, the total being £110,565,955. On the assumption that these people ought to be despoiled and made to share with their less fortunate brethren, let us see what would happen. The population of the kingdom in the year these returns were made was 37,176,464. If the income, then, of people having more than £300 a year were divided among the masses per capita, it would give each individual an income of about £3, or $15, annually. I always wonder, when reading the romances of the ethical economists, whether they have ever taken the trouble to look at these figures. Apparently they have not. If they had, we should assuredly, unless they have gone clean daft, hear less talk about what " the State " or the municipality can and ought to do for the elevation of the poor. The State has no money which it does not wring from the hard earnings of sorely pressed people. If it took, as we see here, every cent they had, it would not be able to make a very noticeable change in the laborer's condition, even for a single year. What the rich spend on themselves is only a drop in the bucket, and they can secure none of their luxuries without sharing with the laborer, through investment.

The notion that there is a reservoir of wealth somewhere, either in the possession of the Government or the rich, which might be made to diffuse

"plenty through a smiling land," is a delusion
which nearly all the writings of the ethical economists tend to spread, and it is probably the most
mischievous delusion which has ever taken hold on
the popular mind. It affects indirectly large numbers of persons, who, if it were presented to them
boldly and without drapery, would probably repudiate it. But it steals into their brains through
sermons, speeches, pamphlets, Fabian essays, and
Bellamy utopias, and disposes them, on humani-
tarian grounds, to great public extravagances, in
buildings, in relief work, in pensions, in schools,
in high State wages, and philanthropic undertak-
ings which promise at no distant day to land the
modern world in bankruptcy. It will be very
well if the century closes without witnessing this
catastrophe in France or Italy, or both—the two
countries in which the democratic theory of the
inexhaustibility of State funds has been carried
furthest. It is diffusing through the working
class of all countries, also, more and more every
day, not only envy and hatred of the rich, but an
increasing disinclination to steady industry, and
an increasing disposition to rely on politics for the
bettering of their condition. The Unions in England have already announced openly that it is no
longer to strikes, but to Parliament, they must look
for elevation, and, of course, all that Parliament

can do for them is either to give them more
money for less labor, or to spend other people's
money on them in increasing their comforts.
This indifference to cost, or unwillingness to say
where the money is to come from to make all the
world happy and comfortable, is not confined, by
any means, to our American and English Socialists.
It is an equally marked characteristic of those of
the Continent. Says the Paris *Temps*, speaking
of that latest scheme of pensioning all old people:

"What are the usual tactics of Radicals and Socialists?
They call with loud cries for reforms of all sorts, and vote
the principle of them, but always refuse to discuss their
financial consequences. More than this, they are among
the first to vote remissions of taxes. On one side they swell
the expenses; on the other they diminish the resources."

At Roubaix, the other day, the mayor proposed
the following resolution: "All invalid laborers and
all children should be supported by the Commune
and the State." Somebody then asked him where
the Commune and the State were to get the money.
His answer was: "The money will be taken wherever it can be found." As Director Ely says, it
was to be done from a "broad social stand-point,"
and "the general social effect" only—not cost—
was to be considered.

Next in importance to the delusion that there is

somewhere a great reservoir of wealth, which can still be drawn on for the general good, is the delusion that there is somewhere a reservoir of wisdom still untapped which can be drawn on for the execution of a new law of distribution. Not only is this current, but some of the philosophers have got into their heads that if our politicians had more money to spend, and more places to bestow, they would become purer and nobler and more public-spirited. This theory is so much opposed to the experience of the human race, that we are hardly more called on to argue against it than against the assertion that there will be no winter next year. We must take it for granted that what is meant is that there is somewhere a class of men whose services are now lost to the world, who would come into the field for the work of production and distribution under the new régime, and display a talent and discretion and judgment, which now cannot be had either for love or money, for the ordinary work of the world. Any salary is, to-day, small for a competent railroad, mining, or mill-manager; but we are asked to believe that when the State took charge of the great work of clothing and feeding and employing the community, men would be found in abundance to see that "ideal justice" was done, at about $3,000 a year. Well, there is no sign of such men at present. Nobody knows of their existence. The probabilities of biology, physiology, psychology, and sociology are all against their existence. The opportunities for display of their talents even now are immense, and yet they do not appear. Nobody says he has ever seen them. Nobody pretends that they could be found, except the ethical economists, and they never mention their names or habitat. In fact, as in Bellamy's case, the writers of the social romances are compelled to make them unnecessary by predicting a change in human nature which will make us all wise, just, industrious, and self-denying.

I think, on the whole, it would not be an exaggeration to say that such a social evolution as the ethical economists have planned could not be accomplished, even for a single year, without doubling the wealth of every country which tried it, while making no increase in the population. And this arrest of the growth of the population is just as necessary as the increase of wealth. For it is the exertions of mankind in keeping up and increasing their numbers which have prevented the poor from profiting more by the recent improvements in production. Statistics show readily that, thus far, subsistence increases more rapidly than population, and this does much to cheer up the optimists and the revilers of Malthus. But to make a man of any use to civilization, he must in some manner be able to pay for his board. If wheat costs only ten cents a bushel, the man who has not and cannot get the ten cents is clearly a bit of surplus population. He has to depend on some one else for his support, and is thus a burden to the community. Employing him at the public expense does not change the situation, for his neighbors are the public. If they really wanted the work done, he would have something to exchange. If they do it in order to keep him from starving, the demand for his labor is not legitimate, and is only a thin disguise for charity. Population and subsistence are equally balanced, in an economical sense, only when there is a full demand for all the labor that offers itself, a state of things which is never seen now in any of the great towns of the world. Let a strike but take place in any branch of unskilled or only slightly skilled labor, and the swarm of applicants for the vacant places, who instantly appear, shows that there is in that spot an excess of people. That is to say, statistics may prove that food has far outrun the population of the United States at large, and yet there will be in New York and Boston and Philadelphia thousands who find it very difficult to purchase it at any price. The Socialists have no plan of dealing with this, except making the successful support the unsuccessful, the industrious the idle, on the same scale of comfort as their own.

I have also learned from my reading that a new "law of distribution" is under consideration in the colleges and ethical schools of the world, and that there is a fair prospect that one which will satisfy all existing needs will be evolved. Now, there are only three laws of distribution of which I can form any conception. One would be a natural law, like the law of gravitation, which automatically divided among all concerned, as soon as completed, the results of any given piece of production, without any care on the part of anybody, and of which nobody could complain any more than of the earth's attraction. Another would be a law formed by some authority, which everybody would acknowledge as final, and to which all would submit, either owing to the overwhelming force at its command, or to the universal confidence in its justice. The third would be the present law, which I may call the law of general agreement, under which everybody gets the least for which he will labor, and the least for which he will save and invest. If there be any other than these, I am unable to think it.

The first of these, I presume, does not need discussion. There never will be any natural distributive force to which we shall all have to submit as

we submit to the law of chemical affinity or proportion. The division of the products of labor
and capital will always be the subject of some sort
of human arrangement, in which the human will
will play a more or less prominent part. So that
the second of these laws would have to be the
result of some kind of understanding as to who or
what the deciding authority should be, to which all
would have to submit without murmuring. Thus far
in the history of mankind it has never been possible to come to such an agreement even on matters
touching the feelings much less nearly than one's
share of the products of one's labor. No government, spiritual or temporal, has ever existed, which
had not to keep in subjection a hostile minority
by the use of force in some shape. The Pope in
the Middle Ages came nearer seeming the voice of
pure justice than any other power that has ever
appeared in the Western world. But Christendom
was never unanimously willing to let him arrange
even its political concerns, and I do not think it
ever entered into the head of the most enthusiastic
papist to let him arrange his domestic affairs—so
far as to say what his wages or his profits should
be. The guilds came near doing this in various
trades, but their authority was maintained by the
power of expulsion. When the whole of civil
society becomes a guild, this power cannot be ex-

ercised, because there will be no place for the
expelled man to go. To make him submit, there
would have to be some sort of compulsion put
upon him. In other words, he would have to be
enslaved by being compelled to labor against his
will for a reward which he deemed inadequate.
Except on the assumption, which the smallest
knowledge of human nature makes ridiculous, that
everybody is sure to be satisfied with what he
gets for his work, any law of distribution emanat-
ing from a human authority would necessarily result in slavery. In truth it is impossible to conceive any plan of State socialism which would not
involve the slavery of some portion of the population, unless we can picture to ourselves unanimity
concerning the things on which men under all previous régimes have been most apt to differ.

It is hardly necessary to discuss the chances of a
"State" composed of men of such acknowledged
wisdom and goodness that nobody would dispute
their ordering of his domestic concerns. But, im-
probable as this is, it is by no means so improba-
ble as a State composed of men competent to meet
the Socialists' demands in their business capacity.
The ethical economists never go into details on
this subject. They assume, as does Schmoller,
that the State—that is, the small body of men
charged with the enormous responsibilities of a

socialist or semi-socialist community, both with its
production and distribution, and the care of its
health and morals—would in some manner be a
sort of concentration of the virtue and morals of
the whole community; that it would, in addition,
have an amount of administrative power, for which
railroads, mines, and mills now vainly offer almost
any salary, and for which nations would give
every conceivable earthly honor and reward —
fame, power, money, and enthusiastic homage —
could they get them for the management of their
finances or the command of their armies.[6] As this
assumption is so gross and bold that there is
curiously little discussion about it, and as its
basis is never explained, it may be dismissed as
chimæra.

Mr. Kidd makes mention, among Socialists' expectations, the expectation that some day the
laborer will have the same "social position" as
the more well-to-do classes, that is, what the
French call the *bourgoisie* — the men who wear
black coats and do no manual labor. "Social
position" is an extremely vague phrase, and yet I
think there is probably more hope for the working
classes in this direction than in any other. The
Socialists mean, I presume, by sameness of social
position, association for purposes of social enjoyment on a footing of equality and with reciprocity

of pleasure. But the difficulties in the way of this consummation, though on the surface trifling, and, like the thing itself, hard to define, are nevertheless likely to prove very troublesome. The old feudal feeling which made the man who employed labor look down on the laborer as an inferior or semi-menial person, has hardly reached this country, or, if it ever did reach it, has died out. Society is consequently divided by what we may call natural lines—that is, by differences of taste, of personal habits, of mental culture, and social experience. People of the same " social position " are, as a rule, people who live in much the same way—that is, with about the same expenditure in clothes, furniture, and cookery, and are drawn together by some sort of community either of ideas or of interests.

But any change which goes on in the way of development or " evolution," in this arrangement, is in the direction of bringing people together socially who do *not* live in exactly the same way, do not belong to the same caste or circle or class. In those countries in which the democratic movement has made most advances and made most impression on the manners—France, Italy, and the United States, for instance—differences of fortune are less and less potent in preventing social intercourse. But in no country has the workingman made his way as yet into anything that can be called "society," that is, into any circle which gives "social position." Nor could he be introduced into it by any sort of legislation or any species of compulsion. "Social position" is something beyond the reach of armies or fleets or parliaments. It must be won in some manner. It cannot be accorded or decreed. The difference between a lady's drawing-room full of guests, and a wigwam packed with squaws and warriors, tells better than even science, or art, or laws, or government, the distance the community has travelled in its upward course.

THE POLITICAL SITUATION IN 1896[1]

THE country is suffering to-day from two sequelæ of the civil war. One is the currency question, and the other the tariff question. Of neither
of them, as national questions of momentous interest, had anybody the smallest idea before the
war. What the political prophets thought would
follow it, were great disorder in the South and
great difficulty in persuading the army to go back
to civil life and peaceful industry, and, possibly, in
persuading the people to pay the national debt.
None of these perplexities has come upon us. The
troubles which have come upon us are a strong desire to debase the currency and to levy heavy taxation for protective purposes. These two problems
to-day constitute almost the sum total of our politics, and they present themselves in an extremely
unmanageable form.

The plan of making money go farther, by debasing
or depreciating it, is a very old one. It is not quite
as old as metallic money, but it is as old as legal
tender. There was no use in debasing the medium

of exchange so long as nobody was obliged to take
it in return for his goods, or in payment of what
was due to him. But so soon as the issue of money
became a governmental function, the practice of
adulteration, or clipping, or in some manner alter-
ing it, so as to retain its purchasing or liquidating
power, while lowering its real value, became very
general. The Greeks resorted to it; so did the
Romans. So have nearly all modern nations.
But until our time it has always been a device
for the easy payment of public debts. It was
the favorite resort of embarrassed governments
before the days of public loans. It was the government that was to get the benefit of it, not private individuals. That it was a fraudulent device,
and that it was a thing, if possible, to be concealed,
nobody ever denied. History may be searched in
vain for any assertion of its morality. To see that
it must always have been looked upon as dishonest,
one has only to ask one's self why men invented
money, and why it has continued in use. They invented it, and have clung to it, simply as a measure
of value ; that is, a small portable memorandum
of the worth of something they have parted with,
which shall procure them, on presentation, something as valuable as that thing. This is the
explanation of the practice of hoarding, or hid-
ing gold and silver coins, which has prevailed

in all ages. People have buried them in the ground, or concealed them in holes and corners, in the belief and expectation that no matter how long they might be kept out of sight and out of use, their purchasing power would remain unchanged. Sovereigns traded on this popular belief in the steadiness of their value, by lowering this value secretly. But, as I have said, it was only sovereigns who resorted to this mode of raising the wind, and it was so easy that down to the seventeenth century nearly all sovereigns resorted to it. They were the official keepers of the national measure, and they privately shortened it for their own benefit. They enlarged the power of regulating the currency into the power of " scaling " their own debts.

During our civil war we followed their example. We issued debased currency—that is, dollars that were of inferior value to real dollars—and, in our distress, not only paid the public debts with them, but authorized all debtors to do the same thing to their creditors. We excused this on the same ground on which we excused our killing people or destroying property at the South, namely, that it was necessary to save the life of the nation. Congress had the right of every government to preserve its own existence by any means necessary for the purpose. The country accepted this view of

the matter. Our Government, we said, has issued
debased money as a matter of necessity. There
has been no concealment about it, and it will all
be made right in the end. Its dollars are bad dollars. The reason it issued them was the same as
that for which it has destroyed thousands of lives
and vast amounts of property.

When the war was over, however, a very curious
thing happened. Some people came forward and
said : " We see these dollars of yours are really
not money, in the strict sense of the term, but
promises to pay money. You say you issued them
during the war on the plea of necessity. The war
has now been over for some years, and the necessity has disappeared. Is it not time that you paid
them, or at all events cease to compel people to
take them in payment of their debts ? " The answer
to these questions came from the Supreme Court in
what were known as the Legal Tender Cases.[1] The
court said that the power to regulate the currency,
which every government must have, was really a
power to make any kind of money it pleased ; that
it had power not only to stamp and weigh the metal
or metals which mankind has in all ages agreed to
regard as the only true money, the only safe measure
of value, but to make money out of any metal or

[1] The effect of these decisions will be found summed up in
Chap. lvii. of Hare's " American Constitutional Law." [2]

other material, to issue it instead of the money actually current, to raise or lower its value in the
market, and to give it any name it thought proper—
to call, for instance, a piece of paper ten inches
by four " One dollar," or to declare a piece of cop-
per or platinum to be of the same value as a circu-
lar piece of gold weighing $25\frac{8}{100}$ grains, and usa-
ble for the same purposes ;—that therefore its
paper promises to pay money were, to all intents
and purposes, money. All the discussion which
has raged among lawyers over this decision has
turned upon the constitutionality of it, not on the
justice or honesty of it. The court judged of the
power of Congress in this matter of currency by
analogy. It said that Congress must have the
power over the currency as an "incident of sovereignty," which all the old governments have had,
and the definition of sovereignty was obtained by
observing the practice of sovereigns. Turning to
history, it found that all the older governments
had depreciated the currency for their own benefit,
but I do not believe it found one champion of the
right to do it, or that any one of these governments
ever publicly claimed such a right for itself. So
that we have clothed our Government with a power
which no other government has ever possessed in
the forum of morals. The right to punish people
for their religious opinions might in fact be recog-

nized, with more force, as an "incident of sovereignty" on the same grounds. "*Cujus regio ejus religio*" was an accepted maxim of European public law for a thousand years.

Out of this decision has grown our currency question, as we see it to-day. So soon as the people of the United States heard from the mouths of their judges that their Government had the power not only to regulate money,—that is, to weigh, stamp, and give it a name,—but to choose the material for it, and fix its value, a large party sprang up, commanding a majority in Congress, and demanded that the Government should go to work to make money out of paper, and pay its debts with it. This party was beaten, after a hard struggle, by the aid of various arguments, of which the foremost was that, paper having no intrinsic value, Congress might increase it to any extent it pleased, and it would thus soon become worthless, —witness the Continental paper, the French assignats, and the Confederate money. The greenbackers then abandoned the field, or were in the fair way of abandoning it, when silver began to fall heavily. It at once seemed to them that here was something cheap, comparatively easy to get hold of, and therefore peculiarly suited to the needs of the poor, which was already in use as currency in many countries, and would be nearly as good as greenbacks as a means of restoring prosperity. It could not be said of it, as had been said of the greenback, that it had no intrinsic value. It had value, apart from its use as money. It was a metal. Moreover, Congress could not increase the quantity of it at pleasure, as it could increase the quantity of greenbacks. Its amount was fixed by nature.

Then there grew up about silver a remarkable amount of legendary matter. The ancient idea that money was a measure of value seemed to fade away. To the demand of those who insisted that gold should be retained in circulation, and that silver should, as money, bear some fixed ratio to it, the answer was made that we could, by legislation, make the ratio anything we pleased,—15 to 1, or 16 to 1, or 20 to 1. Some preferred 15 to 1 because this was the ratio fixed by the Almighty when placing the two metals in the ground. Others did not think any ratio was necessary because gold ought not to be retained in circulation in a country of poor or plain people. Silver ought to do all the work of money. If it was too heavy, as some said, for daily use, let it be stored and have paper issued against it. Paper money, by the by, could be issued "against" anything. It did not need to be exchangeable for a thing provided it were "based" on it, that is, if the

issuer of the paper owned something of value
which he had in his mind when he issued it.
Therefore, silver did not need to be mined or
coined in order to "base" paper on it. We need
only, one member of Congress said, have our
engineers calculate how much silver there was in a
mountain, and we could then "base" paper on it
to that amount. Silver, too, was gradually per-
sonified into something almost human. It was
entitled to "a place of honor." It was the friend
of the poor, and stayed with people in times of
misfortune when gold fled to the rich, or to foreign
countries. You could be ungrateful, or indifferent, to silver as to a human friend. Very recently,
a member of Congress reproached a newspaper in
this city with "never having said a kind word of
silver." Silver came to have a "cause" of its own,
to be degraded or betrayed. It had triumphs to
achieve and defeats to sustain. You could insult
silver, or slight it, or slander it, or humiliate it, or
snub it. I do not believe that it would be easy to
find, in the discussions of the past ten years, the
smallest recognition, on the silver side, that money
is, or ought to be, a measure of value simply. It
has been treated throughout as a commodity which
it was the duty of the Government to make as
plentiful as possible, and put within easy reach of
as large a number of people as possible. On this

view of the duty of the Government, what we call the silver party, which is now in the field, has been founded.

Now, the founding, in a country of universal suffrage, of a party which looks on money not as a measure of value but as a commodity, is a new thing and a serious one. The aberrations of the human mind on the subject of currency have, as I have already said, been many since the dawn of history, but I do not recall any aberration in which the pretence, at least, of regarding money as a standard by which to regulate the exchange of commodities, was not kept up. This pretence often covered fraudulent alterations of the standard, but it was never laid aside, and the alterations were concealed. The adulterators and debasers never said, "Never mind about the purchasing power of this ; the more there is of it the better for you." They always said, "This is just the same as what you have got already, and will purchase you just the same amount of anything you desire." Moreover, like most other functions of government in times past, the regulation of the currency was always left in the hands of a few experts, that is, of men who made the currency a matter of scientific observation, and who sought, according to their lights, to make money a measure, as well as a medium, of exchange. For the currency question is not altogether, as many suppose, a question of material or of quantity. It is, essentially or mainly, a question of psychology. What they study, who study it aright, is the way the human mind plays around exchange. The merits or demerits of gold or silver or paper as money are to be found not in the things themselves, but in the way in which the people who use them look at them. Take Gresham's Law for instance. It says that, when there are two kinds of currency,—one inferior in value to the other, but both legal tender,—the more valuable one will leave the country. Well the more valuable one does not walk off of its own accord; it is sent away by men who see profit in exporting it. The objection to silver— the great overwhelming one—is that the men who make most use of coin prefer gold. And what all statesmen or economists who make a specialty of currency try to get at, through tables of prices, and movements of bullion, is how people feel about the different kind of medium in which they make their purchases and pay their debts.

The transfer to the newspaper, the caucus, the convention, and the popular vote, of this extremely delicate task of deciding what kind of money in any given country makes the best measure of value, while furnishing the most convenient medium of exchange, is, as I have said, something new.

The problem before the country now is almost as
much how to take the measure of value out of politics, as how to get at the right measure just now.
For there will be little use in establishing the gold
standard or any other standard, unless politicians
can be induced to let it alone, and leave it in the
hands of men who will change it only to secure
greater steadiness, and not to help debtors or to
stimulate a particular branch of industry.   Until it
is well established that the currency will not come
up as a question to be settled by the popular vote
at every Presidential election, there cannot be any
industrial or commercial peace or tranquillity. The
questions of ratio or no ratio, of one metal or another, of government paper or bank paper, of elas-
ticity or fixity,—have all to be considered with reference to the effect on the standard of value, and
this class of problem is no more capable of being
settled at the polls than are parallels of latitude or
of longitude.   The debating of it on the stump, except to prevent the commission of some great folly,
or to procure their transfer to experts, is a patent
absurdity.   The one thing which the popular vote
can safely do for the currency, is to direct its committal to a few men who are familiar with it, both
from the theoretical and the practical side.   This,
too, is the main object of the championship of the
gold standard which we now witness.   What the

"gold bugs" really demand is not the gold standard, so much as assimilation in currency matters to the other great commercial nations, and the absolute abandonment of the currency question as a political issue. That we shall secure these things at one election is not likely, but the election of a President on a sound-money platform will be the first step toward it, and a great one.

The currency problem is made all the more complicated by the attitude of the West toward the East. That there is a line dividing the two regions has been for a long time vaguely perceived, but it was never so clearly defined as by the war feeling and by the silver question. Speaking generally, the bulk of whatever there was of pugnacity toward England after Mr. Cleveland's message was to be found west of the Alleghanies; and, speaking generally, also, it may be said that the principal support of the silver standard is to be found west of the Alleghanies.[3] It is accompanied in both cases by a dislike or distrust of the East, which is partly social and partly financial, and covers also European countries, but principally England. The social dislike or distrust would need an article to itself. The financial one is, in the main, that of a borrowing for a creditor community, and that of a new agricultural community for one which is devoted mainly to the business of selling commodities and exchanging money. It is composed, in part, of the old dislike of the farmer for the financier, and in part, that of the poor debtor for the rich creditor. Behind it all lies great ignorance about foreigners and foreign relations, and of the other forms of society than those by which western men are surrounded, combined with an immense sense of power. It is difficult to make a western man understand that a country of 70,000,000 of inhabitants cannot do anything that it has a fancy to do, including the circulation of silver at a fixed ratio. It is also difficult to persuade him that a well-dressed man with superfine manners, does not cherish evil designs of some sort. He does not see how the great fortunes he hears of in the East have been honestly acquired, and he, therefore, would hear with equanimity of the bombardment of eastern cities. He brooks very ill the unconscious assumption of superiority which the long cultivation of the social art brings with it in older countries, and thinks it the main business of the American abroad to resent this by threats and defiance.

Among the mass of western people, a knowledge of the conditions of foreign exchange is scanty. The notion that a nation with $1,600,000,000 of foreign commerce can be a law unto itself in commercial matters, and that it is easy to create financial conditions which will cut us off from the rest

of the world, is still rife in that part of the
country. In fact, it would not be too much to say
that, in spite of a high degree of culture at certain
points, the West is suffering all the observed consequences of too great isolation,—that is, want of
more contact with other social conditions and other
forms of civilization. All genuine and steady progress thus far has come from intercourse with foreigners and familiarity with their point of view,
and readiness to adopt whatever is best and most
suitable in their ideas, manners, or customs. This
has been true from the earliest times, is, in fact,
the most familiar phenomenon of advancing civilization. The greatest danger the Valley of the
Mississippi runs to-day, is the danger of living in
its own ideas,—the belief that Providence still
creates peculiar peoples.

Escape from the silver idea is not likely to be
easy. The protective idea is incorporated with it.
The belief that silver is a commodity, not simply a
measure of value, has taken possession of the western mind. The notion that it is, therefore, as
much entitled to protection as any other commodity, by any means within reach of the Government, is not easily dislodged, so long as the protective theory prevails at the East. It is not easy
for an eastern protectionist to face the arguments
by which a western man refuses to help the East

to support its industries by heavy duties so long
as the West, and more especially the mining
States, have no share in the blessings derived from
the national policy. The western man is a protectionist, too, but he wishes to push the plan
farther, and he has concocted a theory of currency
to go along with it. A self-supporting Europe-
defying country, producing everything it wants for
its own use, including its own money, is his idea
of a state. The eastern man goes only half way.
He wishes to be independent of Europe indus-
trially, but to keep up his connection with it pecu-
niarily, which is not thorough and complete "Americanism."

That these ideas will be overcome, except by actual experiment, seems unlikely. If the currency
should, by the next election, fall into the hands of a
Government dominated by the ideas of the silver-
ites, we must be prepared for deliverance through
a panic of very great magnitude. This is the way,
as a general rule, the financial heresies of a democracy are dissipated. Books are not read, or
theorists much listened to. The thing has to be
tried. Nevertheless discussion has produced a
great deal of effect in the great cities where commercial considerations tell, and the chances are
that, if the sound-money men shall get hold of the
Government in 1897, the cult of silver will gradu-

ally retreat, like paganism in the early ages, to remote country districts, and linger rather as a
superstition than as a financial theory. Several
things are working against it, and the most powerful is the great increase in the production of gold;
but its greatest support, that which will probably
last longest, is patriotic belief in the power of the
nation to do what it pleases.

Much the same things are true, *mutatis mutandis*, of the tariff question. I am quite aware
that there is a great deal to be said for a tariff that
shall fairly protect native industries from foreign
competition. The theory of protection has been
defended by many able men, and is held by many
honest ones. But the protective tariff, as enacted
by legislation either in this or in any other democratic country, is never the protective tariff which
publicists or economists work out in their libraries.
The latter takes a general view of the whole field
of industry, and endeavors to impose duties with
such impartiality that no one industry shall profit
at the expense of another, or interfere with another's freedom of action. Moreover it insists
above all things on permanence, or, at all events,
on sufficient permanence to enable the legislator
to see the result of his own experiments, as regards
the amount and the incidence of his duties. This
is the sort of tariff which protectionists write

books about, and lecture about land laud on the stump.

The actual tariff of legislation is a totally different affair. It is made up not so much on a general view of the needs of all industries, as on the account each industry gives of the amount of duty it needs to make it profitable. It favors, too, those which are able to make the largest contributions to electioneering expenses of the party which enacts it, without regard to the general effect. Permanence is the last thing it thinks of. Our tariff has undergone twenty-five changes since the war, all in the direction of higher duties. All but one of these changes were made on the demand of manufacturers, who claimed more assistance, and got it without any inquiry into the reason why they needed it, or why they had failed to make sufficient profits under the existing duties. So that the tariff of the scientific protectionists is never seen and probably never will be seen in practice, nor is it at all likely that any tariff can ever have much stability — and this for reasons which apply to all, or nearly all, governmental interferences with trade and industry.

No such interference can in modern society ever be isolated or confined to one object or class of objects. Its effects are always vastly more far-reaching than the promoter ever imagines. One

of the most marked of these is to stimulate competition at home by bringing more capital into
every protected industry—thus diminishing the
advantages of protection to each beneficiary, while
tempting people to start new industries without a
special fitness for them, in reliance on protection.
So that, like all stimulants, its influence diminishes as time goes on, and the cry for more duties or new duties is constant.   There have been,
as I have said, twenty-five changes in the tariff
since 1861, and only one of them has been due
to the so-called free-traders.   All the others were
made on the demand of dissatisfied protectionists.
And yet, as any business man will tell you, nothing
is more necessary to prosperous industry than
stability in the conditions under which it is carried
on.   That is, business can flourish under either a
high or low tariff, if the business man can make
his calculations with certainty.   But of any steady
tariff there is no more promise, apparently, to-day
than there was ten years ago.   If the Republicans elect the President and have a majority in
both Houses, they will probably pass something
like the old McKinley tariff bill, and they generally suppose that this will bring in an era of
prosperity; but it will not do so any more than
the old McKinley tariff which led to the terrible
defeat of 1890.   It will be full of excesses and

abuses which will bring about another reaction, and there will then be in a few years another kind of tariff with a similar result. Prosperity will wait for a settlement of the currency question.

Another objection to the protective system, perhaps in the long run the most serious of all, is its effect on public life. No contemporary observer can fail to be struck with the disappearance from Congress and the State Legislatures of men prominent for eloquence, character, or the weight of their opinions. It is no exaggeration to say that there is hardly one left in the political world who is listened to for doctrine or instruction on any great public question. There are in Congress no orators, no financiers or economists, no scholars whom people like to hear from before making up their minds—no Clays, no Websters, no Calhouns, no Wrights, no Marcys, no Everetts, no Sewards, no Lincolns, no Fessendens, no Trumbulls, no Sumners, no "illustrations," as the French call them, in any field. The talent of the country in fact seems to have taken refuge in the great business corporations, and in the colleges, just as in the Middle Ages it took refuge in the monasteries. In the late attempts of Congress to get up a war there seemed to be no one in either House capable of drafting a resolution which would present its designs in respectable shape.

We cannot recall any case in modern times in which a government seemed so completely abandoned by the adepts and experts.

Now why is this to be ascribed to the tariff? Well, in this way : Business—the making of money by the production or sale of commodities—is the greatest interest of life to the bulk of the American community. As soon as government is presented to men as an instrument for the addition to their income of a sum in dollars and cents which they can enter in their ledgers every year, as they can profits from a speculation, they cease to think of it as an instrument for the promotion of the general welfare. Their mind gets fixed on it wholly as a means of increasing their own revenues. When a man has once entered in his accounts a good sum as the result of a piece of legislation procured by his own exertions, he is never again the same man as a citizen. He takes an entirely different view of the State, of the objects of government, of the nature of patriotism, and of the functions of the legislator. Politics becomes business to him. The duty of getting high-tariff men into Congress who will put the right duty on his commodity becomes a duty which he owes to his partners, to his creditors, to his family. The expediency of paying any sum necessary to elect such men becomes as plain as the expediency of paying the expenses of his drummers. Opponents of his tariff become to him assailants of property and order. A speech against the tariff is an instigation to communists to wreck his mill or his workshop. Free-trade books become quasi-incendiary publications. Free - trade professors and editors are corrupters of youth. All the mental influences which create orthodoxy on any subject, work for the conversion of defence against foreign industrial competition into the highest duty of a citizen.

Once fill the country with this idea, as with a religion, and the effect on politics soon becomes manifest. Men who believe in freedom of thought and expression, and who think that government has other and higher duties than seeing that the business of the private citizen is profitable, are generally the fittest men for public life. Such men are rarely good tariff men, and they are, therefore, sedulously discarded by caucuses and conventions. Bosses are hostile to them because money cannot readily be obtained to promote their election, and because they are too independent to be easily disciplined. When this process has lasted a number of years, the thoughts of the *élite* of the nation naturally turn away from politics to fields in which a man may speak the thing he wills, and be the master of his own career.

With more space at my disposal illustrations of this would be easy. There is one before us to-day, however, which cannot be passed over. That this tendency to eliminate men of ability and independence of thought from public life should end in making Major McKinley the Republican candidate for the Presidency, is what is now called "the logic of the situation." If this sifting process continued very long, it was inevitable that it would at last discard from the list of qualifications for the Chief Magistracy everything but devotion to a high tariff, and put in nomination for it a man who had nothing else to recommend him. All the Republican candidates since the foundation of the party— Lincoln, Grant, Hayes, Garfield, Blaine, Harrison —have had some solid claim for the place, apart from the tariff. Lincoln was a considerable orator and valiant opponent of slavery when he was nominated. Grant was a great soldier. Hayes was a good soldier, a sound financier, and a highly respectable local administrator. Garfield was a scholar, an orator, and a publicist of distinction. Harrison was a distinguished soldier, and had considerable eminence at the bar of his own State. Blaine was admired for a good many things which had no connection with protection for native industry. But, as the tariff becomes more prominent in the party councils, the standard of talent or achievement necessary for the place steadily declines. There was a strong note of warning on this subject in General Harrison's remark that a "cheap coat made a cheap man," and in the preposterous doctrine which many of the Republican leaders began in 1890 to preach on the stump, that dearness of commodities was a good thing for the poor. The intellectual descent made by the party at that time cleared the way for a far poorer sort of candidate than any it had ever had, nay, worse than any party had ever had since the foundation of the Government, for we are ready to allow any one who has looked into the published volume of Major McKinley's speeches, or has examined his record as Governor of Ohio, to compare him with any President, or Presidential candidate, in our history. Any such examination will show that the party has, in its search for a suitable standard-bearer, reached a region of extraordinary intellectual poverty and moral weakness, but still a region toward which it has for many years been steadily marching.

The financial situation is simply this: Partly under the influence of the silver craze, partly under the influence of a renewal of the greenback craze —which makes greenbacks a sacred relic of the war to be preserved in spite of their defects as money —we have undertaken to keep about $900,000,000 of mixed silver and government paper at par with gold. This is the most tremendous task any civilized government has ever imposed upon itself. The Bank of England only agrees to keep $80,000,-000 of paper at par. The Bank of France has only $700,000,000 to look after, at the most, for this is all the paper it is allowed to issue, and keeps gold for nearly half of this. The German Bank has only to keep its paper at par in securities, bank-notes, discounted bills, and legal-tender notes of the government. But we undertake to see that every-body who wants it shall get gold for more than $400,000,000 of silver, which brings only 58 per cent. of intrinsic value in the market, and for about $500,000,000 of paper which has no intrinsic value whatever. In order to do this, we borrow gold whenever our stock of it runs short, and every successful loan is greeted as a great financial triumph.

Upon this borrowed stock of gold, too, Gresham's Law plays incessantly. I have recalled the meaning of this law in an earlier part of this article. It means for us that any one who finds it necessary to settle a balance with a foreign creditor, and who is unable to settle it with silver or paper, may settle it with gold drawn from the Treasury. So that the Government stock of gold is sure to undergo incessant diminution from these drafts.

Now the protectionist, or I may say McKinley, remedy for this is to procure larger revenue by putting higher duties on foreign imports. Granting that this would increase the revenue, the only difference would be that we could purchase our reserve of gold with our own money, instead of borrowing it. But it would not diminish the drafts on this reserve. These drafts arise out of the fact that with a dollar in silver worth only 58 cents, I can go to the Treasury and get a dollar worth 100 cents. This demand will not cease until silver becomes worth 100 cents on the dollar, or the race of money-changers dies out, or until the volume of our currency is so reduced that we shall need gold for other uses than bolstering up our silver and greenbacks. If all this be true, it is easy to see that the declarations in favor of the gold standard in the Republican platforms will profit us little, unless some means are devised to stop the drain of our gold caused by our periodical announcements that we mean to keep our silver and paper at par with gold, or perish in the attempt. So long as this continues, it matters not whether we buy the gold for our reserves, or borrow it, we shall be constantly on the edge of a silver basis, and consequently of a frightful panic.

The work of currency reform, therefore, consists in following the example of the other great nations

of the earth and leaving silver to do the best it can
as token-money or small change—that is, limiting
its legal tender quality—and in reducing the volume of the greenbacks, or wholly redeeming them,
and discharging the Government from the duty
of keeping anything at par, except its own credit.
But this involves the substitution, for the greenbacks and silver, of some sort of banking system
whose paper shall be secure and whose circulation shall contract and expand with the wants of
trade.   No Legislature since 1815 has had a more
serious task before it than this, and we doubt if
any Legislature has ever had.   It will need a Congress either of remarkable intelligence or of remarkable docility.   It will need a first-rate financier to direct the operation, one who is intimately
acquainted with currency problems both as affected
by home trade and by foreign exchange—such a
man in truth as Alexander Hamilton or Albert
Gallatin.

THE REAL PROBLEMS OF DEMOCRACY

MR. JOHN MORLEY, in replying to some of Mr. Lecky's charges against the liberal movement of the last fifty years in England, expresses his regret that in his recent book, " Democracy and Liberty," Mr. Lecky has not devoted himself to a discussion of democracy in all its aspects; its effect not only on government, but on social relations of every description, on science, on art, on literature—on the whole of life, in short, as we see it in the western world to-day. He says:

"We can hardly imagine a finer or more engaging, inspiring, and elevating subject for inquiry than this wonderful outcome of that extraordinary industrial, intellectual, and moral development which has awakened in the masses of modern society the consciousness of their own strength, and the resolution, still dim and torpid, but certain to expand and to intensify, to use that strength for purposes of their own. We may rejoice in democracy or we may dread it. Whether we like it or detest it, and whether a writer chooses to look at it as a whole or to investigate some particular aspect of it, the examination ought to take us into the highest region of political thought, and it undoubtedly calls for the best qualities of philosophic statesmanship and vision." [2]

The task suggested is not easy, and Mr. Lecky, perhaps wisely, has not attempted it.   He devotes himself mainly, in the first volume, at least, to describing the objectionable tendencies of democracy, more particularly as illustrated by the history of the last half century in England and America.   The second volume may be called a series of essays on the topics now most frequently discussed in democratic countries; Mr. Lecky gives the pros and cons of each without committing himself to very positive opinions on any of them. All authors who touch at all on democracy in our day recognize in it a new and potent force, destined before long to effect very serious changes in the social structure, and to alter, in many important respects, the way in which men have looked at human society since the foundation of Christianity. But they handle it very much as we handle electricity; that is to say, tentatively.   They admit they are dealing with a very mysterious power, of which they know as yet but little, and on the future manifestations of which they cannot pronounce with any confidence.   The great difficulty in the way

of discussing it philosophically or scientifically is
the one which doubtless Mr. Lecky himself has
experienced—that thus far all investigators have
been themselves part of the thing to be investi-
gated. Every man, or nearly every man, who
takes up a pen to examine the questions what
democracy is, and what effect it is likely to have
on the race, is himself either an earnest advocate
or an earnest opponent of it. He sees in it either
the regeneration of mankind or the ruin of our
civilization. This is true of nearly every writer of
eminence who has touched on it since the French
Revolution. The most moderate of its enemies
seldom admits more on its behalf than his own
ignorance of what it promises. Its defenders are,
as a rule, too enthusiastic to make their predictions of much philosophic value.

In England, the historic background has enough
social gloom in it to make the glorification of
democracy comparatively easy work for the faithful thus far. In America its success seems so
closely connected with the success of the government itself that praise of it and prediction of
its complete sufficiency, have become the part
of patriotism. Doubts about its future seem
doubts about the future of the nation, which no
lover of his country is willing to entertain lightly.
Tocqueville is the one man of eminence who in

modern times has attempted for democracy what
Montesquieu attempted for all government—the
discovery and exposition of the principle on which
it rests. His work on " Democracy in America " is
so well known that it is hardly necessary to say that,
treating the base of democracy as equality, he has
sought to foretell what the effect of this principle
would be, in the end, on manners and institutions.
Some of his predictions have come true. Some
are very erroneous, and the fact is that, as the
years roll by and American development continues,
his work becomes less valuable. It will always be
interesting as what the French call an *étude,* and
was the first glimpse Europe got of the effect of
democratic institutions on character and manners, but it has not maintained its earlier fame.
Tocqueville fell more and more, before he died,
into an attitude of partisanship, and his later political essays are too deeply tinged with melancholy
about the future, for an impartial investigator.

No one, since his time, has taken the subject up
with more authority than Sir Henry Maine. In a
book on Popular Government, published in 1886,
he ventures on a broad characterization of democratic society, which bears the mark of insufficient
observation. The only thing he has to rely upon
in the way of experience is the Athenian democracy and that of America. There was not in the

ancient world any democracy at all in the sense in which we understand the term, and the working of the system in the United States has been too short, the disturbing elements have been too numerous, and Sir Henry's acquaintance with it is all too slight, to make it possible for him to speak about it with philosophic positiveness. To crown all, he was essentially an aristocrat, an authority who, rightly or wrongly, felt his position in some sort menaced by the new régime.

Mr. Lecky suffers from the same disadvantages. He is a gentleman in the old sense of the term, who feels that his weight as such is in some sort menaced. In the new régime he expects men of his sort to count for less in some way, probably in many ways. He is fresh, too, from a revolution in his own country, much more searching and deep-seated than revolutions used to be—one of the first democratic revolutions, in short, that we have had since that of France, one hundred years ago. The recent Irish land laws are the dethronement of a great class, the apparent sacrifice of the few to the many, on a large scale; this is what democracy calls for, but it is never accomplished without seemingly serious violations of natural justice. Mr. Lecky took a prominent part in opposing these recent changes in Ireland. Whether they are bad or good, no man could share either in

defending or in advocating them without considerable damage to his judicial-mindedness, to his
philosophic insight, so to speak. He cannot approach them as a Cavour or a Beaumont.[3] He is
part of the revolution. He cannot wholly like
them, and he cannot help ascribing them in some
way to the great movement which, for better or
worse, is plainly upturning the world, putting
down the mighty and exalting the humble. If,
therefore, one were disposed to be ill-natured, one
might call Mr. Lecky's book an attempt to pay
democracy off for suggesting or assisting the Irish
land laws and home-rule movement. It is essentially an address to the opponents of democracy, written with his usual narrating ability and
fulness of reading; but, for the reasons I have
stated, it cannot do much to convince those who
are not fellow-sufferers and do not share his prejudices. In short, it is not the book on democracy of which the world is just now in need and
in search.

The chief objection to it, and to most recent
writings of the same sort, is that, while nominally
discussing democracy, it really only points out the
apparently bad tendencies of democracy. It does
not treat democracy as a whole. It errs in this
respect somewhat as Burke's Reflections on the
French Revolution do. One could not get from

Burke any idea of the objections to the *ancien régime.* The Revolution seems, according to him, the work of mocking devils who could give no reason for their mischief. That anybody in France had anything serious to complain of, anything which could not be removed by means of a little patience and good will, anything which was likely to have an educating influence, which was likely to mould character and breed defects, does not appear. The whole outbreak seems gratuitous, uncaused, and therefore against the order of nature. Mr. Lecky singles out and makes prominent nearly everything that can be said against democracy, by means of partial comparison—the least fair of all methods of judging either a society or a régime, and yet it is the commonest method of travellers and essayists. For my part, I never read a description of the evils of democracy at the present day without inquiring with what state of society or with what kind of government the writer compares it. When and where was the polity from observation of which he has formed his standard? When and where was the state of things, the "good estate," from which we have declined or are declining? This is extremely important, for all we know or can say about government must be the result of actual observation. "Ideal government," as it is called, such as is described in Plato's "Republic," or More's "Utopia," or Bellamy's "Looking Backward," is interesting to read about, as the play of an individual mind, but no one considers any of these books very helpful to those who are actually contending with the problems of to-day.

To enable any reformer to make his impress on the age in which he lives, or to win any considerable number of his countrymen over to his way of thinking, the state of things he seeks to bring about must commend itself to his contemporaries as capable of realization. He must have some model in his mind's eye, not too far removed, either in time or in distance, from the popular imagination. This is an essential condition of the advance of all great multitudes. Every man's standard of civilization is drawn from what he has seen, or thinks he may readily reach. Nearly all differences touching governments, between various peoples or between various classes of the same society, came from differences of standards. Some are extremely content with a state of things that others think impossible. An Indian, for instance, cannot understand the white man's eagerness to get him to give up the tepee, in which he has been so happy, for the log cabin or the frame house. The spoils politician is puzzled by the Mugwump's passion for competitive examinations, and government based on party distribution of the offices as spoils seems to him most natural and thoroughly successful. Probably few or no Tammany men can to this day quite understand the objection of reformers to their style of government. They see that tens of thousands apparently like it and are satisfied with it. What is the need of a change? The cause of all the discussion is that the Mugwump has a different standard of government from the politician, and is not satisfied until the government he lives under comes up to it. In like manner, when a monarchist or conservative begins to complain to a democrat of the defects of his system and of the gloominess of its prospects, in order to produce any effect he must point out from what period or from what system there has been a falling away. When and where were things any better, taken as a whole? And how much better were they? This is a question which every writer on democracy is bound to answer at the outset.

I have said "taken as a whole," because the fatal defect of all attacks on democracy of recent years, like Mr. Lecky's, is this defect of partial comparison. When we undertake to compare one régime with another, old with new times, it does not do to fasten on one feature of either. In our day this is sure to be ineffective. If we judge American society, for instance, solely from the point of view of legislative purity and ability, it will certainly

suffer in comparison with that of Great Britain.
If we judge it from the point of view of judicial
learning and independence, we shall probably reach
the same conclusion. It would be quite easy to point
out certain losses which it sustains from the absence of an aristocracy, as contrasted with any
European country. If, too, we undertake, as Mr.
Lecky does, to compare the England or Ireland of
to-day with the England or Ireland of some by-
gone period, known or unknown, it does not do to
say that at that period Parliament was better, or
county government was better, or legislation was
more deliberate and impartial, or other statesmen
were better than Mr. Gladstone. To produce any
real effect the comparison has to be complete.
You have to compare the general happiness from
all causes. You have to treat the two contrasted
communities as places for the poor and friendless
man, or for the industrious, enterprising, and
thrifty man, to live in, as well as for the wealthy
and cultivated man. Otherwise you make no
headway. Every reader will think instantly of the
things you have overlooked. You cannot compare
the England of to-day with the England of 1800
or 1867 without destroying or greatly weakening
your case. There is not a poor man in England
who is not conscious that he is vastly better off, as
regards all the things furnished him under the

name of "government," than his grandfather was. The same thing is ludicrously true of Ireland. A proposal submitted to the people in either country to go back fifty or one hundred years, would be rejected almost unanimously with derision. You might give them fifty reasons for thinking them mistaken, but not one of them would produce any impression. Why is this? An adequate book on democracy would answer the question. It would not only give these reasons, but state fully and fairly why they were certain to be disregarded.

The truth is that democracy is simply an experiment in the application of the principle of equality to the management of the common affairs of the community. It is the principle of equality which has conquered the world. That one man is as good as another is an outgrowth of what may be called social consciousness, and as soon as it has got possession of the State, democratic government follows as a matter of course. The theory of the social contract is an offspring of it. This theory made no impression on the masses when Locke preached it. It did not reach the people till Rousseau took it up, in the middle of the last century. Since then it has made great strides. Rulers have become the mere hired servants of the mass of the community, and criticism of them has come naturally with the employment of them as agents. The

notion that all men are alike, and are entitled to
an equal voice in the management of the common
affairs, is democracy.   It is the effort of all to
assert this, and to see how the thing can be done,
which forms the democratic experiment that is being tried in so many countries.

Many things have occurred which seem to warrant the belief that it will not succeed. What constitutes the success of a government? The very
first answer to this question is that we cannot tell
whether a government is successful or not without seeing how long it lasts. The first duty of a
government is to last. A government, however
good, which does not last is a failure. The Athenian republic, the Roman republic and empire, the
Venetian republic, the French monarchy, the English monarchy, and the American republic, have
all to be tried by this test. To say that a government is a very good government, but that it was
overthrown or changed in a few years, is almost a
contradiction in terms. All we know of any value
about any government is derived from observation
of its working. It must be confessed, therefore, that
nearly all that we read in our day about democracy
is pure speculation. No democracy has lasted long
enough to enable one to write a treatise on it of
much value. Almost everything that Mr. Lecky
says of the working of democracy in America, or

that he has got from Mr. Bryce, though all true,
fails to throw much light upon the future.

The men who first began to write on democracy,
toward the close of the last century and the beginning of this, had really a very small notion of its
working on the scale which the modern world wit-
nesses. Their only opportunities of observation
lay in the history of the small Greek communities,
of early Rome, of Venice and the minor Swiss cantons, and of the early New England States. They
had not for a moment pictured to themselves the
government by universal suffrage of communities
numbering tens of millions. Their democracies all
met in the forum or market-place; their leading
men were known to every citizen. Nothing seemed
easier than to fill the public offices by a mere show
of hands. Every man was supposed to be intensely
occupied with public affairs, to be eager to vote on
them, and to be quite able to vote intelligently.
The work of management had not a prominent
place in any former democratic scheme. The
" demagogue "—that is, the man who leads people
astray by specious schemes, by hostility to the
rich, or eagerness for war, or profuse prodigality,
or winning eloquence—was well known. But the
man who does not speak, who makes no public impression, who is not rich or eloquent or in any
manner distinguished, yet who leads the voters and

holds legislation in the hollow of his hand, had still to make his appearance.

In the new, unforeseen, enormous democracy, 40,000,000 to 100,000,000 in England, or France, or America, he is indispensable. In these large democracies, the work of bringing the popular will to bear in filling the offices of the government, or in performing any act of government, is one of great difficulty, which needs almost constant attention from a large army of "workers." To influence, persuade, or inform this immense body of persons is no easy matter, as two antagonistic forces are always engaged in pulling it in different directions. The diffusion among it of any one view of anything would be a serious task. To insure the triumph of either view is still more serious. Then, a very large proportion of the voters are not interested in public questions at all, or their feeble interest has to be aroused and kept awake. Another large proportion do not desire to give themselves the trouble to vote. They have to be, in some manner, induced to go to the polls, or have to be prepared to go by numerous visits. The business of what is called the "canvass" in modern democracy is, in fact, something unlooked for and unprovided for by theoretical democrats. It has produced a profession whose sole occupation is to get people to vote in a particular way. As the mass of voters in-

creases, this profession, of course, becomes larger
and more important. In my own opinion, its importance constitutes the strongest argument against
woman suffrage. The doubling of the number of
votes to be influenced or managed in any community is a very grave consideration; for not only
have you to find such workers, with the certainty
that their character will not be very high, but you
have to pay them, and no provision for their payment has ever been made in any scheme of democratic government. The duty of remunerating
them is thrown on the victorious parties at elections; in America, for a long time, this duty was
discharged by distributing among them the smaller
offices. There has been an escape from it here by
what is called civil service reform, or, in other
words, by competitive examination. In England,
the aristocracy, finding the government patronage
passing out of their hands, judiciously introduced
the merit system, in time to save it from the in-
coming democracy, but in France and Italy the
tendency is still in the direction of " spoils." The
passion for government places is strong, and the
difficulty of getting anything done for the State,
except in return for a place, grows apace, on the
whole. If I said that the reluctance of a democracy
to vote at all, or to vote right, was not foreseen by
the early democratic advocates, and that they made

no provision for it in their system, I should not be very far wrong. This was the greatest mistake of the theoretic democrats. They never foresaw the big democracies. The working of democracy in America is something of which they had no conception. They did not anticipate the necessity of organizing and directing the suffrage, nor of the intervention of the boss and his assistants.

When you come to examine this mistake, you find it consists really in the absence of provision for the selection of candidates by the multitude, or, in other words, in the absence of a nominating system. None of the books contain any direction for the performance of this work of nominating by a large democracy. The founders of the United States had apparently never thought of it. In their day, a few leading men met and chose one of their own number as a good person to fill, say, a legislative or other important place ; or a prominent man proposed himself to his fellow-citizens to fill it. For some time after the foundation of the government, a committee of Congress named candidates for the presidency. But it was soon seen that this would not do. The voters would not allow any one to do this work for them. An elected assembly had to do it, and the nominating convention, in its various stages, was started. In other words, the business of electing officers was doubled by having another election to elect the people who were to select good people to elect. This work of nominating has added to the boss's, or manager's, power by adding to his duties. He has to see not only that people vote for the various candidates, but that they vote for those who have to choose them. More complication, more patience, more watchfulness, more dexterity.

Under this régime, the nominating system, of which no theoretical writer had the least idea, has grown into a piece of machinery more complicated than the government itself. The man who manages it, who says who must compose the body which selects the candidates—that is, who designates the delegates to the nominating convention —is really the most powerful man in the community. Every one who wishes to enter public life bows before him. No one who, being in public life, wishes to rise higher, no Representative who wishes to be Senator, no Governor who wishes to be President, will gainsay him or quarrel with him. Everybody but the President in a second term is at his beck. For similar reasons, he holds the legislators in his power. If they do not legislate as he pleases, he will not allow them to come back to the legislature. He has to be consulted, in fact, about every office. He may be boss of a district, a city, or a state. The larger his dominion and the denser its population, the more powerful he is. The people, being busy, are not willing to go to the trouble of voting at two elections. As a rule, they do not vote at all for the nominating convention. This is, therefore, almost completely in the boss's hands. As he decides who shall compose it, he also decides what it shall do. In fact, in ordinary times and in the absence of great public excitement, he is the great man of a democratic community; and yet neither he nor the nominating system which has made him what he is, was foreseen by any early political thinker. There was no foreshadowing of the difficulty that democracy would experience in filling office, and no one has as yet devised any good plan for the purpose. Any person who to-day described the government, say, of New York, or Pennsylvania, or any other large American State, out of the books, would give no real idea of it. He would miss the real source of power, and the way in which it was infused into the machinery. If there be anything seriously wrong with democracy in America to-day, it lies in the nominating system, yet this attracts comparatively little attention.

Another new phenomenon which has greatly affected the development of democratic government, and has received no attention, is the growth of corporations. These aggregations of capital in a few hands have created a new power in the State, whose influence on government has been very grave. They employ a vast number of voters, over whom their influence is paramount; a single railroad company has in its service thousands of men. They own immense sums of money, which they think it but right to use freely for their own protection. In some States, men make a livelihood in the legislature by "striking" them, — that is, threatening them with hostile legislation, and getting themselves bought off by the agent of the corporation; for each corporation is apt to keep an agent at the seat of government to meet these very demands, and makes no secret of it. Latterly the bosses have taken charge of this business themselves. They receive the money, and see that the legislature is properly managed in return. The companies have, in fact, created a code of morality to meet this exigency. The officers say that they are the custodians of large amounts of other people's property, which they are bound to defend, by whomsoever attacked. That wrong does exist in the State is not their affair. The reform of the legislature or of the State is not their affair. It is their business to keep safely what has been placed in their charge. Indeed, the levying of blackmail on companies, either as a contribution to campaign ex-

penses or as fees to pay for protection, is now one
of the principal sources of a boss's revenue, and, in
States like New York, goes a good way toward enabling him to defy hostile sentiment. It furnishes
him with funds for subsidizing the legislature and
the press. How to bring these corporations under
the law, and at the same time protect them from
unjust attacks, is one of the most serious problems
of democratic government. But it can hardly be
said to have received any discussion as yet. Corporations are as powerful as individual noblemen
or aristocrats were in England in the last century,
or in France before the Revolution, but are far
harder to get at or to bring to justice, from their
habit of making terms with their enemies instead
of fighting them.

This brings me naturally to two other serious
and significant changes which have occurred within fifty years in democratic societies. I mean the
decline of the legislatures, and the transfer of
power, or rather of the work of government, from
the rich to the poor.

That this decline of the legislatures is not a
mere decline in manners seems to me undeniable.
It is a decline in the quality of the members in
general respect, in education, in social position, in
morality, in public spirit, in care and deliberation,
and, I think I must add, in integrity, also. Legis-

lation is more hasty and more voluminous, is drafted with less care, and enacted with less deliberation and with much greater indifference to public opinion, particularly to instructed and thoughtful public opinion. This is said to be true of France and Italy, and in some degree of England, but it is especially true of America. Congress and the State legislatures are not what they were forty years ago. Both the Senate and the House contain fewer men of prominence and ability. The members are more slenderly instructed, but much more eagerly interested, in questions of political economy, finance, and taxation than they used to be, and more disposed to turn to account what they conceive to be their knowledge. They are more difficult to lead, and yet are more under the domination of their own cliques or sets. In the State legislatures, the boss is far more powerful than he was. But little legislation originates with the members themselves. It is generally concocted outside and passed under orders. Few of the members are really chosen and elected by the people. They are suggested and returned by the boss of the State or district. They feel accountable to him, and not to the public. The old machinery of agitation, the public meeting and the press, produces little effect on them. Their motives are rarely made known. Many of their acts, if not corrupt, are open to the suspicion of corruption; some of them are bold attempts to extort money. All this is true, as I have said, in some degree or other, of all the countries in which democratic institutions have taken or begun to take root. These bodies have not answered the earlier expectations of democratic philosophers. The men who were expected to go to them do not go to them. The men who have served the public well in them do not return to the service. The influence on them of the intellectual, cultivated, or instructed world is small.

To account for this, or to say how it is to be mended, is, I admit, very difficult. Few subjects have done more to baffle reformers and investigators. It is the great puzzle of the heartiest friends of democracy. The matter is growing more serious in America as society is becoming richer and more complicated. As commerce increases, credit expands and interests multiply, of course the machinery of government increases in delicacy. Derangement becomes easier, repair more difficult. The effect, for instance, of instability in taxation, or of adventures in foreign policy, upon foreign trade, or upon investment and the movements of capital, is very great; so that already merchants, bankers, and dealers in money are beginning to ask themselves whether it will be long possible to carry on the financial affairs of a great nation under a government so unskilful, and possessed of so little knowledge of the machinery of credit, as democratic governments generally are. This gives great importance to the question, What prospect is there of any change for the better? What sign is there of anything of the kind? As to this I confess I think the dependence of the optimist, if he descends to argument at all, must be on the general progress of the race in self-restraint, in love of order, and in a better knowledge, through experience, of the conditions of successful government. Any such process must necessarily be slow, and no results can be looked for until after the trial and failure of many experiments.

In other words, I do not look for the improvement of democratic legislatures in quality within any moderate period. What I believe democratic societies will do, in order to improve their government and make better provision for the protection of property and the preservation of order, is to restrict the power of these assemblies and shorten their sittings, and to use the referendum more freely for the production of really important laws. I have very little doubt that, before many years elapse, the American people will get their government more largely from constitutional conventions, and will confine the legislatures within very narrow limits and make them meet at rare intervals. The tendencies all over the Union are in this direction, and Switzerland, the most democratic country in Europe, is showing the way distinctly toward less law-making and more frequent consultation of the people at large. I believe, for instance, that after a very few years' experience of the transfer of the currency question, which has now begun, to the management of popular suffrage, the legal tender quality of money, which is now behind the whole trouble, will be abolished, and the duty of the government will be confined simply to weighing and stamping. The usefulness of the legal tender now is ludicrously disproportioned to the noise made about it. Except as a rule for fixing the denomination in which debtors must pay their debts in the absence of an agreement—which rarely causes any dispute—and for enabling debtors to cheat their creditors by paper money or the adulteration of coin—which is not infrequent—it is difficult to see what good purpose legal tender serves. It is almost certain that the day will come when it will be seen that no democratic government is fit to be entrusted with the power of giving any substance legal tender quality, and that the very best solution of the money problem is to be found in letting people make their own bargains—a solution which will be hastened by the increasing tendency to settle contracts, make purchases, and pay debts by check or draft.

The other corrective of which I see signs, though of less importance, is the increasing ability or willingness of business men to separate their business from their politics, and to refuse any longer to put money into the hands of party agents to do as they please with it. This use of money, especially since the growth of the tariff question in importance, has been one of the great sources of the degradation of American politics, because it supports the excesses or abuses of the nominating system by strengthening the hands of the boss; for it is he who generally receives the funds. But it would be absurd to build great hopes of progress on the mere cessation of an abuse. It is a thing to be noted rather than dwelt on. All that we can say with certainty is that no Western society is likely, in modern times, to let itself run completely down, as the ancient societies often did, without vigorous attempts at recovery and improvement. The general belief in progress which now prevails, the greatly increased desire to extract comfort out of life (and comfort includes quiet and order), the more scientific spirit of the time, the disposition of all classes to assume social responsibility, and the sense of what the

French call "solidarity" diffused by the press, assure us that every means of progress will be tried, that no defect will be submitted to indefinitely; but what means of improvement will be most effective, and what safeguards will be found most reliable, he would be a rash man who would venture to predict in detail.

As to the transfer of the government to the poor, it should be remembered that, except during very short periods in ancient democracies, the world has been governed by rich men; that is, by the great landholders or the great merchants. This is true of all the ancient republics and of all the modern monarchies. The unfitness of poor men for the important offices of legislation and administration has been generally acted on in the modern world, as a State doctrine. Every government has been a rich man's government. It is only in some of the smaller Swiss cantons that departures from this rule have been made. But, as a rule, in democratic societies in our day, government has been transferred to poor men. These poor men find themselves in possession of very great power over rich communities. Through the taxing power rich corporations and rich individuals are at their mercy. They are not restrained by tradition; they are often stimulated by envy or other anti-social passions. If it were not for the

restrictions imposed in American States by the
Constitution, the lives of rich men and of companies would be full of difficulty. There has
grown up around this change the foreshadowing
of a code of morality in which men's right to be
rich is called in question, and the spoliation of
them, if done under forms of law, is not an offense
against morality. This, again, is counterbalanced
or neutralized by the general popular tendency to
make the accumulation of wealth the one sign of
worldly success, and to estimate men by the size
of their income, from whatever source derived.
There is probably in America to-day a nearer approach to a literal rendering of the English term
"worth," as measuring a man's possessions, than
ever occurred elsewhere; that is, the term is more
fully descriptive of the fact than it has ever been.
Inevitably, there has appeared side by side with
this a certain distrust of the opinions of persons
who have not made money, which has naturally
had an injurious effect on the government, and
has, along with several other causes, contributed
to the exclusion of the learned or professional
class from the work of administration. A faithful
description of the position of the wealthy class in
America to-day would probably say that the accumulation of wealth by a man's own exertion is admired by the public, and greatly respected if he

gives it fully to public objects, but that his attempt to participate in the work of government is viewed with a certain jealousy, while contributions for party purposes are eagerly received by the bosses, and offices are occasionally given in return for them by regular bargain. It is in this way, in fact, as well as through lower forms of corruption, that individual wealth protects itself against the consequences of the change to which I have already called attention, the transfer of the government to the poor and obscure. Property still has weight in public affairs, but not open weight, and the power of persuading the legislators has been taken from the public orator, or writer, who wielded it in the beginning of the century, and turned over to the successful man of affairs, who has schemes to carry out, but cannot waste time in arguing about them with anybody.

Among the minor illustrations of the failure to foresee, afforded by the early founders of democracy and speculators on it, is the virtual abolition of the board of electors who were to elect the President. They are now a mere formal body of registrars, who have no more to do with the results than a voting machine. Another is the total loss of the power of choice by the legislatures in electing Senators of the United States. The legislatures no longer choose them. They are chosen by

the managers of the party outside, and the legislators are, in fact, elected to carry out this choice.
A more complete disappointment than these two
modes of bringing great care to bear on two important operations of government could hardly be
imagined, and yet it is a disappointment which
does not appear to have been suspected as likely
to come. The present generation of reformers are
nearly as eager to abolish the Electoral College
and the legislative election of Senators, after a
century of experience, as the framers of the Constitution were to establish them. The prevailing
desire is to remit the work in both cases to the
popular vote.

This brings to our notice two tendencies, apparently, but only apparently, opposing, in American opinion. One is to throw as much of the
nominating or canvassing or preparatory work as
possible on individual men, like bosses and workers ; the other is to make the constituency of each
important office as wide as possible. The whole
people of the Union would like to vote directly for
the President, the whole people of a State would
like to vote for a Senator, and the whole people of
a city would like to vote for an almost despotic
mayor, but few want to take any trouble in creating or arranging machinery for choosing them.
The work of " getting delegates " to nominating

conventions, and making other preparations for elections, is left to professionals ; that is, to men who do little else, and who get a living out of this work. The exhortation of political moralists to "attend the primaries" has become almost a joke among the class to whom it is mainly addressed.

The discussion of all these matters—that is, the observation of the working of democracy on a large scale during the past century—should be the work of any writer on democracy from the philosophic point of view in our day. Mr. Bryce's book is mainly descriptive.[4] He does not foreshadow consequences or suggest remedies. Mr. Lecky is, to a certain extent, right in drawing illustrations from him, but we can read Mr. Bryce as well as Mr. Lecky can, and we know better than he what corrections or allowances to make. There are tens of thousands of Americans more troubled by many American phenomena than any European observer, and far more intelligently ; yet it is difficult for any American to deal with them adequately as yet, for obvious reasons.

In the first place, political speculation is somewhat discountenanced or discouraged in America by the excessive cultivation of what is called "patriotism," not unnatural in a young people, whose growth in wealth and numbers has been prodigious beyond example. This "patriotism"

has been made by the multitude to consist in holding everything that is, to be exactly right, or
easily remedied. A complaining or critical man,
as a speculator is apt to be, is therefore set down
as a person "unpatriotic," or hostile to his country. He may object to the other party, but he
must not find fault with the workings of his
government. The consequence is that any man
who expects to make his way in politics, or even to
succeed comfortably in a profession or business, is
strongly tempted to proclaim incessantly his great
content with the existing order of things, and to
treat everything "American" as sacred. Criticism
of the government or of political tendencies is
apt to be considered a sign of infidelity to the
republic, and admiration for something foreign.
More than this, an American is himself part of
what he discusses or proposes to amend. He has
his prejudices, some of them hereditary; he has
tastes and associations, few of which are corrected
by contact with or knowledge of different forms of
society; and his range of possibilities is therefore
narrow.

What is most serious of all is that we have not,
as England or France or Germany has, one great
capital, in which all the philosophers and speculators, and in fact men of education, live and make
a philosophical or political atmosphere, are influ-

enced by each other's opinions, enjoy each other's society, profit by each other's criticism, and transmit to the provinces, as from a court of last resort, final judgments on literature, art, and politics, and snap their fingers at country denunciation and grumbling. Our thinkers are scattered all over the country, hundreds or thousands of miles away from their congeners. They brood rather than speculate. They live among "plain people." They have a human desire to be comfortable and happy with their neighbors, to receive their approval and respect. They have but few opportunities of intercourse with their fellows in other parts of the country. Even in cases like the Venezuelan affair, or like the greenback or silver "craze," it is so easy to fall in with the crowd, or still easier to be silent, so hard to be generally denounced as "unpatriotic" or as a "Mugwump," or to be accused of foreign tastes or leanings, that attempts to point out a "more excellent way" are somewhat under a cloud. Only men of marked ability or strong character make them, and even for these the work is wearisome and a little disheartening. In short, the influence of the scholarly, thinking, philosophical class is nót felt in American progress nearly as much as it ought to be.

This is the more regrettable because no rational observer can suppose that the government of the

United States is destined to retain indefinitely its
present form. It is sure, like all governments
which have preceded it, to change, and probably
change from century to century. The history of
all republics and of all monarchies, like the history
of man himself, is one of incessant change. The
Greek republics, the Roman republic and empire,
the Venetian republic, the French and English
monarchies, have all undergone modifications from
generation to generation, in institution, laws, and
manners. Since Elizabeth the English monarchy
has experienced at least four enormous changes,
involving complete transfer of power and a complete revolution in political ideas. Even China is
succumbing to what is called "the spirit of the
age." To suppose that we, with forty-five republics, indulging in annual experiments in government, shall be exempt from the general law is
absurd. These changes consist, too, as a rule, in
adaptation of the institutions of the country to
an altered condition of popular sentiment, to the
revelation of new dangers, to the decline or
deterioration of some law or custom. The English in 1649 would not submit to a monarch like
Charles I. In 1688 they would not submit to a
monarch like James II. In 1832 they would not
submit to a Parliament like that in which Pitt
thundered and Burke reasoned. In other words,

the history of nations is the history of incessant attempts, fortunate or unfortunate, to better themselves.

For these reasons and many others, all disquisition on the phenomena of modern democracy in any community as final, or as certain to result in despotism or in any other great calamity, appears to me exceedingly inadequate. Democracy in America, like democracy and monarchy elsewhere, is following the course of other political societies. It is suffering from unforeseen evils, as well as enjoying unforeseen blessings. It will probably be worse before it is better. It is trying a great many experiments in laws and manners, of which some, doubtless, will be hideous failures. The régime of " crazes " through which it is now passing is very discouraging, but it is engaged, like most other civilized societies, in a search after remedies.

To illustrate my meaning, let me cite the case of civil service reform. One of the unforeseen evils developed by the new democracy not long after the foundation of the government was the practice of offering all the places, high and low, in the government service, to the victors at each election as " spoils." It took fifty years to bring this evil to what I may call perfection; that is, to reveal in practice exactly how it would work, how it

would affect legislation and administration and
public life. It was something novel at first,
because although, under European monarchies,
places were given away as rewards to favorites,
and were even sold, they were permanent, and the
field of distribution was small. It became deeply rooted in the political manners of the people,
and by large numbers was looked on as the true
American system of appointment,—the only one
suited to a democratic republic. Two generations,
at least, had never seen any other system. A full
discussion of its injurious effects on public life and
on the public service was not begun till after the
civil war. The advocates of a change were met
at first with intense hostility and ridicule from the
politicians and from members of Congress, and
were received with great indifference by the
general public. Yet, in five years they succeeded
in making some impression upon the President.
Within ten years after the war they had secured
some favorable legislation. Every President since
then has made further concessions to them, and
this year the final transfer of the whole federal
service, including 85,200 places, to the merit
system has been made. I do not believe that,
at the time when the agitation for civil service
reform began, there was any evil or abuse in the
government, an attack on which seemed so hope-

less, and yet this evil has disappeared within one generation. I cite it as an illustration of the danger or error of treating any democratic failure as permanent or hopeless, or denying to any democratic society the capacity and determination to remedy its own defects in some direction or other by some means or other. No society in our time is willing to deteriorate openly, or ever does so long, without struggling for salvation.

THE EXPENDITURE OF RICH MEN [1]

FROM the earliest times of which we have any historical knowledge rich men have had to exercise a good deal of ingenuity in expending their income. The old notion that wealth is desired for the sake of power was never completely true. It has always been desired also, as a rule, for the sake of display. The cases have been rare in which rich men have been content to be secretly or unobtrusively rich. They have always wished people to know they were rich. It has, also, from the earliest times, been considered appropriate that display should accompany power. A powerful man who was not wealthy and made no display, has, in all ages, been considered a strange, exceptional person. As soon as a man became powerful, the world has always thought it becoming that he should also be rich, and should furnish evidences of his riches that would impress the popular imagination. As a rule, he has sought to make this impression. He has liked people at least to see what he could do if he would. Of course, except in the case of rulers, he could not put his money into armies or fleets. Consequently, as a private man, he has put it into tangible, visible property, things which people could see and envy, or wonder over. A rich man who did not do this was always set down as a miser, or something very like it, in some way queer or eccentric. He, too, has been held bound to spend his money in ways in which the public in general expected him to spend it, and in which it had become usual for men of his kind to expend it. His expenditure was, therefore, in a certain sense, the product of the popular manners. If a man in England, for instance, expends money like a rich Turkish pacha, or Indian prince, he is frowned on or laughed at. But if he keeps a great racing-stable, or turns large tracts of land into a grouse moor or a deer forest, in which to amuse himself by killing wild animals, it is thought natural and simple.

But one of the odd things about wealth is the small impression the preachers and moralists have ever made about it. From the very earliest times its deceitfulness, its inability to produce happiness, its fertility in temptation, its want of connection with virtue and purity, have been among the commonplaces of religion and morality. Hesiod declaims against it, and exposes its bad effects on the character of its possessors, and Christ makes

it exceedingly hard for the rich man to get
to heaven. The folly of winning wealth or car-
ing for it has a prominent place in mediæval
theology. Since the Reformation there has not
been so much declamation against it, but the rich
man's position has always been held, even among
Protestants, to be exceedingly perilous. His
temptations might not be so great as they used to
be, but his responsibilities were quadrupled. The
modern philanthropic movement, in particular
has laid heavy burdens on him. He is now allowed to have wealth, but the ethical writers and
the clergy supervise his expenditure closely. If
he does not give freely for charitable objects, or
for the support of institutions of benoficence, he is
severely criticised. His stewardship is insisted
on. In the Middle Ages this was his own look-
out. If he endowed monasteries, or bequeathed
foundations for widows, or old men, or orphans,
it was with the view of making provision for his
own soul in the future world, and did not stand
much higher in morals or religion than that old
English legacy for the expenses of burning here-
tics. But in our times he is expected to endow
for love of his kind or country, and gifts for his
soul's sake would be considered an expression of
selfishness.

In Europe, as I have said, the association of

displays of wealth with political power has lasted
since states were founded. It was largely made
possible in the ancient world through slavery.
From what we know through architectural remains,
or historic record, there was no length, in that
world, to which a great man could not go in the
display of his possessions. What we hear or see
of Hadrian's villa, or Diocletian's palace at Spala-
tro, makes Versailles seem a mere bauble. The
stories told of the villas of Lucullus, or Mæcenas,
even if half true, show that our modern rich men
know but little of the possibilities of luxury.
Pliny's description of his own villa in his Letters
shows that they were far more than half true, that
not one of our modern rich men has done one-
quarter of what he might have done for material
enjoyment. Undoubtedly the non-existence of
slavery has been the greatest check on his extravagance. Could he have the same absolute control
over domestic servants, he would probably treat
himself to more extraordinary varieties of luxury
in the matter of habitation and clothing and equipages. The traditions of the Roman Empire in
this matter perished with the Empire. When the
modern rich man came into possession of the
means and appliances of civilization, he found
himself in a new world, in which it was vastly
more difficult to secure steady, uncomplaining per-

sonal service, and in which money was harder to
get hold of. But what was within his reach, he
readily used. The mediæval noble all over Europe
after the Renaissance, transferred himself to mag-
nificent abodes, and surrounded himself with a
small army of servants. But he did this in obe-
dience, I will not say to public opinion, for there
was no such thing, but to popular notions of the
fitting. It was held, as I have said, but becoming
that a man who occupied his political place, who
counted for so much in the state, whose descent
was considered so illustrious, who owned such
vast tracts of land, should live in a very great
house, and be followed by a great retinue, should
have his gentlemen and pages, and his numerous
servants to wait upon him. When Madame de
Sevigné travelled in the seventeenth century to
Paris from her château in the country, she went
with two carriages, seven horses, and four men
on horseback, and each carriage had four horses;
yet she was only a person of moderate fortune.
Madame de Montespan, when she went to Vichy,
had six horses in her coach; another behind with
six maids. Then she had two *fourgons*, or bag-
gage-wagons, six mules, and a dozen men on horseback, forty-five persons in all. Once when Madame
de Sevigné's son came home from the army, her
man of business had fifteen hundred men under

arms to receive him in the court of the château.
When the Marquis de Lavardin came to see her,
he had officers and guards and trumpets and
twenty gentlemen. The Montmorencis and Roh-
ans and Soubises and Colignys made still greater
display. The same thing went on in England.
The rich men lived and travelled surrounded by
splendor, because they were really great men.
They had power over hundreds and thousands of
fortunes, if not of lives. They had a share in the
government. They were largely above the law.
"God Almighty," as a pious but well-born French
woman said, "thought twice before damning one
of them." Down to the end of the last century the
enmity of a peer, as was recently remarked, was
enough to ruin a man in England.

All this is now changed in Europe. As power
has left the upper classes, display has ceased. To
be quiet and unobserved is the mark of distinction.
Women of Madame de Sevigné's rank travel in
dark-colored little broughams. Peers in England
are indistinguishable when they move about in
public, from any one else. Distinction is sought
in manners, in speech, in general simplicity of demeanor, rather than in show of any kind. An attempt to produce on anybody, high or low, any
impression but one of envy, by sumptuousness of
living or equipage, would prove a total failure. It

may be said, without exaggeration, that the quietness of every description is now the "note" of the
higher class in all countries in Europe—quietness
of manner, of voice, of dress, of equipages, of, in
short, nearly everything which brings them in contact with their fellow-men. Comfort is the quest
of the "old nobility" generally. Ostentation is
left to the newly enriched, but there can hardly be
a doubt that this is largely due to loss of power.
Wealth now means nothing but wealth. The European noble was, in fact, everywhere but in Venice, a great territorial lord. It was incumbent on
him as a mark of his position, as soon as he came
out of his mediæval "keep," to live in a great
house, if only for purposes of entertainment. His
retinue required large accommodation ; his guests
required more, and more still was added for the
needs of the popular imagination. But the system
of which he was the product, which made his château or mansion grow out of the soil like his crops,
was never transferred to this country. The few
large grants which marked our early history never
brought forth large mansions or great retinues.
The great houses of that period, such as those of
the Van Rensselaers or Livingstons on the Hud-
son, or of the planters on the James River, are
simply moderate-sized mansions which, on most
estates in England or France, would be considered

small.   Hospitality was in none of them exercised
on anything like the European scale.   None of
them was ever occupied by anybody who exercised
anything more than influence over his fellow-citizens.   In fact most of them are to-day mainly interesting as showing the pains taken to put up
comfortable abodes in what were then very out-of-
the-way places.

All this amounts to saying that the building of
great houses was, down to our own time, a really
utilitarian mode of spending wealth.   It was intended to maintain and support the influence of
the ruling class by means which was sure to impress the popular mind, and which the popular
mind called for.   The great territorial owners had
a recognized place in government and society,
which demanded, at first a strong, and later, an extensive, dwelling-place.   It was, in short, the product and indication of contemporary manners as
dwelling-places generally are.   If we travel through
a country in which castles and fortified houses
are numerous, as they used to be prior to the four-
teenth century all over Europe, we conclude in-
fallibly that the law is weak, and that neighbors
make armed attacks on each other in the style described in the Paston Letters.[2]   If we find, coming
down later, as in the Elizabethan period, strong-
holds abandoned for extensive and ornamental res-

idences with plenty of unprotected windows, we conclude that the government is omnipotent and the great men live in peace. If we go through a democratic country like Switzerland, and find moderation in the size of houses and in the manner of living, the custom of the country, we conclude that the majority is in power, and that every man has his say in the management of the state. In short it may be truly said that dwelling-places, from the Indian's tepee up to the palace of the great noble, indicate, far more clearly than books or constitutions, the political and social condition of the country.

It is only of late years that we have had among us a class capable of equalling or outdoing the European aristocracy in wealth. American fortunes are now said to be greater than any of those of Europe, and nearly, if not quite, as numerous. But the rich American is face to face with a problem by which the European was not, and is not, troubled. He has to decide for himself, what is decided for the European by tradition, by custom, by descent, if not by responsibilities, how to spend his money. The old rich class in Europe may be said to inherit their obligations of every kind. When a man comes of age, if he inherits wealth, and is of what is called " good family," he finds settled for him the kind of house he shall live in, the number of horses and servants he shall keep, the extent to which he shall entertain. His income is, in truth, already disposed of by will, or settlement, or custom. There are certain people he is expected to maintain in a certain way, a certain style in which he is to live. This has led to, what appears to the American, the curious reluctance of the Englishman " to lay down his carriage." To certain families, houses, and properties, to certain social positions, in short, is attached the obligation of " keeping a carriage." It is one of the outward and visible signs of the owner's place in the state. To the American it is generally a mere convenience, which some years he possesses and other years he does not, and the absence of which excites no remark among his neighbors. If an Englishman of a certain rank gives it up, it indicates the occurrence of a pecuniary catastrophe. It advertises misfortune to the world. It says that he has been vanquished in a struggle, that his position is in danger, and his friends sympathize with him accordingly, partly because the women of his family do not, as with us, use public conveyances in the cities.

From all these responsibilities and suggestions the American, when he "makes his pile," is free. He can say for himself how the owner of millions in a country like this ought to live. He may have

one servant, eat in the basement, sup on Sunday
evenings on scalloped oysters, and sit in his shirt-
sleeves on his own stoop in a one-hundred-thou-
sand-dollar house, and nobody will make any remark. Or he may surround himself with lackeys,
whom he treats as equals, and who teach him how
the master of lackeys should behave, give gorgeous
entertainments to other rich men like himself,
at which his wife will eclipse in finery all other
wives, and nobody will express interest or surprise
except people who long for invitations from him.
Or he may, after a period of such luxury, "burst
up," sell everything out, and go live in Orange or
Flushing. Or his wife may "tire of housekeeping,"
and they may retire to an expensive apartment in
the Waldorf, or Savoy, after storing their furniture, or selling it at auction. What this indicates
is simply that great wealth has not yet entered
into our manners. No rules have yet been drawn
to guide wealthy Americans in their manner of
life. Englishmen, Frenchmen, Prussians, Austri-
ans, Swiss, of rank and of fortune, have ways of
spending their money, notions of their own of
what their position and personal dignity require.
But nothing of the kind is yet national in America.
The result is that we constantly see wealthy Americans travelling in Europe, without the slightest
idea of what they will or ought to do next, except

get rid of their money as fast as possible, by the payment of monstrous prices and monstrous fees, or the committal of other acts which to Europeans are simply vulgar eccentricities, but which our countrymen try to cover up by calling them "American" when "irrational" would be a more fitting appellation. Some of this confusion of mind is due, as Matthew Arnold has suggested in one of his letters, to the absence among us of an aristocracy to set an example of behavior to our rich men.[3] In European countries the newly enriched drop easily into the ranks of the aristocracy by a mere process of imitation. They try to dress and behave in the same way, and though a little fun may be made of them at first, they and their sons soon disappear in the crowd.

Ours do not enjoy such an advantage. They have to be, therefore, their own models, and there are finesses of manners and points of view in an aristocracy which are rarely got hold of except by long contact. By aristocracy I do not mean simply rich or well-born people, but people who have studied and long practised the social art, which is simply another name for the art of being agreeable. The notion that it consists simply in being kindly, and doing pleasant things for people, and having plenty of money, is one of the American delusions. The social art, like all other arts, is only carried to perfection, or to high excellence, by people who carefully practise it, or pay great attention to it. It consists largely in what are called "minor morals," that is, in doing things in society which long custom has settled on as suitable for the set of people with whom one associates. But it is full of what seem trifles, and which often become absurd if practised as a branch of learning acquired out of books. Like a large number of other things in civilized life, to be well practised it needs to be practised without thought, as something one is bred to. It is better obtained from books, or by study, than not at all, but it is most easily learned by observation. Ease of manner, taste in dress, tone of voice, insight into the ways of looking at small things of well-mannered people, are most easily acquired by seeing them in others. The benefit of watching adepts in this art have been enjoyed by but few rich men in America, and the result is that the rich world with us can hardly be called a social world at all. There can hardly be said to be among us what is called in Europe a "world" or "monde," in which there is a stock of common traditional manners and topics and interests, which men and women have derived from their parents, and a common mode of behavior which has assumed an air of sanctity. Our very rich people are generally sim-

ply rich people with everything in the way of social life to learn, but with a desire to learn which
is kept in check by the general belief in the community that they have nothing at all to learn, and
that it is enough to be rich.

That, under these circumstances, they should, in
somewhat slavish imitation of Europe, choose the
most conspicuous European mode of asserting
social supremacy, the building of great houses, is
not surprising. But in this imitation they make
two radical mistakes. They want the two principal reasons for European great houses. One is
that great houses are in Europe signs either of
great territorial possessions, or of the practice of
hospitality on a scale unknown among us. A very
large house in the country in Europe indicates
either that the owner is the possessor of great estates, or that he means to draw on some great
capital for a large body of guests whom he will
amuse by field sports out-of-doors, or who will
amuse each other in-doors. These are the excuses
for great houses in England, France, or Austria.
The owner is a great landholder, and has in this
way from time immemorial given notice of the
fact. Or he is the centre of a large circle of
men and women who have practised the social art,
who know how to idle and have the means to idle,
can talk to each other so as to entertain each

other, about sport, or art, or literature, or politics,
are, in short, glad to meet each other in luxurious
surroundings.

No such conditions exist in America. In the
first place, we have no great landholders, and there
is no popular recognition of the fact that a great
landowner, or great man of any sort, needs a great
house. In the second place, we have no capital to
draw on for a large company of men and women
who will amuse each other in a social way, even
from Friday to Monday. The absence of anything we can call society, that is, the union of
wealth and culture in the same persons, in all the
large American cities, except possibly Boston, is
one of the marked and remarkable features of our
time. It is, therefore, naturally what one might
expect, that we rarely hear of Americans figuring
in cultivated circles in England. Those who go
there with social aspirations desire most to get into
what is called " the Prince of Wales's set," in which
their national peculiarities furnish great amusement among a class of people to whom amusement
is the main thing. It would be easy enough to fill
forty or fifty rooms from " Friday to Monday " in
a house near New York or Boston. But what
kind of company would it be ? How many of the
guests would have anything to say to each other ?
Suppose " stocks " to be ruled out, where would

the topics of conversation be found? Would there
be much to talk about except the size of the host's
fortune, and that of some other persons present?
How many of the men would wish to sit with the
ladies in the evening and participate with them in
conversation? Would the host attempt two such
gatherings, without abandoning his efforts in disgust, selling out the whole concern, and going to
Europe?

One fatal difficulty in the way of such modes of
hospitality with us is the difference of social culture between our men and women. As a rule, in
the European circle called "society" the men and
women are interested in the same topics, and these
topics are entirely outside what is called "business;" they are literary or artistic, or in some degree intellectual, or else sporting. With us such
topics are left almost entirely to women. Whatever is done among us for real society is done by
women. It is they, as a general rule, who have
opinions about music, or the drama, or literature,
or philosophy, or dress, or art. It is they who
have reflected on these things, who know something and have something to say about them. It is
a rare thing for husbands or sons to share in these
interests. For the most part they care little about
them; they go into no society but dinners, and at
dinners they talk stocks and money. A meeting

of women for discussion on such subjects would
be a dreadful bore to them. The husband feels
better employed in making money for his wife
and daughters to spend seeing the sights abroad.
This difference in the culture of the sexes, and
in the practice of the social art, is in fact so
great in some parts of the country as to make
happy marriages rare or brief. It makes immense
houses, with many chambers, in town or country,
almost an absurdity in our present stage of progress.

Another, and the most serious reason against
spending money in America in building great
dwelling-houses, is, as I have already indicated,
that the dwellings of leading men in every country
should be in some sort of accord with the national
manners. If there be what is called a "note" in
American polity, it is equality of conditions, that
there should neither be an immoderate display of
wealth, nor of poverty, that no man should be
raised so far above the generality in outward seeming as to excite either envy, hatred, or malice ;
that, above all things, wealth should not become
an object of apprehension. We undoubtedly owe
to suspicion and dislike of great wealth and displays of it, the Bryan platform, with its absurdities
and its atrocities. The accumulation of great fortunes since the war, honestly it may be, but in

ways mysterious or unknown to the plain man, has
introduced among us the greatest of European
curses—class hatred, the feeling among one large
body of the community that they are being cheated
or oppressed by another body. To erect "palatial
abodes" is to flaunt in the faces of the poor and
the unsuccessful and greedy the most conspicuous possible evidence that the owner not only has
enormous amounts of money, but does not know
what to do with it. We know that from the earliest
times there has not been, and we know that there
is not now, the smallest popular dislike to the successful man's "living like a gentleman," as the saying is, that is, with quiet comfort, and with a reasonable amount of personal attendance. But the
popular gall rises when an American citizen appears, in the character of a Montmorenci, or a
Noailles, or a Westminster, in a gorgeous palace, at
the head of a large army of foreign lackeys. They
ask themselves what does this mean? Whither
are we tending? Is it possible we are about to re-
new on this soil, at the end of the nineteenth century, the extravagances and follies of the later Roman Empire and of the age of Louis XIV.? What
it does mean, in most cases, is simply that the citizen has more money than he finds it easy to dis-
pose of. Consequently the only thing he can think
of is building a residence for himself, which, like

Versailles, shall astonish the world, if in no other way, by its cost.

All this may be said without denying in the least the great liberality of American millionnaires. What colleges, schools, museums, and charities owe to them is something new in the history of the world. They have set Europe an example in this matter which is one of the glories of America. It is a pity to have them lessen its effect or turn attention away from it, by extravagance or frivolity, the more so because there is a mode still open to them of getting rid of cumbersome money, which is untried, and is full of honest fame and endless memory. We mean the beautifying of our cities with monuments and buildings. This should really be, and, I believe, will eventually become, the American way of *displaying* wealth. Considering what our wealth is and what the burden of our taxation is, and, as shown by the Chicago Exhibition, what the capabilities of our native architecture are, the condition of our leading cities as regards monuments of sculpture or architecture, is one of the sorrowful wonders of our condition. We are enormously rich, but except one or two things, like the Boston Library and the Washington public buildings, what have we to show? Almost nothing. Ugliness from the artistic point of view is the mark of all our cities. The stranger

looks through them in vain for anything but population and hotels.   No arches, no great churches,
no court-houses, no city halls, no statues, no tombs,
no municipal splendors of any description, nothing
but huge inns.

I fear, too, of this poverty we are not likely soon
to be rid, owing to the character of the government. It will always, under the régime of universal
suffrage, be difficult in any city to get the average
tax-payer to do much for art, or to allow art, as we
see in the case of the Sherman Monument, to be
made anything but the expression of his own admiration for somebody. It is almost impossible to
prevent monuments or buildings being jobs or cari-
catures, through the play of popular politics on a
subject which was no more meant for its treatment
by majorities than the standard of value. Governments in all European countries do much for art.
They erect fine public buildings under the best
artistic conditions.   They endow and maintain
picture-galleries and museums.   In fact the cultivation of art is one of their accepted functions.
Nothing of the kind is known among us. It would
infuriate Populists and Bryanites to know that our
Treasury was putting tens of thousands of dollars
into books and paintings, or bric-à-brac, or even
into art-education.   An École des Beaux Arts, or
National Gallery, seems to be an impossibility for

us. Whatever is done for beauty in America, must,
it seems, at least for a long time to come, be done
by private munificence. If we are to have noble
arches, or gateways, or buildings, or monuments of
any description, if our cities are to have other attractions than large hotels, it is evident our rich
men must be induced to use for this purpose the
wealth which it seems often to puzzle them to
spend. Such works would be a far more striking
evidence of the owner's opulence than any private
palace, would give his name a perpetuity which
can never be got from a private house, and would
rid him completely from the imputation of selfishness. For our experience with regard to great
houses, hitherto, is that the children of the men
who cause them to be built rarely wish to live in
them, and often have not the means to do so. Such
buildings become after their death either hotels or
some kind of charitable institutions. They are in
no sense memorials in men's minds of anything
but somebody's folly or extravagance. All they
say to coming generations, if they are not pulled
down, is that So-and-so made a fortune.

In erecting public monuments a rich man would
have the great advantage of doing what he pleased.
If the thing were more than a building, were, for
instance, an arch or a fountain, all he would have
to get from the public would be permission to

build, which would be seldom difficult. To obtain
from a popular government large expenditure of
money in a way which artists would approve, especially a government resting on a public as little
instructed in art matters as ours, is likely to be for
a long time to come at least almost an impossibility. Men in office are rarely experts in such matters, and if thoroughly honest, are apt to plume
themselves on their economy and rigid devotion to
utility, rather than on any regard for beauty. The
banker in New York who refused, some time ago,
to give in aid of an Academy of Design, money
which might be used, he said, in setting "a young
man up in the grocery business," fairly represented
the state of mind of any official class which we
are likely to have for a good while. Our reliance
for the ornamentation of the new world must therefore be mainly on our rich men. They can choose
their subject and their architect, without let or
hindrance, and they have thus far shown themselves fully alive to the value of professional ad-
vice and criticism. They have, in fact, before
them a wonderful opportunity, of which we trust
the next generation at least will avail itself, without
servile imitation of a society which is passing away
in the places in which history produced it.

NOTES

INDEX

Notes

ARISTOCRATIC OPINIONS OF DEMOCRACY

1. From *North American Review*, 100 (1865): 194–232. Godkin wrote the piece at the instance of his friend Charles Eliot Norton, who then edited the *Review*. In its original format it was a discursive review of Francis Bowen's edition of Alexis de Tocqueville, *Democracy in America* (Henry Reeve, trans., Cambridge, Mass., 1863), and John Stuart Mill's 1840 review of Tocqueville's work (reprinted in Mill's *Dissertations and Discussions, Political, Philosophical, and Historical* (New York, 1874), II, 79–161. Godkin sent a copy of his article to Mill, who responded warmly to its spirited defense of democracy as a way of political and social life. Mill to Godkin, May 24, 1865, in Hugh S. R. Elliot, *The Letters of John Stuart Mill* (London, 1910), II, 35.

2. Godkin is referring here to the substantial literature critical of the political theory and the social practice of democracy that emanated from Victorian England. The most significant of these works were by Sir Henry Maine, W. E. H. Lecky, Thomas Carlyle, John Ruskin, Matthew Arnold, and James F. Stephen. (See Benjamin E. Lippincott, *Victorian Critics of Democracy*, Minneapolis, 1938).

3. Sir Archibald Alison was the author of a Tory *History of England* widely read during the 1840's; the *Quarterly Review* was the most distinguished Tory periodical of the time. Together, they represented the English antidemocratic sentiment that Godkin attacked in "Aristocratic Opinions."

4. The passage in fact is in vol. I, bk. III, chap. X, para. 8 of Mill's *A System of Logic* (7th ed., London, 1868), pp. 504–505.

5. The references are to vol. II, first book, chaps. X, XIII, XVIII, XXI, and second book, chap. XIII, of *Democracy in America*.

6. There was a widespread awareness of the frontier's formative effects on American life before Frederick Jackson Turner's classic formulation in 1893; see, for example, Wirt A. Cate, "Lamar and the Frontier Hypothesis," *Journal of Southern History*, 1 (1935): 497–501. Nevertheless, Godkin offers here an early and vigorous statement of the thesis.

7. The *Saturday Review* of London during the Civil War years gave its readers a detailed and strongly anti-Northern account of American affairs. It spoke for a segment of British opinion that Godkin attempted to counter in wartime articles for the *London Daily News*.

8. Godkin examines the development of Australian political institutions at greater length—and with less sanguine conclusions—in "The Australian Democracy," *Unforeseen Tendencies of Democracy* (Boston, 1898), pp. 226–265.

9. The quotation is from Seneca's *Ad Helvium Matrem de Consolatione*, VII, 4–5.

10. Godkin cleansed the quotation of the darker line that Milton put into it:

> Fame is the spur that the clear spirit doth raise
> (That last infirmity of noble mind)
> To scorn delights, and live laborious days.
> (*Lycidas*, ll. 70–72)

11. Mill, "Democracy in America," *Dissertations and Discussions*, II, 146–147. Godkin's tone here is a reminder of the ideological distance that he would travel by the century's end. Soon the *Nation* insisted that literature was a declining form of expression in the American democracy. In the 1890's Godkin observed of Tocqueville: "as the years roll by and American development continues, his work becomes less valuable," and declared that "the English radicals of the earlier part of the century" badly needed correction. Richard C. Sterne, "Political, Social, and Literary Criticism in the New York *Nation:* 1865–1881; A Study in Change of Mood" (unpub. diss., Harvard University, 1957), pp. 303f; *below*, p. 278; *Unforeseen Tendencies of Democracy*, p. iii.

12. The reference is to Sir Henry Maine's *Ancient Law* (London and New York, 1864), a work which had a profound influence on educated men on both sides of the Atlantic. See Mark De Wolfe Howe, *Justice Oliver Wendell Holmes: The Shaping Years, 1841–1870* (Cambridge, Mass., 1957), pp. 193–195.

POPULAR GOVERNMENT

1. Originally "An American View of Popular Government," *Nineteenth Century*, 108 (1886): 177–190. Sir Henry Maine's *Popular Government* (London, 1885) was an attempt to apply to political institutions the historical method with which he examined legal institutions in *Ancient Law*. The result was a markedly hostile examination of democracy. The American institutions that won Maine's approval were those that checked democratic impulses. He warned against the dire effects on American life of party politics, nationalism, and imperialism. It is questionable if Godkin a decade later would have taken issue with Maine's arguments.

2. The passage is in bk. VI, chap. VII, para. 1 of Mill's *System of Logic*.

3. The Bland-Allison Act of 1878 required the Treasury Department to make substantial monthly purchases of silver for dollar coinage. The bill failed to have the inflationary effects that its advocates hoped for. But it did absorb

America's silver production, and thus served as the sort of subsidizing measure best calculated to infuriate Godkin.

4. Richard Cobden and John Bright, British manufacturers, statesmen, and publicists, were the leaders of the Manchester school of economics. They were the great spokesmen of free trade in the years of Godkin's youth. Henry Fawcett was the author of *Free Trade and Protection* (London, 1878), a critical analysis of the persistence of protectionism on the Continent, in the United States, and in the Empire. Fawcett also wrote a *Manual of Political Economy* (London, 1863) that was a faithful rendering of Manchesterian economic doctrines.

SOME POLITICAL AND SOCIAL ASPECTS OF THE TARIFF

1. Originally appeared in *New Princeton Review*, 3 (1887): 164–176.

2. Godkin refers here to Augustus Mongredien, an advocate of free trade whose work included *The Western Farmer in America* (London and New York, 1880) and a widely read *History of the Free-Trade Movement in England* (London, 1881).

3. Writing in 1857 to Henry S. Randall, the biographer of Jefferson, Macaulay said: "I have long been convinced that institutions purely democratic must, sooner or later, destroy liberty, or civilization, or both." He predicted that low wages and poor living conditions in the industrial cities would lead to social anarchy, and warned: "Your Constitution is all sail and no anchor." Southern publicists made much of the letter in the years just before the Civil War. It was reprinted in *Harper's Magazine*, 54 (1877): 460–462. See also "What Did Macaulay Say About America?" in *Bulletin of the New York Public Library*, 29 (1925): 459–481.

CRIMINAL POLITICS

1. Originally appeared in *North American Review*, 150 (1890): 706–723. In April 1890 Godkin directed an anti-Tammany publicity campaign in the New York *Evening Post.* He ran devastating biographies of Tammany leaders, including Mayor Hugh Grant, who was up for re-election. Suits for criminal libel were brought against Godkin by some of his victims, and he was harrassed by midnight process servings and a night or two in jail. Tammany won the election despite his efforts.

2. In 1867 New York's Protestant Irish established the Loyal Orange Institution. Parades of the Orangemen led to clashes with Irish Catholics, especially in 1871, when about 50 people were killed and over 100 were wounded.

3. John J. O'Brien was the New York City Republican leader in the 1880's. He often served state boss Thomas C. Platt as an intermediary for arrangements with Tammany.

4. Universal white male suffrage in fact came to New York with the 1821 constitutional convention and a constitutional amendment in 1826. The chief work of the 1846 convention was to limit the powers of the legislature and to change many offices from appointed to elective positions.

5. Tammany in 1884, bitterly opposed to Grover Cleveland's presidential

nomination, ran an anti-Cleveland ticket for city and county offices and organization man Hugh Grant for mayor. The County Democracy and Irving Hall, anti-Tammany Democratic organizations in the city, united behind the candidacy of former Mayor William R. Grace. Grace was elected, but the existence of a separate Republican candidacy made his victory over Grant a narrow one. In 1888 Tammany ran "Hughie" Grant once again. The County Democracy offered Abram S. Hewitt, who had been the victorious Democratic candidate against Henry George in 1886. Grant beat Hewitt by a 2 to 1 margin. But if Hewitt had had the vote that was cast for the Republican candidate, he would have won.

"THE ECONOMIC MAN"

1. Originally appeared in *North American Review*, 153 (1891): 491–503.

2. John N. Keynes, *The Scope and Method of Political Economy* (London, 1891), was an introduction to the subject particularly influenced by the economist Alfred Marshall. It sought to present economics as a highly professional and scholarly form of academic inquiry more than as a form of social analysis.

3. Godkin refers here to Wilhelm Roscher, *Principles of Political Economy* (John J. Lalor, trans., New York, 1878). Roscher, a professor at the University of Leipzig, was the father of the historical school of German economics. Scholars of this persuasion viewed economic institutions in relative and in historical terms—much as Sir Henry Maine viewed legal and political institutions. For Roscher's impact on American economic thinking, see Joseph Dorfman, *The Economic Mind in American Civilization* (New York, 1949), III (1865–1918), 88–92.

4. "The Tide of Economic Thought," *Publications of the American Economic Association*, 6 (1891): 20–21. See also Dorfman, *Economic Mind*, III, 101–110.

5. Godkin refers here to several of the benchmarks in the development of the historical school. The new German economists were university professors, and they were nicknamed *Katheder-Sozialisten*—Socialists of the Chair—by their critics. John Kells Ingram's article on "Political Economy" in the 9th edition of the *Encyclopaedia Britannica* was a notable statement of the historical school. (Dorfman, *Economic Mind*, III, 87–98, 265.) Auguste Comte deals with political economy in his *Positive Philosophy* (Harriet Martineau, ed., London, 1853), II, 60–65.

6. After boss Kelly's death in 1886, four leaders ran Tammany: Richard Croker, Hugh Grant, Thomas F. Gilroy, and Bourke Cockran. But by 1888 Croker had emerged as Kelly's true successor.

7. The Presbyterian minister Lyman Beecher was called to Litchfield, Connecticut, in 1810 at the instance of Tapping Reeve, founder of the town's famous law school. Judge James Gould was the school's principal teacher at the time. Beecher scored a great success in Litchfield, conducting a continuous revival until he went to Boston in 1826.

IDLENESS AND IMMORALITY

1. Originally appeared in *Forum*, 13 (1892): 334–343.

2. Gladstone, "Locksley Hall and the Jubilee," *Nineteenth Century*, 21 (1887): 16. There is some poignancy in the fact that the optimism pervading Gladstone's article is not unlike that of Godkin's own "Aristocratic Opinions of Democracy" twenty-odd years before.

3. The scientist Charles Darwin, the English historian George Grote, the Italian statesman Count Camillo di Cavour, the English statesman William E. Gladstone, the eighteenth century English philanthropist and prison reformer John Howard, and the American historian John Lothrop Motley followed their careers with the aid of considerable family wealth—the lack of which, one suspects, at times sorely troubled Godkin.

THE DUTY OF EDUCATED MEN IN A DEMOCRACY

1. Originally appeared in *Forum*, 17 (1894): 39–51.

2. The reference is to an article by President Charles W. Eliot of Harvard, "One Remedy for Municipal Government."

3. In 1884, while ambassador to Great Britain, Lowell spoke at the Birmingham and Midland Institute on "Democracy" (Lowell, *Works*, Boston, 1890, *Literary and Political Addresses*, pp. 7–37). His was a notable defense of democracy before an English audience. Lowell also shared Godkin's view of politics and labor unrest in the Gilded age. See Lowell to Godkin in Charles Eliot Norton, ed., *The Letters of James Russell Lowell* (New York, 1893), II, 31, 77.

4. Isaac H. Maynard, a stalwart in the state Democratic organization led by David B. Hill, was appointed by Governor Roswell Flower to the Court of Appeals in 1892. He stood for election to the Court in 1893. Maynard's political past was unsavory enough to evoke much opposition to his campaign. A committee of the New York Bar Association condemned his candidacy, and he was defeated by over 100,000 votes.

5. The New York State Democratic convention of 1892 was known as the "snap" convention because of the haste with which Hill convened it—the object being to lessen Cleveland's influence therein. Anti-Snappers thus were anti-Hill, pro-administration Democrats.

6. W. E. H. Lecky, *History of the Rise and Influence of the Spirit of Rationalism in Europe* (New York, 1866), I, 34–35.

WHO WILL PAY THE BILLS OF SOCIALISM?

1. Originally appeared in *Forum*, 17 (1894): 394–405.

2. Benjamin Kidd's *Social Evolution* (New York, 1894) was the widely read work of an English sociologist. Its theme was that religion and emotion, rather than reason, were the prime determinants of human conduct. The work's millennial tone, and its mystical insistence that the individual self must give

way to the common good, made it for Godkin yet another instance of the new and unpleasant ways of social thinking that were coming into their own at the century's end.

3. Godkin now has additional developments in economic thought to concern him: the moderate Socialism of the British and American Fabian Societies, the Christian Socialism of the American economist Richard T. Ely.

4. W. T. Stead was an English journalist who wrote *If Christ Came to Chicago!* (London, 1894), an exposé of conditions in the city that was influential in the development of the social gospel and of urban reform.

5. Stanton Coit was Felix Adler's assistant in the Society for Ethical Culture during the 1880's. He spent some time in London's Toynbee Hall, the first settlement house, in 1886, and on his return to New York established the first such institution in the United States. This was first called the Neighborhood Guild. In 1891, under the sponsorship of President Seth Low of Columbia, it became the University Settlement.

6. Gustav Schmoller, professor of economic history at the University of Berlin, was one of the *Katheder-Sozialisten,* the historical school of German economic theorists whose work challenged Godkin's Manchester Liberalism.

THE POLITICAL SITUATION IN 1896

1. Originally "The Political Situation," *Forum,* 21 (1896): 257–270.

2. Godkin is referring to Lecture LIX of John C. J. Hare's *American Constitutional Law* (Boston, 1889), II, 1288–1310. The Legal Tender Cases, 12 *Wall.* 457 (1871), affirmed the constitutionality of the acts by which the government issued greenbacks during the Civil War.

3. Cleveland's message to Congress on December 17, 1895, reviewed the heated controversy with Great Britain over British claims to Venezuelan boundary territory. Cleveland reaffirmed the Monroe Doctrine, and spoke of resisting British aggression if necessary.

THE REAL PROBLEMS OF DEMOCRACY

1. Originally appeared in *Atlantic Monthly,* 78 (1896): 1–13.

2. Morley's critique of W. E. H. Lecky's *Democracy and Liberty* (New York, 1896), "Lecky on Democracy," is in his *Works* (London, 1921), XV, 1–22. He wrote a similar analysis of Sir Henry Maine's *Popular Government* (*ibid.,* pp. 23–58).

3. Cavour, the statesman most responsible for the unification of Italy, had a political outlook shaped primarily by the precepts of English Liberalism. Gustave de Beaumont, Tocqueville's companion in America, interested himself as well in Irish problems, and wrote *L'Irlande, Sociale, Politique, et Religieuse* (Paris, 1839).

4. James Bryce's *The American Commonwealth* had been published a few years before, in 1888.

THE EXPENDITURE OF RICH MEN

1. Originally appeared in *Scribner's Magazine*, 20 (1896): 495–501.

2. The Paston letters are the detailed and revealing correspondence of a substantial English family in the fifteenth century. They have been printed in many editions.

3. In the Preface to *Culture and Anarchy* (*Works*, London, 1903, VI, xxvi), Arnold makes the observation that Godkin ascribes to him.

Index